395 -

Without Fear

Without Fear

The Life and Trial of Bhagat Singh

Kuldip Nayar

HarperCollins *Publishers* India
a joint venture with

New Delhi

Published in India in 2007 by
HarperCollins *Publishers* India
a joint venture with
The India Today Group

First published by Har-Anand Publications Pvt. Ltd. in 2000
as *The Martyr Bhagat Singh-Experiments in Revolution.*

ISBN 13-978-81-7223-692-2
3rd impression, 2008

Kuldip Nayar asserts the moral
right to be identified as the author of this work.

HarperCollins *Publishers*
A-53, Sector 57, Noida, Uttar Pradesh-201301, India
1A Hamilton House, Connaught Place, New Delhi 110001, India
77-85 Fulham Palace Road, London W6 8JB, United Kingdom
Hazelton Lanes, 55 Avenue Road, Suite 2900, Toronto, Ontario M5R 3L2
and 1995 Markham Road, Scarborough, Ontario M1B 5M8, Canada
25 Ryde Road, Pymble, Sydney, NSW 2073, Australia
31 View Road, Glenfield, Auckland 10, New Zealand
10 East 53rd Street, New York NY 10022, USA

Typeset in 11.5/14.7 Aldine401 BT
Mindways Design

Printed and bound at
Thomson Press (India) Ltd.

*This book is dedicated
to my grandchildren
Mandira, Kartik and Kanika*

Preface to the New Edition

I HAVE BROUGHT OUT A REVISED EDITION OF MY BOOK ON Bhagat Singh on two accounts: one, the chapter on the tribunal proceedings of Sukhbir, Rajguru and Bhagat Singh, in which they were sentenced to death by hanging, was left out of the earlier edition and two, I wanted to incorporate some more information in the text. This also gave me the opportunity to rewrite certain portions and arrange them in the proper context. My feeling is that you will find the present edition absorbing and comprehensive even if you have read the edition I released a few years ago.

Kuldip Nayar
September, 2007

Foreword

THE MINARET OF AN ELEGANT MOSQUE RISES FROM ACROSS the spot where Bhagat Singh's cell 'Phansi ki Kothi' once stood, but no arch, no plaque, not even a stone, marks the spot where Bhagat Singh and his two comrades, Sukhdev and Rajguru, were executed.

Today, Lahore Central Jail, where the three young revolutionaries were hanged on 23 March, 1931, is in a state of ruin. The cells that housed these three martyrs are falling apart. The scaffold on which they were hanged is now a traffic roundabout. Vehicles careen around it as waywardly as they do through the rest of Lahore. Noise, smoke and dust shroud the crossing. The road between the mosque and the ruins of the jail leads into the gateway of a mental hospital. It is as if the establishment does not want any sign of them to remain. Ironically, the authorities have named the colony that has sprung up around it 'Shadman' – the abode of happiness.

On a visit to Pakistan, I asked the residents of Shadman if they knew who Bhagat Singh was. Not many had heard the name. A few had a vague idea of his imprisonment and hanging. 'When we came here, there were only police quarters, which were pulled down as the colony expanded,' said a man in his fifties. But there is a story about the roundabout that has been retold many times after the execution of Prime Minister Zulfikar Ali Bhutto in 1979, almost three decades ago. It was the spot where Nawaz

Mohammad Ahmed Khan, father of Ahmed Raza Kasuri, then a member of Pakistan's National Assembly, was shot. Bhutto had reportedly ordered his killing. When the guns were fired Kasuri had been negotiating the roundabout. Sitting beside him in the car, his father was fatally wounded. Kasuri's grandfather had been one of the officials on duty called upon to formally identify the bodies of the three revolutionaries. Old-timers believe that nemesis caught up with the Kasuri family when Mohammad Ahmed Khan was killed at the same spot.

In the eighties, Lahore was the venue of the World Punjabi Conference. The hall where the conference was held had only one portrait on its walls – that of Bhagat Singh. I asked the organizers why they had chosen to felicitate Bhagat Singh at the cost of ignoring another distinguished Punjabi freedom fighter, Mohammad Iqbal, the renowned Urdu poet and visionary, who had first dreamed of a land called Pakistan. 'Only one Punjabi laid down his life for the country's independence, and that man was Bhagat Singh,' they replied.

Soon after my trip to Pakistan, I had the opportunity to travel through the towns of southern India. I was surprised to find Bhagat Singh's statue in many small towns in the south and I wrote an article on him on my return to Delhi. Shortly thereafter I received a letter from Harjinder Singh and Sukhjinder Singh – both of whom had been given the death sentence for assassinating General A.S. Vaidya, former chief of army staff, in Pune. What they wrote made me think. They questioned my judgement. Why did I hail Bhagat Singh and call him a 'revolutionary' while condemning them as 'terrorists', they asked. They said that they too had served a cause. Bhagat Singh had avenged the death of Lajpat Rai, the Lion of Punjab, at the hands of a British police officer, while they had settled scores with Vaidya for having planned the attack in 1984 on the Golden Temple, their Vatican.

Fearing that more and more militants would compare themselves with Bhagat Singh, I thought it worthwhile to trace his life and philosophy, and explain the difference between a terrorist and a revolutionary. What does killing mean to a revolutionary? Bhagat Singh explained it in his own words:

> We attach great sanctity to human life, we regard man's life as sacred...We would sooner lay down our lives in the service of humanity than injure anyone.

There was no revenge, no vendetta, on Bhagat Singh's mind:

> These actions (killings), have their political significance inasmuch as they serve to create a mentality and an atmosphere which shall be very necessary to the final struggle. That is all.

A revolutionary believes in the complete overthrow of any established government or political system that does not give economic equality to the people. In his scheme of things, citizens should be empowered against economic powerlessness and given individual dignity. On the other hand, a terrorist is motivated by personal revenge against a particular person, who is a mere instrument in the hands of rulers. So, while one transcends hatred, the other is a victim of it.

Researching this book was an arduous task. Work continued sporadically for more than seven years. The Archives of Pakistan is the best, most comprehensive, source for material on the life and times of Bhagat Singh but it is not open to Indians. New Delhi and Islamabad have no agreement that allows nationals of one country access to the archives of the other. I approached the Pakistan government through a friend. A lame excuse was dug up to deny me access. They said they were afraid they might get entangled in the Sikh problem. I could not fathom the connection between the Sikh problem, fifty years later, with the 1931 execution, except for the fact that Bhagat Singh was a Sikh.

The India Office Library in London has practically nothing on Bhagat Singh. In any case, the library has distributed its books, reports and documents in different libraries all over the UK. This is meant to dissuade India, Pakistan and Bangladesh and other ex-colonies of Great Britain, from ever staking claim to what should have rightfully come to them after Independence. After the partition of the subcontinent, India and Pakistan could not agree upon a formula for the division of the library, thus giving the UK a pretext to usurp it entirely.

Some information on the appeal in the privy council in London against the death sentences of the three revolutionaries is available. This material is in our archives as well. My feeling is that crucial files have been destroyed or withheld. I'm sure that telegrams and documents, as yet uncovered, indicating that the British establishment was determined to hang Bhagat Singh and his two comrades to smother revolutionary ferment, must exist somewhere.

Bhagat Singh's revolutionary ideas had been fed by the French Revolution, the American Declaration of Independence, and the Bolshevik Revolution in Russia. The struggle against social evils, the awakening of oppressed castes and the rise of peasants and workers against social oppression and inequality all became an integral part of the freedom struggle. In the course of my research, I found that Bhagat Singh had written as many as four books in jail. *The History of the Revolutionary Movement in India, The Ideal of Socialism, Autobiography* and *At the Door of Death.* I tried in vain to locate them. I was told that the manuscripts, which had been smuggled out of jail before Bhagat Singh's execution and kept by the revolutionaries in custody, were handed over, in the forties, to Kumari Lajyavati, who later became the principal of Kendriya Mahavidyalaya, Jalandhar. Lajyavati, who is now dead, reportedly gave them to someone in Lahore, just before Partition, to send them back to India. This someone, not identified, is said to have told her that he burnt all the manuscripts in panic before immigrating to India in August, 1947. The story is not credible. I still believe the manuscripts will surface some day.

The first thing I did while collecting material for my book was to locate Bhagat Singh's brothers. Unfortunately, Kulbir Singh, died before I could meet him. Kultar Singh, the younger brother, lived in Saharanpur, UP. His memory of Bhagat Singh's last meeting with his family was poignant and evocative. I learnt that others in Bhagat Singh's family also had a nationalistic streak. His uncle, Ajit Singh, was sharing a prison cell with Lajpat Rai in Burma when Bhagat Singh was born, while his grandfather openly contributed to the Congress party.

In December 1992, I was able to trace Mathura Das Thapar, Sukhdev's younger brother. I wrote him a letter that very month. Thapar replied to me in March, 1993. His story was touching. He said he had to leave Lyallpur (modern-day Faislabad) 'due to the constant troubles created against me by the Punjab Police on account of my being the blood brother of Sukhdev'.

Mathura Das Thapar, then eighty-two, was bitter. In his reply to my letter, he said:

> Allow me the indulgence to add that the other political sufferers like Dr Kichloo's son, got a monthly packet of Rs. 5,000 and a flat, free of cost. Against Dr Kichloo's son, compare our clan's sacrifice.

He drew my attention to a copy of the 'Proceedings Book of the Lahore Conspiracy Case' which he had brought from Pakistan and had deposited with the National Archives in New Delhi. This copy had comments scribbled in the margins by

Sukhdev, who was allowed to read it before he was executed. Pakistan has a record of the original proceedings in Urdu, which I have gone through.

Thapar's letter, which I retain (see Annexure 1), ends with the remark: 'Hoping to be of use in your great task of writing the masterpiece of great historical importance.' He too died before we could meet. I do not know what he would have thought of this book. My work may not be a masterpiece, but I have tried my best to present Bhagat Singh as he lived, thought and died.

I read the correspondence between Mathura Das Thapar and Hans Raj Vohra – who later turned informer in the Lahore Conspiracy Case – in a private collection. The correspondence, particularly Vohra's letter explaining his decision to turn informer, along with Thapar's rejoinder to the letter, form the epilogue of this book.

Also, through Kultar Singh, I learnt that Durga Devi, wife of Bhagwati Charan, a leading revolutionary in those days, lived in Ghaziabad with her son. Although she suffered frequent memory lapses, she was able to reconstruct the story of Bhagat Singh's escape from Lahore after the assassination of deputy superintendent of police J.P. Saunders, in which she played a major role. She too died a few years ago.

Several books on Bhagat Singh and his own writings have helped me narrate the story and philosophy of his life. Words attributed to him have been culled from his letters, statements and speeches. I have not taken any liberties with the facts.

The police records of those days gave me an insight into the methods used by the British to suppress the revolutionaries. Intelligence reports, very few in our archives, have also been of some assistance. A repository of information is Amiya K. Samanta'a six-volume collection of documents, *Terrorism in Bengal,* brought out by the Government of West Bengal. I have made use of some information from the collection.

Many of Mahatma Gandhi's writings throw light on his attitude towards the revolutionaries. He admired their courage but not their use of guns and bombs. He did not doubt their commitment but he was definite that the use of force could not release India from the clutches of British power. Gandhi and Bhagat Singh were diametrically opposed to each other in their approach. Bhagat Singh believed in violence and did not flinch from using it to achieve independence. Gandhi, on the other hand, remained wedded to non-violence all his life and brooked no other approach.

It was a tribute to Bhagat Singh's remarkable achievement when Dr Pattabhi Sitaramayya wrote in his *History of the Indian National Congress* that Gandhi and Bhagat Singh were equally popular – the first for his experiments with truth and the second for his essays in bravery. Bhagat Singh was twenty-one when he first met Gandhi; the Mahatma was fifty-nine.

I have gone through the newspapers of those days. I have also talked to a few people who knew Bhagat Singh. There are not many left. My main source was a friend, Virendra, editor of the *Pratap,* Jalandhar. He died seven years ago. He was in Lahore Central Jail when the trial of Bhagat and his comrades was underway. Virendra too was a suspect but nothing credible was found against him. He was released after a stint in prison.

Many people have helped me complete this book. They include Kavita, my younger daughter-in-law, who researched the trial; and R. Ramachandaran, Subramanyam and Gopal, who typed and retyped the draft before keying it into a computer. I thank them all.

I am going to sacrifice my life for a cause. What more consolation can there be? A God-believing Hindu may expect to be reborn a king; a Muslim or a Christian might dream of the luxuries he hopes to enjoy in paradise as a reward for his sufferings and sacrifices. What hope should I entertain? I know that it will be the end when the rope is tightened around my neck and the rafters moved from under my feet. To use more precise religious terminology – it will be my moment of utter annihilation. My soul will come to nothing. If I have the courage to take the matter in the light of 'Reward', I see that a short life of struggle with no such magnificent end shall itself be my 'Reward.' That is all. With no selfish motive or desire to be awarded here or hereafter, quite disinterestedly, have I devoted my life to the cause of independence, because I could not do otherwise.

– Bhagat Singh, 'Why I Am an Atheist'

1

Koi din ka mehman hun ai ahle mehfi,
Chiragh-e-sehar hun bujha chahta hun
MIRZA GHALIB

23 MARCH, 1931 BEGAN LIKE ANY OTHER DAY IN LAHORE CENTRAL Jail. As usual, the political prisoners were let out of their cells in the morning. They normally stayed out during the day and were locked back in after sunset. So that day, when Warden Charat Singh came around at four p.m. and asked them to return to their cells, the inmates were surprised. They often lingered outside, long after dusk, despite the warden's gentle chiding. But this time he was adamant. He would not say why. All he muttered was, 'Orders from above.'

The prisoners were fond of Charat Singh. They always referred to him with respect, calling him 'Charat Singhji' because of his caring and paternal attitude towards them. On his part, the warden sympathized with the prisoners and did not harass them, turning a blind eye when books banned by the British were smuggled into Lahore jail. If he was asking them to get back to their cells, he must have a valid reason, the prisoners told themselves. One by one, all of them complied with his orders. But they were restive. They couldn't help wonder what was afoot. It was then that the prison barber, Barkat, going from cell to cell, informed them in a subdued voice that Bhagat Singh, Sukhdev and Rajguru were going to be hanged that night.

The prisoners were devastated. Though they all knew that Bhagat Singh and his comrades were going to die, the finality of the moment shook them. They asked Barkat if he would try and smuggle out Bhagat Singh's comb, pen, watch – any small remembrance of the fiery young revolutionary whose courage had inspired a nation; it would be a lifelong treasure for them to cherish. Barkat went into Bhagat Singh's cell and returned with a comb and a pen. All seventeen prisoners staked their claim and a draw was organized. Then they grew quiet again. Their eyes were now riveted to the passage outside their cells. Bhagat Singh was expected to pass that way on his way to the gallows. Once, when he was being led through the passage past their cells, Punjab Congress leader, Bhimsen Sachar, had asked Bhagat Singh why his comrades and he had not defended themselves during the Lahore Conspiracy Case.

'Revolutionaries have to die,' Bhagat Singh had said to him, 'because the cause they represent is strengthened by sacrifice – not by an appeal in court.'

Sentenced to death by a British tribunal nearly six months ago, on 7 October, 1930, Bhagat Singh sat behind the high walls of Lahore Central Jail waiting for Charat Singh. Even though both knew their friendship was doomed to be short-lived, the head jail warden and he had developed a deep fondness for each other, often breaking into Punjabi, their mother tongue, when they were together. That day, sitting chained and alone in his cell, he recognized his slow, shuffling footsteps. A stint in the army and a long innings with the police had affected Charat Singh's health and, coupled with his prematurely white beard, made him look older than his age. Bhagat Singh smiled to himself. Life was strange, he thought. And the shorter it was, the more poignant its intensity.

Charat Singh had been kind to him. He had allowed him to smuggle in all the books he had wanted to read. Mostly Marxist literature, strictly banned by the government and devoured by him. Hardly would a book on Marx, Lenin or Russia arrive that he would put in a demand for it. His secret source – the local Dwarka Das Library founded by progressive nationalists – could barely keep pace with his voracious reading. So ferocious was his appetite for books that he once wrote to his schoolmate, Jaidev Gupta, to issue, among others, *Militarism* by Karl Liebknecht, *Left-Wing Communism* by Lenin, *Why Men Fight* by Bertrand Russell, and the novel *The Spy* by Upton Sinclair from the library, and to send them to him through his brother Kulbir.

Books had been his passion from childhood. 'Study' was the cry that reverberated in his mind. Study – to enable him to refute the arguments advanced by the opposition. Study – to arm himself with reasons in favour of his cult of revolution. Study – to find methods to change the age-old systems in India. He taught himself Marxism, communism and revolutionary philosophy. It was this wide study that broadened his mind. This, that gave him strength and the courage of conviction.

He had grown used to a harsh life. His cell, No. 14, was a filthy pit with grass on the floor and a smelly hole in a corner. When he stretched, there was just enough space to accommodate his 5 foot 10 inch frame. Though he had learnt to live in solitude he was impatient. Not because he was isolated but because it had been a long and purposeless wait. At times he wished they would carry out the execution quickly. But at other times he felt his life of twenty-three years had been too short. He once wrote to a friend that he had not accomplished even a thousandth of what he had proposed to do. Another time he told a comrade, Bijoy Kumar Sinha, who met him a fortnight before the execution:

It would be a calamity if I am spared. If I die, wreathed in smiles, India's mothers would wish their children to emulate Bhagat Singh and thus, the number of formidable freedom fighters would increase so much that it would be impossible for the Satanic powers to stop the march of revolution...

Circumscribed in space and time, he could not see the change in weather. When a tattered blanket was thrown at him to fight the minus three degrees centigrade temperature, he sensed rather than saw autumn change to winter. Now the advent of March had lessened the rigour. There was the promise of spring in the air. But the very name given to his cell, 'Phansi ki Kothi' (The Hanging Cell), blighted any pleasant thoughts.

Bhagat Singh was perceptive enough to realize that his execution was linked with political developments in the country. The British had drawn a blank at the Round Table Conference that they had convened in London in November, 1930. They wanted to ladle out limited powers for 'self-governance' but had found no takers. India was seething with discontent. The Congress party, which led the national struggle for independence, had boycotted the conference. Other parties had also followed the Congress.

Bhagat Singh was not opposed to compromise. He believed it was not a deplorable thing to do and was an integral part of political strategy. Any nation that rose against its oppressors was bound to fail in the beginning but would later gain partial reforms through compromise. The Russian Revolution, which inspired India's revolutionaries, was an example. When the Bolsheviks were forced to sign the Peace Treaty of Brest-Litovsk after the 1917 revolution, everybody except Lenin was opposed to it. He had famously declared 'Peace and again peace: peace at any cost' – even at the cost of yielding many of the Russian provinces to German war lords. When criticized, he admitted that since the Bolsheviks could not face the German onslaught, he had to compromise.

London favoured some sort of agreement with the Indians through another Round Table Conference. But it did not want the corpse of Bhagat Singh lying between England and India when the talks took place. The British had therefore deferred the hanging till they had explored all avenues to reach a settlement, primarily with the Congress and with Gandhi.

To Bhagat Singh the struggle for independence in India was basically a struggle for economic betterment. Freedom would provide an opportunity for improvement. An independent India, without removing poverty, would be free only in name. Bhagat Singh did not want to substitute one status quo with another. Coming as Bhagat Singh did from a clan of freedom fighters, the urge to participate in the struggle for independence was natural; but he also came from a family of zamindars. Books made him realize that social disparities were created by man and perpetuated by man. Karl Marx was his guru. The German thinker said that a change in the balance of economic power was the rationale upon which all other changes of human history depended. How could political freedom mean anything without economic freedom? What use was freedom if the poor remained poor? And how would disparities between the rich and the poor end? Awakening to socialist ideas was something new to him. Political history, the history of thought, of religions and the rest were born in the womb of economic circumstances. Never before had he so keenly appreciated dialectical materialism's contention that political theory was not prior, but posterior, to political fact. Marx made him feel that political actions were not the cause; they were the product of economic forces.

He had once written to his mother, Vidyavati Kaur:

Ma, I have no doubt that my country will be one day free. But I am afraid that the brown sahibs are going to sit in the chairs the white sahibs will vacate.

Bhagat Singh believed that the plight of the people would remain the same if the end of British rule was to mean only a change of masters. No improvement was possible without the destruction of India's antiquated system – it was this system that stood like a wall in the way of progress. Philosophers had interpreted the world in different ways, but the real point was to change it. Revolution alone could do so.

He was not alone in his thinking. There were hundreds of revolutionaries like him who had come together and reinvigorated the dying Hindustan Republican Association. Bhagat Singh had added the word 'socialist' to its name and re-named it the Hindustan Socialist Republican Association. The HSRA had also constituted an armed wing lead by Chandra Shekhar Azad, a senior revolutionary and the best shot in the party. The armed wing's job was to collect arms and ammunition and arrange mass protests. Then there were sympathizers propagandizing the cause, raising money and arranging shelter for members of the armed wing. Locked in adjoining cells, his comrades Sukhdev Thapar and Shivaram Rajguru cherished the same dreams.

He had seen daylight creep into No. 14, linger, and then recede into the twilight of the evening. When the sun was down, the darkness was really thick, with no electric bulb, no lantern, not even an earthen lamp to light his cell. Somewhere in the distance a searchlight revolved to provide a semblance of illumination to the area where he, along with his two comrades, awaited execution. He had listened to the sounds of silence endlessly, interrupted only by the hourly tolling of a jail gong and the clang of an iron door as it opened and closed.

Charat Singh stood outside his cell, fumbling for the right key from the bunch he dug out of the deep pocket of the uniform he wore.

Saying he wanted to ask him if he had a last wish, Bhagat Singh's lawyer, Pran Nath Mehta, managed to meet him two hours before the hanging. Bhagat Singh who was pacing up and down his cell like a caged lion welcomed Mehta with a broad smile and asked him whether he had brought him the book he had asked for: *The Revolutionary Lenin*. Bhagat Singh had sent Mehta a message asking him to bring the book because its review in a newspaper had impressed him. When Mehta gave him the book, he was very happy and began reading it immediately as though conscious that he did not have much time left. Mehta asked him if he had any message for the nation. Without taking his eyes off the book, Bhagat Singh said: 'Just the two messages – "Down With Imperialism!" and "Long Live Revolution!".' When Mehta asked him how he felt he replied, 'Happy, as always.' And when he asked if there was anything else he desired he said, 'Yes, I want to be born again in the same country so that I can serve it again.' Then Bhagat Singh asked Mehta to thank Pandit Nehru and Babu Subhash Chandra Bose because both of them had shown great interest in his case.

After meeting Bhagat Singh Mehta met Rajguru whose last words to him were, 'We shall meet soon.' While Sukhdev simply reminded Mehta to take back a carrom board, that Mehta had given him a few months earlier, from the jailor.

Soon after Mehta's departure, the authorities told the three revolutionaries that the time of hanging was being advanced by eleven hours. Instead of six the next morning, they were to be executed at seven p.m. the same day.

Bhagat Singh had barely finished a few pages of the book. 'Won't you allow me to finish one chapter?' he asked.

The three young revolutionaries were moved out of their cells to prepare them for the hanging. Bhagat Singh, Sukhdev and Rajguru locked arms and strode behind the sentries and broke into their favourite freedom song:

Kabhi woh din bhi ayega
Ke jab azad hum honge
Yeh apni hi zamin hogi
Yeh apna aasman hoga
Shahidon ki chitaon par
Lagenge har baar mele
Watan par marne walon ka
Yahi nam-o-nishan hoga.

(Someday that day will come when we are free/ This will be our land and our sky/ People will gather in the grounds where once/ Martyrs' pyres were lit/ A tribute to all those who/ Gave their lives for their land.)

The three men were weighed one by one – they had all gained weight – and asked to take their last bath. They were then dressed in black robes. Their faces were left uncovered. Charat Singh whispered into Bhagat Singh's ears to pray to Wahe Guru.

'All my life I have never prayed. As a matter of fact, I have many a time abused God for the miseries of the poor. If I were to ask now for His forgiveness, He will say, "Here is a coward who seeks forgiveness because his end has come",' Bhagat Singh said, declining with a smile.

Dusk fell as the prisoners waited to hear the sound of footsteps in the passage outside their cells. Nobody had come that way for more than two hours, not even the warden to re-check the locks. When the jail gong struck six they heard muffled voices in the distance accompanied by the thud of heavy boots and faint snatches of a familiar song, '*Sarfaroshi ki tamanna ab hamare dil me hein…*' And then sounds of 'Inquilab Zindabad!' and 'Hindustan Azad Ho!' rent the air. The prisoners began to sing '*Mai rang de mera basanti chola...*' (Mother, prepare my clothes for martyrdom) and fervently shouted 'Long Live Revolution!' and 'Down with Imperialism!' their urgent voices resounding through the corridors of Lahore Central Jail.

The scaffold was old, but the hefty hangman was not. The three men sentenced to death stood on separate wooden planks, with a deep ditch running below them. Bhagat Singh stood in the centre. He wanted to fulfil his mother's last wish and shout 'Long Live Revolution!' from the scaffold.

The noose was tightened around the necks of the three young revolutionaries. Their hands and feet were tied. They kissed the rope that looped their necks. Then the hangman asked who would go first. Sukhdev said that he would. The hangman pulled the ropes one by one and kicked the rafters from under their feet.

The bodies remained hanging from the scaffold for a long time. Finally they were brought down and examined by a doctor. Bhagat Singh, Sukhdev and Rajguru were pronounced dead. One jail officer was so moved by the courage of the young revolutionaries that he refused the order to identify the dead. He was suspended on the spot. A junior officer did the job instead. Two British officers, one of them the superintendent of the jail, certified the deaths.

Outside the prison walls, hundreds of people kept vigil. The problem the jail authorities now faced was how to dipose of the bodies. The idea of cremating the bodies inside the jail was dropped when the authorities realized that the large crowd outside would attack if it saw smoke or the glow of fire. So they broke a part of the jail's rear wall. Late in the night a truck was brought in and the bodies were thrown into it unceremoniously, like pieces of luggage. Initially, the cremation was planned by the banks of the Ravi but the water in the river proved too shallow so they decided to head to the Satluj instead. British soldiers escorted the truck on the drive to Ferozepur, near the Satluj. Once there, they had barely managed to set the bodies aflame, when they were discovered.

People in the countryside, particularly those living in village Gandha Singh Wallah, saw the pyres burning and rushed to the spot. The soldiers ran to their vehicles, leaving the half-cremated bodies and sped back to Lahore. Through the long night the villagers sat reverently by the remains of their heroes...

News of the execution spread like wildfire in Lahore and the other cities of Punjab. Young men took out processions through the night shouting 'Inquilab Zindabad!' and 'Bhagat Zindabad!' There was a hartal in the city. Shops downed their shutters. All schools and colleges – except the toady government college – remained closed. Police pickets were set up to guard government buildings and the posh Civil Lines area, where the white officers lived.

Around noon, notices signed by the district magistrate were put up in various parts of Lahore, announcing that the bodies of Bhagat Singh, Sukhdev and Rajguru had been cremated according to Hindu and Sikh rites on the banks of the Satluj. This news was challenged in several gatherings where it was said that the bodies had not even been properly cremated. The magistrate issued a denial but nobody believed him.

A mourning procession started from Neelagombad, not far from the place where Saunders had been shot dead. Thousands of Hindus, Muslims and Sikhs participated in the over three-mile-long procession. The men wore black bands while the women draped themselves in black saris. The processionists shouted 'Inquilab Zindabad!' and 'Bhagat Singh Zindabad!' The entire place was a sea of black flags. Passing through the Mall, the procession stopped in the middle of Anarkali Bazaar. The crowd was hushed into silence by the announcement that Bhagat

Singh's family had reached the city from Ferozepur with the remains of the three martyrs.

Three hours later, three flower-bedecked coffins, accompanied by Bhagat Singh's family, joined the procession. Loud cries rent the sky. People wept profusely, openly. The procession, ironically, came back to the banks of the Ravi, where the authorities had first brought the bodies for cremation. A mammoth meeting was held in Lahore, condemning the execution and calling it murder. There was outrage over the manner in which the authorities had disposed of the bodies. Maulana Zafar Ali Khan, the renowned editor of an Urdu daily, recited a poem describing how the half-charred remains of the dead bodies had been left callously unguarded under the open sky.

Warden Charat Singh dragged himself slowly back to his room and burst into tears. In his thirty years of service he had witnessed many executions but never had he seen anyone mount the gallows as courageously as Bhagat Singh and his two comrades. The lives of three of the nation's finest and bravest young men had been brutally cut short by the British imperialists.

Little did anyone realize then that the saga of their bravery would write the epitaph of British rule. On 15 August, 1947, some sixteen years after Bhagat Singh, Sukhdev and Rajguru laid down their lives, the last English soldier left Indian shores for ever.

As Bhagat Singh had predicted, the cause would triumph one day. So what if he and his comrades had to die in the process to keep the torch of freedom burning?

It was a sacrifice on the altar of independence.

2

Kucchh arzoo nahin hai, hai arzoo to yeh
Rakhde koi zarasi khak-e-watan kafan mein

ASHFHAQULLA KHAN

IN THE FIRST DECADE OF THE TWENTIETH CENTURY A revolutionary fire had spread all over the country. People were determined to wrest freedom from the British. The Punjab had many leaders who had joined the struggle. Two such leaders were Sardar Ajit Singh and Sardar Kishen Singh, Bhagat Singh's paternal uncle and father. Both of them were members of the Ghadar party founded in the US in the early twentieth century to oust British rule in India. Both were jailed for alleged anti-British activities. Ajit Singh had twenty-two cases against him and was forced to flee to Iran. Thereafter he went to Turkey, Austria, Germany and finally to Brazil to escape Black Water (Kalapani) punishment – which was where practically every freedom fighter ended up. This was a high-walled jail in an island in the middle of the sea. (The African leader Nelson Mandela was confined in a similar jail near Cape Town but the jail could be seen from the city.) The jail in the Andamans was deep in the sea, making escape well-nigh impossible.

Interestingly, although middle-class and leading lives of comfort and plenty, both brothers were opposed to the mainstream leadership of the Indian National Congress and particularly persons like Lala Lajpat Rai. Both brothers were consistently radical in attempting to mobilize the masses to oppose the British at every opportunity that arose.

Bhagat Singh's birth, on 28 September, 1907, coincided with the release of his father Kishen Singh and his uncle Swaran Singh from jail. There was also the news that Ajit Singh would be freed. As he brought good fortune to his family, the child was named Bhaganlal ('bhag' means the future). The young Bhagat began his primary education at the District Board Primary School in Banga. In 1916-17, his father moved to Lahore to be able to organize relief work for the victims of a severe earthquake in Kangra. Bhagat Singh was now shifted to the DAV High School, Lahore. Writing about these years, Bhagat Singh said that it was his father's teachings that inspired him to devote his life to the cause of freedom.

In 1923, Bhagat Singh joined the National College, Lahore, which was affiliated to the Punjab Quami Vidya Pith and was founded and managed by Lala Lajpat Rai and Bhai Parmanand. The college was set up to provide an alternative to the institutions run by the government, bringing the idea of swadeshi to the field of education. The philosophy behind the establishment of this college was to produce self-reliant and progressive men and women that new India needed.

Bhagat Singh had an impressive academic record in college. The principal of the college, Chhabil Das, recalled in his memoirs that as there were no books available the teachers selected books from the libraries and gave the relevant portions to the students to read. The talk was about Mazzini and Garibaldi and about the Russian Revolution. Bhagat Singh was also a member of the College Dramatics Society and was prominent amongst the students and teachers, not only of his own college but of other local colleges. 'He was particularly impressive because of his youthful physique and commanding voice,' one of his biographers, S.R. Bakshi tells us (*Bhagat Singh and his Ideology,* 1981). Bhagat Singh was fluent in Urdu, Hindi, Gurmukhi, English and Sanskrit. In his pamphlet, 'Why I Am an Atheist' Bhagat Singh wrote about his days in college:

Though a favourite with some professors and disliked by certain others, I was never an industrious or studious boy. I could not get any chance of indulging in such feelings as vanity. I was rather a boy with a shy nature, who had certain pessimistic dispositions about (my) future career.

By the age of sixteen, Bhagat Singh was completely dedicated to the cause of national liberation. Nothing illustrates this better than his attitude to marriage. In 1924, Bhagat Singh was being pushed by his father to get married. Unable to convince his parents of his determination not to marry, Bhagat Singh left his house in Lahore and reached Kanpur armed with an introduction from Jai Chandra Vidyalankar for Ganesh Shankar Vidyarthi. In the note left behind for his father Bhagat Singh wrote,

My life has been dedicated to the noblest cause, that of the freedom of the country. Therefore there is no rest or worldly desire that can lure me now. If you remember, when I was small, Bapuji (Arjun Singh) declared at my thread ceremony that I had been dedicated to the service of my country. I am, thus waiting to fulfil that commitment. I hope you will forgive me.

On being asked why he did not want to get married, Bhagat Singh told Jaidev Gupta, his classmate and friend, that he had chosen a path which was full of many adversities. Two of his uncles had gone that way and both had left behind widows. Should he leave behind a widow too? Chhabil Das has left us an account of how, when he was to get married, Bhagat Singh admonished him about it. Das said, 'If I could get a really good life companion who, instead of retarding my activities, would invigorate them, what would be your view?' In the same breath he quoted the example of Mrs Sun Yat Sen, the wife of Lenin and the companion of Karl Marx. At this Bhagat Singh replied, 'Guruji, who can vanquish you in any argument?'

From 1923–24, Bhagat Singh worked with Ganesh Shankar Vidyarthi, a great Hindu who died upholding the cause of secularism. Vidyarthi brought out a weekly nationalist newspaper called the *Pratap* in Kanpur. Bhagat Singh worked under the alias, Balwant. It was while living here that he met people like Batukeshwar (B.K.) Dutt, Shiv Verma and B.K. Sinha with whom he would share a close camaraderie in the years to come. Ajoy Ghosh (*Bhagat Singh and His Comrades,* 1945) who was fifteen at the time wrote about his first meeting with Bhagat Singh thus:

> I believe it was sometime in 1923 that I met Bhagat Singh… he was introduced to me by B.K. Dutt in Cawnpore. Tall and thin, rather shabbily dressed, very quiet, he seemed a typical village lad lacking smartness and self-confidence. I did not think very highly of him and told Dutt so when he was gone…

1924 was a seminal year in Bhagat Singh's life. In Kanpur he became a member of the Hindustan Republican Association (HRA), started by Sachindranath Sanyal a year earlier. Chandra Shekhar Azad was the main organizer of the HRA and Bhagat Singh became very close to him. It was as a member of the HRA that Bhagat Singh first began to take the philosophy of the bomb seriously. Armed revolution was understood to be the only weapon with which to fight British imperialism. Bhagat Singh went from village to village recruiting people to activate the villagers in the United Provinces.

In 1925, Bhagat Singh returned to Lahore after his father's letter of apology, and within the next year he and his colleagues started a militant youth organization called the Naujawan Bharat

Sabha. In April, 1926, Bhagat Singh established contact with Sohan Singh Josh and through him the Workers and Peasants' Party which brought out the monthly magazine *Kirti* in Punjabi. For the next year Bhagat Singh worked with Josh and joined the editorial board of *Kirti*. In 1927, he was first arrested on charges of association with the Kakori Case accused, for an article written under the pseudonym Vidrohi (rebel). He was also accused of being responsible for a bomb explosion at Lahore during the Dussehra fair. He was let off for good behaviour against a heavy security of Rs 60,000, which was later waivered.

In 1928, Bhagat Singh and Chandra Shekhar Azad were the sole absconders of the Kakori Case and the other leaders being put behind bars meant that they were the leaders of the Hindustan Republican Association. Ajoy Ghosh remembers:

One day in 1928 I was surprised when a young man walked into my room and greeted me. It was Bhagat Singh but not the Bhagat Singh that I had met before. Tall and magnificently proportioned, with a keen, intelligent face and gleaming eyes, he looked a different man altogether. And as he talked I realized that he had grown not merely in years… All those who met Bhagat Singh then and afterwards have testified to his remarkable intelligence and to the powerful impression he made when talking. Not that he was a brilliant speaker. But he spoke with such force, passion and earnestness that one could not help being impressed. We talked the whole night and as we went out for a stroll… it seemed to me that a new era was dawning for our party. We knew what we wanted and we knew how to reach our goal.

It was 3 October, 1928. Some 5,000 protestors had gathered near the Lahore railway station, demonstrating against a seven-man

Commission led by Sir John Allsbrook Simon. The members of the Commission had arrived from London via Bombay. The task assigned to them was to assess whether and how far India was 'ready for further Constitutional reforms'. It was a statutory obligation that the British had to fulfil every ten years under the Indian Council Act, 1919, known as the Montague-Chelmsford Reforms. The intent was to 'help' India move towards 'self-rule' – whatever that meant.

Mohandas Karamchand Gandhi was not a revolutionary of the Bhagat Singh school. He did not speak the language of fire and brimstone. Nor was he willing to rub the British the wrong way. His was a cooperative approach. He had his own plan of action, to achieve things peacefully without the use of violence either in method or words. Non-violence was the most deadly weapon he had against oppression and brutality and it vanquished the opponent because he promoted it by his own example: to suffer, not to retaliate.

Gandhi was conscious of the limitations of the Congress. Still he believed the British would offer Dominion Status and he was confident that he could bring the Congress around to accepting it, although the party had threatened to go all out for independence if Dominion Status was not granted by 31 December, 1929. But the Commission's appointment was an anti-climax. It meant, Gandhi began to feel, that the British were not serious about giving India any substantial powers. They were only playing with the sentiments of the Indian people.

Gandhi had gone to the farthest limits to cooperate with the British in the step-by-step approach involved in the transfer of power. He felt so let-down that he persuaded the Congress, which looked to him for guidance, to pass a resolution declaring that the only self-respecting course of action for India to adopt was to boycott the Commission at every stage and in every form.

The Congress was his instrument. When founded in 1885 by a Briton, Allan Octavian Hume, the party was Her Majesty's loyal organization. In the earlier years, the party awaited favours from the rulers like crumbs from the dining table of the rich. The Congress was just a tool in the hands of the British, used to manipulate Indian public opinion. The British directed it from behind the scenes. For the Indian elite, the Congress was a club through which they kept contact with those who mattered in the establishment.

Whenever London thought of bestowing the natives with power at some tier of governance, it first sought out the Congress. The elite knew this and flocked to the Congress. The British found the party handy and obedient. But with the passage of time, Congress too had been awakened by liberal ideology. Self-rule whetted the appetite for more self-rule. The Congress showed signs of 'impudence'. But it was still under the influence of the British.

After Bal Gangadhar Tilak, who famously declared 'freedom is my birthright', it was Gandhi who had infused life – and rebellion – into the body politic of India. After his return from South Africa – where he had won several non-violent battles for the rights of Indians settled there – he found the Congress the best platform to experiment with his ideas. The radicals did not accept his philosophy. To them he was a visionary but not a person who could make the British afraid. Yet they had to reckon with his leadership because he had charisma. The teeming millions of India followed him.

The greatest defect in radical socialists, according to Gandhi's next-in-command, Jawaharlal Nehru, was their contempt for what might be called the moral and spiritual side of life. Their philosophy not only ignored something basic in man, but also deprived human behaviour of standards and values. Ethical aspects, he said, 'are ultimately basic to culture and civilization' and give meaning to life. Nehru strongly believed Gandhi's dictum that 'wrong means will not lead to right results'.

The revolutionaries knew that their thinking did not coincide with that of Gandhi's. The experience of a centuries-long and worldwide struggle between the masses and the governing class was the guide to their goal, and the methods they were following 'had never been known to have failed'. Before them the French Revolution had successfully proclaimed the ideas of liberty, fraternity and equality, while the Bolshevik Revolution had introduced the ideas of socialism.

Bhagat Singh and his comrades did not support Dominion Status. Their demand was for full independence. Still, they decided to respond to Gandhi's call to boycott the Simon Commission. As revolutionaries, they believed that any move to stir the people was a step in the right direction. Such a step, however small, would make the nation conscious of the shackles it wore. Action, pro-active and decisive action, was required.

That day, as soon as the Commission members stepped out of the railway station porch, the crowd surged forward. This was the first time that the protestors raised the slogan 'Inquilab Zindabad!' Bhagat Singh had coined the phrase to give the freedom struggle a new edge, a new meaning, that of revolt, of defiance. The crowd shouted: 'Simon Commission go back!' and 'Angrez Murdabad!' (Down with the British). They chanted:

Hindustani hain hum, Hindustan hamara,
Mur jao, Simon, jahan hai desh tumhara.

(We are Indians and India is ours\ Go back, Simon, to the country to which you belong).

Bhagat Singh had joined issue with Lala Lajpat Rai more than once. He disagreed with his chauvinistic Hindu stance. Lajpat

Rai, in turn, had denounced him as a 'Russian agent'; he regarded the revolutionaries as 'irresponsible young men'. Lajpat Rai had authored the idea that India should be divided into two countries: Hindu India and Muslim India. Bhagat Singh could not even contemplate such a partition. Hindus and Muslims had lived side by side in thousands of towns, villages and hamlets for hundreds of years. They shared each other's sorrow and happiness, heritage and history. They toiled together and suffered together. The country belonged to both the communities. When free of the British, they would shape the country's political and economic destiny together, equal participants in the task of nation-building. Bhagat Singh, for one, had many Muslim comrades. Just because the Muslims followed a different religion it did not make them different. They ate the same food, wore the same clothes, spoke the same language and reacted in the same manner. They were not aliens. They were the warp and woof of the fabric that constituted the Indian nation. Why should they give up what was their patrimony and content themselves with a fragment of it? How could religion separate them from the Hindus? Bhagat Singh feared that if Lajpat Rai's idea of a division of the country along religious lines ever took shape, it would be disastrous. There would be a bloodbath. Hindu and Muslim countries would be perpetually at war. All their attention and resources would be diverted towards acquiring weapons to fight one another.

Religion, Bhagat Singh felt, was the prop of a man who had not yet found himself. Yet Bhagat Singh had an abiding respect for Lajpat Rai. Whatever his limitations, he was a great man. Lalaji's life-long fight against the British was a sterling example for the country. He had even been banished to Burma for his anti-British activities. His sacrifices and his defiance of the rulers had blazed a path for the youth of the land. Bhagat Singh was opposed to

Lajpat Rai's parochialism but he truly respected Lalaji's patriotism and devotion to India.

That is why on 30 October, 1928, the day the Simon Commission arrived in Lahore, Bhagat Singh rallied behind Lajpat Rai. When the members of the Commission tried to walk on ahead past the crowd, it blocked them, standing strong as a wall, preventing them from moving forward. A large contingent of policemen tried to push the people back to clear the way but they did not budge. Lajpat Rai, in an impromptu speech, said: 'If the government did not wish the Commission to see the demonstrators, the best thing for it to do was to put blindfolds over the eyes of members and take them straight to the government house.'

Superintendent of police J.A. Scott ordered a lathi-charge. The crowd ran helter-skelter. Some fell by the roadside, some braved the lathi-blows and some were arrested. Lajpat Rai exhorted his supporters to hold their positions like true satyagrahis (truth warriors). Many who had run away returned. They were his flock and he their shepherd. Scott spotted Lajpat Rai from a distance and went for him. The policeman used his baton to beat the Indian leader mercilessly and did not stop hitting the venerable leader till Lalaji fell down bleeding profusely. It was as if Scott was venting an anger and frustration pent up against all those Indians who had dared defy the British. He wanted to teach the natives a lesson, to spell out the fate of all those who challenged the authority of the British.

Only nine years earlier, Brigadier-General Reginald Dyer, an Irishman born in Shimla, had wreaked his vengeance upon the people of Amritsar for heckling a British woman in one of the city's bazaars. He too had been motivated by the desire to set an example, a deterrent, to impress upon the Indians the extent to which the raj could go, to make them fall in line. Dyer, who was given control of Amritsar by the lieutenant-governor of Punjab, Michael O'Dwyer, chose 13 April, 1919, the day of the Punjab harvest festival Baisakhi, to exact revenge. To voice their protest against the Rowlatt Act – which gave the rulers the power to detain anyone without trial – some 20,000 people had gathered in a garden called Jallianwala Bagh, a stone's throw from the Golden Temple.

Dyer had set the police on the gathering like a hunter unchaining his ferocious hounds to bring the pursued animals to bay. He blocked the garden's only exit to prevent anyone escaping from the place. Targeted by machine-guns, men, women and children had no escape or respite from the bullets. They were shot at till the police exhausted its stock of ammunition. As many as 1,650 rounds were fired. Scores of people tried to escape the bullets by jumping into the garden's only well, mute witnesses to this barbarous massacre. Some 400 people died on the spot and more than 1,500 were injured.

When it learned of the incident, London too was horrified by the barbarity of this act. It recalled Dyer who, appearing before an inquiry committee, said that he had only done his duty. He expressed no regret. Nor was he admonished. Some in the British political hierarchy declared he had saved Punjab from 'anarchy'.

Bhagat Singh was then twelve years old; his mind was deeply disturbed by this event. The day after the massacre Bhagat Singh did not return home after school. His family waited and grew anxious. That day, instead of going to school, Bhagat Singh had gone straight to Jallianwala Bagh. Somehow managing to push through the sentries on guard, he had barged into the garden and collected a jar full of mud, wet with the blood of Indians. When he finally returned home his younger sister said, 'Where were you all this time? Mother has been waiting to give you something to eat.' But Bhagat Singh was not thinking of food. Showing her the jar he said, 'Look at this. This is the blood of our people killed by the British. Salute it.' Then he put the jar in a niche and worshipped it with flowers.

Lajpat Rai fell to the ground bleeding profusely. Before he lost consciousness, he shouted: 'Every blow that was hurled at us this afternoon was a nail in the coffin of the British Empire.' How prophetic his words proved to be – Britain's rule over India ended eighteen years later, on 15 August, 1947. Lajpat Rai had warned: 'I wish to warn the government that if a violent revolution takes place in this country, the responsibility for bringing it about will fall on such officers as misbehaved themselves today.'

Seeing Lajpat Rai fall, a wave of horror and indignation swept through the crowd. Nobody could imagine that the British would single out a person of his stature and beat him like a petty criminal. Bhagat Singh was appalled. He could not believe that a gora (white man) could dare take a stick in hand and set upon Lajpat Rai. As news of the attack on Lajpat Rai spread, the country reacted with anger. Gandhi said: 'What I would like the workers to draw from this incident is not to be depressed or taken aback by assault, but to treat it as part of the game. We have to turn the irritation caused by the unwarranted assault into dynamic energy and translate it for future purposes.' Nehru asked the British to take concrete steps to atone for the insult to the nation. He described the savage treatment meted out to Lajpat Rai as a national humiliation.

How helpless the Indians were. They could not even protect the honour of their revered leaders. The Lajpat Rai incident was probably the much-needed spark to ignite the spirit of rebellion. The nation was transformed from a spectator to a participant. The Congress, and for that matter, even Gandhi, found more support from the people. It made the nation more indignant than ever before.

Not far from the railway station ground, where Lajpat Rai was assaulted, was the river Ravi. Jawaharlal Nehru would unfurl the tricolour, the Congress party flag, by the river bank on 26 January, 1930, to unambiguously declare that India would not accept anything less than full independence (Purna Swaraj). By then, Gandhi too, on his own, would have come to the conclusion that the British would not transfer any meaningful power to India. The anger that Bhagat Singh had felt after visiting Jallianwala Bagh welled up again when he saw Lajpat Rai on the ground. Dyer had managed to get away with his barbarous deed, but Scott must not. Bhagat Singh was determined to avenge the attack on Lajpat Rai and make Scott pay for the insults he had heaped on the Indians. But first he wanted to discuss with his comrades the punishment they would mete out to the cruel rulers. His comrades and he had a retreat at Mozang Road in Lahore. It was a nondescript, rented building, close to a burial ground, away from the gaze of the police and the public. They met there practically every day. This time they had to think of taking action; not just issuing a statement or passing a resolution.

Hari Shivaram Rajguru and Sukhdev Thapar, two senior members of the Hindustan Socialist Republican Association (HSRA) were heatedly discussing Scott's arrogance when Bhagat Singh burst in. News of the brutal lathi-charge and the injuries inflicted on Lajpat Rai had spread everywhere. Bhagat Singh narrated the entire incident to them again and expressed fear that the 'Lion of Punjab', as Lajpat Rai was known, might not live long. All three of them were fired with determination to avenge the attack. One suggestion was to involve the police in a pitched battle, much like Jatindra Nath Mukherjee, a revolutionary from Bengal and his four comrades had done.

This incident had occured during the First World War when Jatindra Nath, along with four other young revolutionaries, was taking delivery of arms from the German cruiser *Emden* on the east Indian coast. None of them knew that armed policemen had been following them. When they learnt of it, they confronted the force in Balasore, Orissa. A gunfight ensued, lasting seventy-five minutes, between the five revolutionaries armed with Mauser pistols and a large number of police and army-men armed with modern rifles. It ended with an unrecorded number of casualties on the government side. On the revolutionary side, Chittapriya Ray Chaudhuri died, Jatin and Jatish were seriously wounded, and Manoranjan Sengupta and Niren were captured after their ammunition ran out. Bagha Jatin died, killed by police bullets, in Balasore hospital on 10 September, 1915.

Bhagat Singh said that a pitched battle with the police was no revenge against Scott. 'Blood for blood' was the message they wanted to convey to London. Ten Englishmen would pay with their lives for every Hindustani they killed.

The formal decision was deferred till the meeting of the HSRA. Chandra Shekhar Azad, the head of its armed unit, who was still underground after the Kakori train case, was sent an urgent message to return to Lahore.

Lajpat Rai died on 17 November, 1928. Before dying, he warned the British that if incidents like the one at Lahore continued to happen, 'I would not wonder if the young men go out of hand and do whatever they choose with the object of gaining the freedom of their country'. Indeed, they were already losing faith in Gandhi's methods, which they felt were as naive and nebulous as 'midsummer's night dreams'.

The revolutionaries were in an ugly mood when they met on the night of 10 December, 1928. Durga Devi, affectionately called Durga Bhabi, presided over the meeting. As the wife of the party's ideologue and the author of the HSRA's manifesto, Bhagwati Charan Vohra, she enjoyed great respect among the revolutionaries.

She was also a respected revolutionary in her own right. She had once been to prison for three years in a shooting case.

At the meeting it was unanimously decided to kill Scott. He was responsible for Lajpat Rai's death, he must pay the price with his life. The revolutionaries had several things in mind. They wanted to spread the message that they would not hesitate to use violence when it became necessary. Their task was to awaken the young from the drudgery of slavery and to participate in the revolutionary struggle against foreign domination and economic exploitation. Their goal was not only to oust the British but also to end economic thuggery.

Bhagat Singh and his associates wanted the world to know that India would not accept Lajpat Rai's death lying down. Rajguru reiterated his earlier proposal of challenging the police and to die fighting. Such a heroic, daredevil act would fire the imagination of the youth and swell their numbers in the HSRA, he felt. The proposal was vigorously rejected because the purpose was to target Lajpat Rai's killer.

Reviewing the situation in the country, Bhagat Singh said that an all-pervasive sense of tension prevailed. The Bengal party had done a commendable job. It had killed some British officials, forcing many terror-stricken Englishmen to send their families back to England. 'The blood of the young men is boiling,' he said.

Durga Devi first asked for volunteers to kill Scott and then raised her own hand. While they recognized her commitment to the revolution – she had stood by them through thick and thin – they could not think of exposing her to risk. Nobody was willing to involve her. It was not male chauvinism. She was their bhabhi, the wife of their revered comrade who had gone to Calcutta to attend the All India Congress Committee session. Reluctantly, she put her hand down and asked for volunteers.

Bhagat Singh, Sukhdev, Rajguru and Chandra Shekhar Azad, as well as nearly all the rest present, raised their hands. Sukhdev was their strategist, it was he who provided them with ideas. Sukhdev wanted the assignment for himself but he was ruled out because he was too important; he was the mastermind behind the network that brought together revolutionaries in different parts of the country, particularly the Punjab. He accepted, however, the role of arbiter. He then chose four comrades from among those present: Bhagat Singh, Rajguru, Chandra Shekhar Azad, and Jai Gopal.

Chalking out the operation Sukhdev said that Bhagat Singh would be the one to kill Scott; he was confident that the task would be executed once it was entrusted to him. As soon as Bhagat Singh's name was announced, there were whispers in the room – some among them suspected that Sukhdev wanted to get rid of Bhagat Singh because of his growing popularity; shooting Scott was difficult, but escaping from the police dragnet was impossible. Sukhdev behaved as if he had not heard the whispers. He spelled out the rest of his plan. Rajguru was to stand near Bhagat Singh to give him cover. Azad was to arrange their escape. Jai Gopal, a relatively junior comrade, had a simple errand – to let the three know when Scott arrived at the police station. His car number was 6728; Jai Gopal was asked to memorize the number. 17 December, 1928 was fixed as the date for Scott's assassination.

Two days prior to the date fixed to carry out the attack, on 15 December, the four men met to rehearse their respective assignments. By this time, each one was familiar with the role he had to play. Bhagat Singh had even decided the exact spot from where he would shoot. Azad explained to Bhagat Singh and Rajguru how they would run to the nearby DAV school to escape. Bhagat Singh prepared a red-lettered poster: SCOTT KILLED. Little did he realize then that one day his handwritten poster would be used as evidence against him in the Lahore

Conspiracy Case. Nor did he suspect that Hans Raj Vohra, a quiet and committed young member of the HSRA, who prepared four copies of the poster, would one day turn government approver.

Bhagat Singh was very particular about bringing in the name of the armed wing of the HSRA in whatever action they undertook. Without an armed revolution it would be impossible to push the British out. He said that the notice they issued after Scott's murder would carry the name of the HSRA army. 'Our party has a strong military wing,' he would proudly say. He wanted the armed wing to be a recognizable force in the minds of the youth so that they would put faith in it as the body which would one day challenge the British army and smash the exploitative imperial system.

For his mission with the HSRA, Bhagat Singh had cut his hair and shaved off his beard. This was the party's order to its members in order to defy detection by the police. The decision was taken at the Ferozeshah Kotla meeting when the different units decided to merge with the HSRA. He went to Ferozepur in the middle of September, 1928 and hired a medical practitioner to cut his hair. (Jai Gopal, who also turned approver, was with him when he cut his hair, and spoke of this in the trial as proof of Bhagat Singh's involvement in Saunders' death.)

Jai Gopal had been deputed to identify Scott. But he had never seen the Englishman before. Strangely, Jai Gopal did not tell this to anybody. It was such a prestigious assignment for him that he did not want to lose it. That he made a mess of it was another matter.

On 17 December, 1928, Scott did not come to the police station. He had taken the day off to receive his mother-in-law who was arriving from England. Jai Gopal mistook assistant superintendent of police J.P. Saunders for Scott and informed Azad, Bhagat Singh and Rajguru about his arrival at the police station at 10 a.m. A few hours later, the three of them took their positions outside the police station and waited for Scott to emerge.

In the afternoon, when Saunders came out of the police station and was about to climb on to his motorcycle, Rajguru shot him dead with one bullet from his German Mauser pistol. Bhagat Singh shouted: 'No, no, he is not the man!' but it was too late. By then Rajguru, excellent shot that he was, had killed him. One bullet had done the job. Bhagat Singh too pumped some bullets into the dead body. Then, as planned, Bhagat Singh and Rajguru ran towards DAV College, a few yards away from the police station.

Azad had positioned himself to give them cover. A British officer, Inspector W.J.C. Fern, emerged from the police station on hearing the commotion. But he quickly retraced his steps when two bullets, shot by Azad, whizzed past his head. Head Constable Chanan Singh, who heard the shots, ran out to help Saunders. He was the only one who chased Bhagat Singh, Rajguru and Azad as they ran from the spot where Saunders lay dead. 'No, we do not want to kill an Indian,' Azad shouted to him, trying to get him to back off but Chanan Singh did not stop. Rajguru shot him dead. Many people watched the scene from the windows of nearby buildings. The revolutionary Urdu poet, Faiz Ahmad Faiz, was among them.

The three revolutionaries entered the compound of DAV College and scaled the wall that separated the college from the hostel. They stopped for a while at the hostel and then, finding that no one was pursuing them, they walked out at a normal pace. They picked up their bicycles, which Azad had placed against the hostel toilet wall, looked around in all directions to make sure that they were not being followed, and then pedalled leisurely to their retreat, the Mozang Road house.

A police party appeared long after they had left. The boarding house was surrounded. A roll call of residents was taken. Every room was searched. The police also ransacked the college. But it found no trace of the culprits. The Punjab government informed the home department: 'Saunders, Assistant Superinendent Police, was shot down and killed this afternoon by two youths who escaped into the DAV College and then into the country on bicycles...'

By the time the authorities learned of Saunders' murder, all the three revolutionaries were sitting safely in the Mozang Road house and comparing notes. After informing them that Scott had reached the police station, Jai Gopal had gone home. They could not even tell him that his mistake had led to the murder of Saunders instead of Scott.

Practically every policeman in Lahore was put on duty to find the killers. All roads and railway exits from the city were heavily guarded. The authorities suspected the hand of the revolutionaries. But they could not nail any of the culprits nor even figure out how and where they had vanished.

The news of Saunders' death spread in no time. Posters appeared at several places in Lahore. The most prominent was the one on which Bhagat Singh hurriedly printed Saunders' name over that of Scott. The poster read:

HINDUSTAN SOCIALIST REPUBLICAN ARMY

NOTICE

J.P. Saunders is dead; Lala Lajpat Rai is avenged

Really it is horrible to imagine that so lowly and violent hand of an ordinary police official, J.P. Saunders, could ever dare to touch in such an insulting way the body of one so old, so revered and so loved by 300 million people of Hindustan and thus cause his death. The youth and manhood of India was challenged by blows hurled down on the head of India's nationhood. And let the world know that India still lives; that the blood of youths has not been totally cooled down and that they can still risk their lives, if the honour of their nation is at stake. And it is proved through this act by those obscure who are ever persecuted, condemned and denounced even by their own people.

Beware, Ye Tyrants, Beware!

Do not injure the feelings of a downtrodden and oppressed country. Think twice before perpetrating such diabolical deeds. And remember that despite the 'Arms Act' and strict guards against the smuggling of arms, the revolvers will ever continue to flow in-if not sufficient at present for an armed revolt, then at least sufficient to avenge the national insults. In spite of all the denunciations and condemnation of their own kith and kin, and ruthless repression and persecution of the alien government, the party of young men will ever live to teach a lesson to the haughty rulers. They will be so bold as to cry even amidst the raging storm of opposition and repression, even on the scaffold.

Long Live the Revolution!

Sorry for the death of a man. But in this man has died the representative of an institution which is so cruel, lowly and so base that it must be abolished. In this man has died an agent of the British authority in India-the most tyrannical of government of governments in the world.

Sorry for the bloodshed of a human being; but the sacrifice of individuals at the altar of the Revolution that will bring freedom to all and make the exploitation of man by man impossible, is inevitable.'

Long Live the Revolution!
Dated 18th December, 1928
Sd/-Balraj
Commander-in-Chief.

Hiding in the Mozang Road house, Bhagat Singh, Azad and Rajguru considered their options of escape from Lahore – which they imagined would be swarming with police. They thought they would lie low for some time before surfacing again. After all, the only person who had seen them was Head Constable Chanan Singh and he was dead too. There was no witness to identify them.

Still they were uneasy. The police was sure to tighten its dragnet soon and it was only a matter of time before they would be caught. Bhagat Singh's hunch was that the police would already be combing the city for the revolutionaries and knocking on the doors of sympathizers. Too many of them were scattered across too many places. Someone somewhere might spill the beans and tell the police all about them and their hideout. They could not afford to put others in jeopardy. They had to quit the city immediately.

Strangely, they had planned the killing meticulously but had paid little attention to their escape from Lahore. It spoke well of their bravery but not of their strategy. They had no clue about what to do next. But they were reassured when Sukhdev stepped in. He was conscious of their predicament and told them how to effect their escape. He advised them to go to Durga Devi's house and then to leave from there at the first opportunity. However her house was under police surveillance from 11 p.m. to 5 a.m. Till then, they had to wait at the Mozang Road house.

Bhagat Singh felt confident enough, later the same day, to run up to the main post office to find a friend or sympathizer who would give him some cash. As he walked through the crowd he saw Sohan Singh Josh, an old comrade. Josh commended the job they had done and warned Bhagat Singh not to visit any public place for some days. But he had no money to give him.

It was still dark when he, Rajguru and Chandra Shekhar Azad used the wheat fields behind Mozang Road as cover to go to Durga Devi's house early the next morning. It was numbingly cold. Frost covered the fields, making them appear like a white sheet. And it was so quiet they could hear the sound of their own footsteps, trampling the newly sprung crop. The countryside was beginning to wake to the jingling of cattle-bells, the gurgling of water from Persian wells and the squeaking of poorly-oiled wooden carts. Some farmers were already in their fields, a few pouring water on their bodies and a few at the plough.

The sight of green fields always inspired Bhagat Singh. They reminded him of his roots, his rural background, the land he owned. He thought of the time when wheat and other agricultural produce came to their home. His mother was generous to those who toiled on their land. He had suggested to his father more than once to give the land to those who ploughed it. This always infuriated his father but Bhagat Singh stuck to his belief that the land belonged to those who tilled and tended it.

A little after five in the morning, when the police departed from outside Durga Devi's house, Bhagat Singh and his two comrades knocked at her door. It was too early for visitors. She was a little apprehensive and hesitated before unbolting the door. To her surprise, Bhagat Singh stood before her. He stepped in and Rajguru and Azad followed. She congratulated them on a job well done. They told her that they had mistakenly killed

Saunders instead of Scott, but she already knew. It in no way minimized their act of courage, she said.

Bhagat Singh told her that Sukhdev had suggested they escape from Lahore that very day. When they revealed their plan to travel by train to Calcutta, where her husband had gone to attend the All India Congress Committee's annual session, she wondered whether they would be able to travel by train without being recognized. They too had their doubts, expecting that the police would be out in full strength at the station but then there was no option. Sukhdev had suggested that the Dehra Dun Express was their best bet because it left for Calcutta early in the morning. There was no time to lose. Sukhdev had worked out the details: Bhagat Singh would act as Durga Devi's husband. Durga Devi was to travel under the alias 'Sujata' while Bhagat Singh would travel under the alias 'Ranjit'. Her three-year old son, Sachin, would be their child. Rajguru would act as their servant. But they had no money. Durga Devi promptly brought out 500 rupees that Bhagwati Charan had left with her for household expenses.

Meanwhile, Azad had made separate plans and slipped out of the house on his own. He joined a party of pilgrims going to Mathura to offer prayers at Lord Krishna's temple. Dressed like them, singing bhajans, he effortlessly sailed past a group of policemen who did not even care to stop them and check their identities.

Lahore railway station was like a fortress, swarming with police. A couple, the husband dressed in European clothes and the wife in an expensive sari, clicking along in her heels, walked confidently up to the first class compartment. They were trailed by a servant carrying a child. There was such an authority about the party that the police did not dare accost them. Dressed as a government official, in Bhagwati Charan's overcoat and a felt hat that a visitor had forgotten at Durga Devi's house some months ago, Bhagat

Singh played his role with elan. All their boxes were neatly labelled, as was the practice among government officials. Bhagat Singh was sure that no one had yet connected him or Rajguru with the killing of Saunders. He was right. He and his comrades were not suspects, though there was a strong suspicion in the government that Saunders' death was the handiwork of the revolutionaries. But there was no real evidence to corroborate their participation. Posters by the HSRA army confirmed the hand of the revolutionaries. But that was all.

All first class passengers had to disclose their names before they boarded the train. Bhagat Singh had bought the tickets earlier and simply waved these at the official checking the tickets. As his party approached the compartment the policeman standing outside whispered, 'They are sahibs. A high government official travelling with his family.' After that they settled into their seats and the Dehra Dun Express chugged out of Lahore slowly, under the very noses of the white officials who lingered on the platform, waving their handkerchiefs at their wives and children. They had not aroused even an iota of suspicion. For a short time they were tense, but as the train speeded up, they felt more relaxed. They had managed to elude the police, after all.

As Bhagat Singh looked out of the window at the countryside speeding by he felt one with the spirit of India, a land of struggle and sacrifice, of suffering and subjugation, where people had defended their identity, their being, from countless invaders over the centuries. Raiders came and retreated. Empires were built and destroyed. Dynasties had risen and fallen. India had been conquered and re-conquered, destroyed and disfigured. But it had remained alive. Foreign regimes were like a gale that passed over its head, seldom disturbing the country's rhythm of life, moral codes and traditional values. Kings and kingdoms had never been able to intrude upon the people's privacy, their values or their innate dignity.

Time was a mute witness to the spell that India cast on all those foreigners who came to subjugate it but who eventually made it their home. During the Slave dynasty and during the rule of the Mughals, all were absorbed in a composite society, as the Buddhists and the Jains had been centuries earlier. Over the years, the rulers and the ruled had become a part and parcel of the same tapestry, drawing strength from the different threads that were interwoven into the fabric of the country, resulting in a texture that reflected diverse shades in a smooth and sturdy fashion. What held people together was not religion, race or language but a certain way of life that reflected one's diversity and individuality at the same time. It was a shared experience of involvement and the spirit of tolerance and accommodation.

And as the Ganga had taken into her lap a multitude of streams, whether stormy, placid or dirty, so too had India assimilated the strange and the strong from several lands. Both the river and the country were not defiled, and remained pure. There was music and dance, but also the clash of swords and the exchange of gunfire. Despite this, what filled the atmosphere was a gentle harmony and serenity. To Bhagat Singh's regret, patience made the Indian people accept even their poverty with noble resignation. They attributed their plight to kismet (fate). He blamed Gandhi for encouraging such a sense of resignation among the people, and reinforcing acceptance – the pre-eminent message of the Gita.

Even though they knew they were not being followed, Durga Devi suggested they break journey at Kanpur. They stayed at a hotel near the station. Durga Devi sent a telegram to her husband, informing him of her arrival, accompanied by her brother. The message was meant to convey Bhagat Singh's arrival, because she had no brother. The next morning, they boarded a train for Calcutta.

So far, Bhagat Singh had exchanged just a few words with Durga Devi. He had been preoccupied with the events of the last few days. Now, suddenly, he found himself telling her everything about himself – especially how he had taken the road to revolution. He spoke of his years in the National College in Lahore, founded by some nationalist Punjabis who wished to spread the message of nationalism among the youth of the province. Bhimsen Sachar, who later became the chief minister of Punjab, was the Registrar. The revolutionary-minded Chhabil Das was the principal who lectured the students on patriotism. His favourite quatrain was:

Duniya se ghulami ka mein nam mita dunga
Ik bar zamane ko mein azad kara dunga
Jo log gharibon par kartein hain sitam nahaq
Gar dam hai mera kayam gin gin ke saza dunga

(I shall obliterate the very name of slavery from the world/ One day I will free the universe/ I shall single out and punish while I live all who heap cruelties on the poor.)

Bhagat Singh admitted to Durga Devi that he personally deplored the outrages that accompanied revolutionary violence. But the British were so harsh on them and so cruel that he felt the revolutionaries' aggression was neglible in comparison. The ouster of the British by the revolution was necessary to change the fate of the country. He told her that Sachindranath Sanyal, a Bengali revolutionary, his contemporary at National College, had warned him that he would imbibe the true spirit of revolution only when he left home. Yashpal, a fiery Hindi writer, also at National College, told him that as long as men led purely private lives with their families they would be held prisoner to natural impulses. They could never really be free. The need of the hour was to think of society, in fact of all mankind, as a whole. They must go out into the world and play their role on the stage of history.

Durga Devi knew Sukhdev only as a cold strategist. She wanted to know from Bhagat Singh – whom she found sensitive and emotional – how he had become close to Sukhdev. He told her he had first met Sukhdev at National College and that they were inseparable after their first meeting. Bhagat Singh told Durga Devi how Sukhdev and he would endlessly discuss India's political condition and the lack of revolutionary zeal, without which they did not see an early release from British domination or the capitalist system. They exchanged notes on books which they freely borrowed from the Dwarka Das Library. This privately funded library had the latest books on the history of revolutionary movements in Italy, Russia, Ireland and China. Their primary interests were politics and economics but they also shared a common interest in the aesthetic aspects of life. They found time to listen to music and appreciate art – the only digression from their discussions on revolution and revolutionaries.

The only time they had had a serious difference, Bhagat Singh told Durga Devi, was while discussing a character, Cimourdain, in *Ninety-Three*, the last novel Victor Hugo wrote. Sukhdev condemned the character Cimourdain for committing suicide after deciding in favour of the death penalty for Guivano – the boy he brought up, who was now one of the Republic's finest – since revolutionary principles must be placed before personal feelings. Sukhdev said Cimourdain surrendered himself to sentimentalism, which did not behoove a revolutionary. He should have let Guivano go. But Bhagat Singh defended Cimourdain's action on the grounds that he did his duty towards the revolutionary cause when he sentenced Guivano to death. The reason why Cimourdain committed suicide, Bhagat Singh argued, was because of the love he had for Guivano. He could not reconcile the two – his love for his friend and his duty as a judge. Without realizing it, Bhagat Singh spoke the language of Gandhi. If the means were wrong, the end was bound to be wrong as well.

For Bhagat Singh, matters of the heart were important. A revolutionary could not be devoid of human feelings; it was feelings that made him different from a terrorist. To him, a sensitive compassionate nature helped restrain the radicals and held them back from committing senseless violence. Bhagat Singh did not want the revolutionaries to be devoid of emotion or sentiment and turn into wooden gods. Bhagat Singh's humane approach betrayed a certain romanticism, Sukhdev would say. He felt it made a revolutionary soft and sentimental.

How different were Bhagat Singh and Sukhdev? While one believed deeply in the quality of mercy, the other considered it a hindrance that came in the way of the enemy's elimination. When engaged in a fight, Bhagat Singh favoured as little damage as possible, Sukhdev knew no limits. Bhagat Singh told Durga Devi that with the passage of time, the differences in their approach had become increasingly pronounced. Still, he said, he would still go by Sukhdev's wishes, as he saw things more objectively.

The two days Bhagat Singh spent with Durga Devi made him mellow and relaxed. He found a sensitive listener in her. He found he wanted to share every thought, every emotion, every fear with her. She was surprised by this aspect of his personality because she had known him as a revolutionary – led by his head, not by his heart.

India represented a quest for fulfilment, Bhagat Singh told her. Many outsiders thought the country was steeped in troubles and turbulence. But they missed the point. Its capacity to face problems was tremendous. Its resilience was inexhaustible. Such a nation could never be defeated. It could withstand any vicissitudes. He recited a verse by Swami Ramatirtha:

Ham rukhe tukade khayenge. Bharat par ware jayenge
Ham sukhe channe chabayenge, Bharat ki baat banayenge.
Ham nange umar bitayenge, Bharat par jaan mitayenge.

(We shall subsist on crumbs, but sacrifice ourselves for Bharat/ We shall live on parched gram, but shall live for Bharat/ We shall go naked our whole lives, but offer our lives to Bharat).

Bhagat Singh spoke of how Ramatirtha often wept while watching the sun set in America: 'Now you are rising in my beloved country. Drop my tears like dewdrops over the beautiful waterfed fields of India.'

As he admired Ramatirtha from Punjab, Bhagat Singh also praised Swami Vivekananda from Bengal. He felt proud that both men had earned fame for propagating the glory of Indian metaphysics abroad. He woefully noted that Vivekananda's mission had become a permanent institution in Bengal, while Ramatirtha did not have even a memorial in Punjab.

Both Ramatirtha and Vivekananda believed in the assertion of man but not in selfishness. Indeed, real progress, Bhagat Singh felt, would come only when an opportunity was given to every individual to develop for the good of the whole community. The touchstone should be how far any political, social or economic theory enabled the individual to rise above his petty self and think in terms of the good of all.

How close, Bhagat Singh thought, he had grown to Durga Devi in the last two days. At first he had known her only as Bhagwati Charan's wife, then as a comrade who had presided over the fateful meeting in which they took the decision to kill Scott, and then as the person who helped him escape from the jaws of death. Now the relationship had developed into something more personal. It thrilled him as well as scared him. It was a strange kind of feeling, one that he had not experienced before.

Bhagat Singh was immersed in his thoughts when Durga Devi told him that they were approaching Calcutta. Indeed, the train was slowing down. The greenery of the lush countryside was being rapidly devoured by concrete buildings. A maze of railway lines criss-crossed the station and ran along the train tracks. The platform was full of memsahibs and sahibs, authoritative in their behaviour and loud in their conversation. There was no evidence of the panic that Bhagat Singh had hoped would engulf the British once they learnt of Saunders' murder.

Buggy-type cars were parked at the edge of the platform. A retinue of liveried, but barefoot, servants took the luggage from the upper class compartments. A small contingent of policemen was present, more on regular duty than to search for anyone in particular.

Bhagat Singh, Durga Devi, her child Sachin, and Rajguru got off the train without drawing any attention. Bhagwati Charan met them at the station. He was curious to know who his brother-in-law was because his wife had no brother. He had suspected that Bhagat Singh might be travelling with her. He had read about the murder of Saunders in *The Statesman*, a paper published from Calcutta.

Although no longer India's capital, Calcutta still had a regal splendour about it. New Delhi was only the political centre, but Calcutta remained the real centre of social, economic and cultural activities. Its buildings were graceful and its parks elaborate and varied.

Bhagwati Charan knew that before long the police would be looking for Bhagat Singh. He settled Bhagat Singh at the residence

of a rich Marwari friend, Chajju Ram, who lived in Alipore, a
posh locality where the sprawling bungalows were appreciated,
and never searched. Wealthy people of the establishment lived
here. Both Chajju Ram and his wife, Lakshmi Devi, were great
admirers of Bhagat Singh. In fact, all revolutionaries evoked awe
in the couple: they were amazed at how a handful of them
fearlessly defied the mighty white men!

In Calcutta, Bhagat Singh was depressed to see rickshaws
being pulled by men, a stark reminder of the poverty and
exploitation of India's poor. Still, he enjoyed hopping on and off
the tram-cars. The Victoria Memorial, although hewn in marble,
could not match the beauty of the Taj Mahal at Agra. The
memorial in Calcutta was as stern and cold as the British. He
liked Bengal's gregarious, cosmopolitan and aristocratic
atmosphere. There was music and art in the air. But he also felt
that there was a sense of superiority among the people. He
regretted the cooling of the Bengali revolutionaries' fervour –
that once had inspired idealism and commitment. While Rash
Behari Bose, a great revolutionary, continued to fight for the
cause, he had more of a following in Punjab than in Bengal.

Bhagat Singh recalled how he nearly came to Calcutta instead
of Kanpur, when he ran away from home. Despite the immense
popularity of revolutionaries like Aurobindo Ghosh and Barindra
Kumar, the Bengali youth remained distant from the struggle.
Viceroy Lord Curzon's proposal to partition Bengal had led to a
widespread agitation. But the stir had left little mark on the
people. In fact, the Bengal revolutionaries, when he met them,
looked upon the youthful Bhagat Singh as the person to rekindle
the flame. To escape detection, Bhagat Singh adopted a new name
in Calcutta. He called himself Hari. He also wore a dhoti and
shawl like the Bengalis and learnt Bengali from B.K. Dutt.

Bhagat Singh attended the session of the Indian National
Congress in the city but was disgusted by it. The goal to be

projected before the country was complete independence and a total severance of ties with the British. But Congress leaders were still debating the demand for Dominion Status, which gave London the final say. Power with conditions was no power. How could India ever feel free if it were to remain within the British Empire as a dominion? And no one at the Session spoke of effecting any radical change in the country.

The Congress, he found, was still in the hands of the upper class. It wanted to secure rights for its own class. So far as the millions of workers and farmers were concerned, they figured nowhere in the reckoning of the Congress. 'If we want to fight for the country's independence, workers, farmers and the common man will have to be brought to the fore,' Bhagat Singh had said many a time at the Mozang Road house meetings. He felt that the Congress leaders did not want to broaden the mass base of the party lest the people should talk about big and drastic changes in the Congress' economic policy. The responsibility had fallen on the shoulders of the revolutionaries to liberate the workers and farmers, not only from the yoke of foreign rule but also from greedy owners and placid landlords.

The Congress session bored Bhagat Singh. He went straight from it to a movie hall. To his delight, *Uncle Tom's Cabin* was being screened. He deeply admired Abraham Lincoln, who had fought a civil war to prevent the southern states of America to secede from the northern states over the abolition of slavery. The north-south divide reminded Bhagat Singh of Lajpat Rai's words, wanting to divide India to accommodate Hindus and Muslims in separate countries. He hoped it would never come to that. If it ever did, it would be the end of socialist ideology. The British policy of divide and rule would leave behind a bitter legacy and a divided nation, Bhagat Singh feared.

In Calcutta, Bhagat Singh met revolutionaries like Prafulla Ganguli, Jyotish Ghosh, Trailokyanath Chakraborti, Phonindro

Nath Ghosh and Jatindra Nath Das. Most of the revolutionaries of Bengal were in the city when he was there. They had discarded what they termed 'anarchism', or the path of the bomb and the gun. They felt it was possible to fight for socialism through the mobilization of the masses. They did not believe that the Kakori train dacoity or Saunders' killing had taken the country any nearer the goal of full independence, much less to revolutionary conditions.

The Bengal revolutionaries had, however, come a long way. Their predecessors had approached people in the name of religion. The Anushilan Samiti, which was formed in Calcutta in 1894, had divided revolutionaries into two categories: those who believed in religion and those who did not. Most revolutionaries of Bengal at that time were influenced by Bankim Chandra Chatterjee and Vivekananda. The Samiti members had to read the Hindu scriptures, especially the Gita. Songs and slogans based on Hindu myths inspired Bengal's revolutionaries in the early twentieth century. The Vandematram, a popular prayer song, invokes the blessings of the Devi.

The Chapekar brothers, who were among the first revolutionaries to shoot a Briton, Rand, for his tyrannical rule in Poona during the plague, drew their inspiration from Hindu rites and rituals. They were openly anti-Muslim. Vir Savarkar, who spent years in the Andaman cellular jail, was also a revolutionary of the same brand, staunchly anti-British but fanatically pro-Hindu. Bhagat Singh knew all this. He felt happy that the Punjab revolutionaries were made of different stuff and were secular to the core.

The Hindu Sanrakshani Samiti (Society for the Protection of Hindus), started by the Chapekar brothers of Maharashtra, did not change. But Bengal's Anushilan Samiti did and talked in terms of economic betterment. In a declaration in 1902, it said: 'Humanity cannot progress under inequalities. We shall have to bring equality amongst all men by abolishing inequality of wealth, social inequality, communal inequality and regional inequality. This can be achieved only through a national government.'

Trailokyanath Chakraborti,who had spent thirty years of his life in prison, advised Bhagat Singh to build a volunteer corps of 5,000 young men on the pattern of the corps the Congress had decided to raise. Bhagat Singh found the Bengal revolutionaries quite secular. They enunciated for the first time the belief that religion and politics should not be mixed.

Forming a corps was not a new suggestion. Bhagat Singh and his comrades had constituted the Naujawan Bharat Sabha in April, 1925, a platform for the youth. Its manifesto, written by Bhagwati Charan, exhorted the youth to think independently, calmly and patiently and urged them to adopt India's independence as the sole purpose of their lives.The manifesto asked, 'Was it not the young Russians who sacrificed their lives for Russia's emancipation?' It had warned the youth against religious bias:

A branch of a peepal tree is cut and religious feelings of the Hindus are injured; a corner of a paper, tazia of the idol-breaker Mohammedans is broken and 'Allah' gets enraged, who then cannot be satisfied with anything less than the blood of the infidel Hindus. Man ought to be given more importance than animals and, yet, here in India, they break each other's heads in the name of 'sacred animals'.

Before enrolment, every member of the Naujawan Bharat Sabha had to sign a pledge that he or she would place the interest of the country above that of the community. Halal and Jhatka meat was cooked together and eaten by Hindus, Muslims and Sikhs alike.

But Bhagat Singh had to admit that the Naujawan Bharat Sabha had not yet caught the imagination of the youth. He believed that all great national movements were begun by unknown men without much influence. Except for faith and determination, nothing else counted.

Professor Jai Chandra Vidyalankar, who had initiated Bhagat Singh into revolutionary work at the National College in Lahore, was in Calcutta those days. He took him to meet Professor Jyotish Ghosh, a member of the Calcutta Revolutionary Party. Through him Bhagat Singh met many other revolutionaries who had spent the best years of their lives in jail.

Of all those he met, Trailokyanath Chakraborti impressed Bhagat Singh the most. Chakraborti too was struck by Bhagat Singh's revolutionary zeal. But neither Chakraborti nor any other Bengali revolutionary had any faith in the methods that Bhagat Singh and his comrades followed in Punjab and UP. The killing of individuals, Bhagat Singh argued, was a step meant only to harness the enthusiasm of the youth. It was the means, not the end. The end was revolution, in which both Bengal and Punjab concurred. He wanted bombs, and the know-how to manufacture them. Chakraborti believed in Bhagat Singh's integrity and honesty and gave him revolvers and cartridges, although he had initially refused to do so.

In Calcutta, Bhagat Singh also met Jatindra Nath Das, a staunch revolutionary who played an important role in giving impetus to the activities of the HSRA. Both men immediately struck up a rapport. Das did not, however, agree to teach Bhagat Singh how to make a bomb. His party had abandoned 'acts of individual terrorism', as he put it, and he, for one, refused to violate the party discipline. However, Das changed his mind when he was convinced that the killing of top British officials would instil a sense of bravery in the youth and make them participate in revolutionary activities. He noted the panic that had gripped the British after a couple of killings. The old placid situation had undergone a sea-change.

If nothing else, Bhagat Singh's visit to Calcutta revived the sagging spirits of the revolutionaries in Bengal. Once again, there were animated discussions on how to bring about a change in the social structure. The Russian revolution of 1917 had enthused all of them. It had taken time for its ideas to percolate but it was becoming increasingly popular to be progressive and to be a sympathizer of the poor.

Democracy was theoretically a system of political and legal equality. But in concrete and practical terms, it was inadequate. There could be no equality in politics and before the law as long as there were glaring economic inequalities. So long as the ruling class controlled jobs and the press and the schools of the country and all organs of public opinion; so long as it monopolized all trained public functionaries and disposed of unlimited funds to influence elections; so long as laws were made by the ruling class; so long as lawyers, who were private practitioners, sold their expertise to the highest bidder and litigation was exclusive and costly, there would be only nominal equality before the law. So the revolutionaries believed and talked.

The British were beginning to feel the heat. Sir David Petrie, assistant director of criminal intelligence who served in the Indian Police from 1900 to 1936 warned London about the 'Bolshevik menace' in India. In a report, he said:

> The Bolsheviks are convinced that in the British Empire the most vulnerable point is India... and they cherish it as an article of faith that till India is liberated, Russia will not be rid of the menace of England.

Sir James Crerar, then home member of the governor-general's executive council, said that India was 'getting contaminated by the doctrine and practice of communism'.

Confident that some Bengali revolutionaries would step forward to teach the Punjabi revolutionaries how to manufacture the bomb, Bhagat Singh left Calcutta for Agra in UP. This was to be the new centre for the activities of the revolutionaries.

3

Duniya se ghulami ka mein nam mita dunga
Ik bar zamane ko mein azad kara dunga

IN AGRA, BHAGAT SINGH AND HIS TWO COMRADES RENTED TWO houses in Hing ki Mandi, a nondescript neighbourhood. All the revolutionaries who had escaped from Punjab after Saunders' killing gathered here. Like the house on Mozang Road in Lahore, the Agra houses came to be both their refuge and their rendezvous. Chandra Shekhar Azad, Bhagat Singh, Rajguru and Sukhdev, all were in hiding here. Jatindra Nath Das and Lalit Mukherji, also a Bengal revolutionary, joined them in Agra to teach them how to make and assemble bombs. The Jhansi forests nearby were an ideal place to test their ammunition.

It was a spartan life in Agra. The revolutionaries did not have enough cots to sleep on, not enough utensils to cook and not enough money to buy food. There were days when a few of them would skip an afternoon meal or dinner in order to manage within their limited resources. Austerity was a trait that the revolutionaries had acquired perforce over a short period of time. Hardship did not matter to them. They had opted for this life, away from the comfort of their homes and the love of their dear ones. It was not for fame or self-applause, but for the glory of the cause.

Azad, who managed the finances, tapped many important people for money. Motilal Nehru and Purshottam Das Tandon, senior UP Congress leaders, were regular contributors. Some

Indian officials sent money through messengers. On one occasion Azad was surprised to get a bearer cheque from Bengal's Advocate-General. He encashed it immediately so as not to leave any trace of his whereabouts.

Holed up in their hideaway the revolutionaries would debate every issue on earth – whether it was economic, political or social. They believed that the state was not really an end in itself and that man was not there for the sake of law or the state, but that the state and law existed for man. The touchstone was how far any political or social theory enabled man to rise above his petty self and think in terms of the common good.

Often their long debates made the atmosphere heavy and tense. To bring some relief, Rajguru one day tore out a picture of a girl in a bathing suit from a magazine and pinned it on the wall. When Azad saw the picture he was furious and ripped it off. He said the revolutionaries did not have the time to indulge in trivial entertainment; theirs was a long and arduous life. Rajguru was not present when Azad lost his temper over the picture but when he returned, he noticed its absence. Before Rajguru could ask what had happened to the picture Azad told him what he had done. To add to Rajguru's hurt, Azad said that he would destroy anything beautiful, even the Taj Mahal. 'We are out to make the world beautiful. How can he talk like this?' Rajguru remarked in anguish.

But Azad was talking only in anger. Lack of action – and progress – was telling on the revolutionaries. As tempers cooled, Azad apologized for his remarks and said he was not against beauty but they could not afford to lose their focus.

The incident made the meetings even more serious and businesslike. Bhagat Singh would go to a local library in the morning and share with his colleagues the information he had culled from his reading in the afternoon. One day he declared that despite his best efforts, he could not find any revolutionary party that had any clear idea about what it was fighting for. The only exception, he said, was the Ghadar (rebellion) party which, having been inspired by the US form of government, clearly stated that it wanted to replace the existing system of government with a republican form. All the other parties, Bhagat Singh contended, consisted of men who had only one idea: to fight the alien rulers. It was a laudable idea, he said, but could not be termed a revolutionary idea.

'We must make it clear that revolution does not mean an upheaval,' said Bhagat Singh.

> Revolution necessarily implies the programme of systematic reconstruction of society on a new and better adopted basis, often necessitating complete destruction of the existing state of affairs. It was one of the illusions of each generation that the social institutions in which it lived were natural and permanent. Yet for countless years social institutions had been superceded by others adapted to temporary needs.

The Ghadar party was one of Bhagat Singh's inspirations. It was the first militant group that had tried to liberate India by force – something that he and his comrades had also vowed to do. The party was constituted in 1913 by Indians living in Canada and the US to wage war against the British raj. The party's objective was clear in its manifesto: 'What is our name? *Ghadar.* What is our work? *Ghadar.* Where will *Ghadar* break out? In India. The time will soon come when rifles and blood will take the place of pen and ink.'

The party was strongly secular, an idea that was dear to Bhagat Singh's heart. One of the booklets which the Ghadar party issued, had the following poem:

No Pundits or Mullahs do we need
No prayers or litanies we need recite
These will only scuttle our boat
Draw the sword: this time to fight.
Though Hindus, Mussalmans and Sikhs we be,
Sons of Bharat are we still
Put aside your arguments for another day
Call of the hour is to kill.
While we were all sunk in stupor
The foreigners took over our government
In pointless disputes we got involved
Like quarrelsome whores our time we spent
Though born we were in one land
By caste we became high and low
These foolish factions we did create
And seeds of discord ourselves did sow.
Some worship the cow; others, swine abhor,
The white man eats them at every place;
Forget you are Hindu, forget you are Mussalman,
Pledge yourselves to your land and race.

At a time when Maharashtra and Bengal were in the grip of Hindu revivalism (the first answering the call of Shivaji and the second answering the call of Kali, the goddess of destruction), and the Muslims had been kept away from the uprising, as even the nationalist leader Bal Gangadhar Tilak called them mlechhas (unclean) – the Ghadar party sustained its faith in secularism.

The Sikhs were the backbone of the Ghadar party. Gurmukhi was its language and the gurudwara its venue. The party brought Sikhs back into the political mainstream and washed away a stigma on the community for having supported the British in the first national uprising in 1857.

The Ghadar party's rebellion started when its party leader Gurdit Singh, who was from Amritsar, chartered the *Komagata Maru,* a Japanese merchant ship to travel from Hong Kong to Canada in 1914. It carried 376 Indians, mostly Sikhs, to Canada. There was no bar against Indian immigrants to that country at that time. When the ship arrived in Canadian waters, it was cordoned off and the passengers were told that they did not have the right to land. Gurdit Singh was pressurized to pay charter dues at one go. He said he would do so after selling the cargo but the ship was not allowed to unload. Indians in Vancouver agitated for the release of the ship. The most prominent among them was Hussain Rahim, a lawyer. Some Canadians also joined them. Fitzgerald, a socialist, gave a call which Bhagat Singh repeated to his comrades: 'Get up and arm yourselves and fight to regain liberty. Inspire your countrymen to return and sweep all the whites from India.'

In Delhi the viceroy showed no sympathy for the stranded passengers, nor did he intervene on their behalf to end the nightmare. Eventually, Canadian guns forced the *Komagata Maru* to return after about two months. The ship was not permitted to berth at any port all the way to Calcutta.

Mewa Singh, an unknown local priest, avenged this humiliation by shooting William Hopkinson dead in the Vancouver court where he was waiting to denounce the ideology that the Ghadar Party was trying to expound. This incident naturally raised tensions among the members of Vancouver's Sikh community. Some had a particular enmity for Yorkshire-born William Hopkinson, a local immigration official, who had once served on the Calcutta Police Force. He spoke Hindi fluently, and could get by in Punjabi. Hopkinson had come to Vancouver in 1907, and was hired by the Canadian Government as an immigration inspector and interpreter. He was also monitoring the activities of East Indian extremists living in British

Columbia, and developing a network of pro-British Sikh informants. Before Mewa Singh was executed, he issued a statement: 'My religion does not teach me to bear enmity towards anybody, no matter what class, creed or order he belongs to. Nor had I any enmity with Hopkinson.'

Ultimately, the *Komagata Maru* docked at the Hooghly's Budge Budge Harbour. The police searched the ship but found no arms. The passengers were herded in a train and sent to Punjab. Some of them insisted on depositing a copy of the *Granth Sahib* at a Calcutta gurudwara. The police opened fire on the procession carrying the holy book from the harbour and killed eighteen people. Over 200 of them were put in jail.

The *Komagata Maru* incident provided the spark that lit the fire of defiance among Indians abroad. The *Ghadar,* the party's organ, wrote relentlessly to exhort people to revolt. Several thousand men living abroad caught the earliest boat to India.

The *Portland Telegram* of 7 August gave a communal angle to the report:

HINDUS GO HOME TO FIGHT REVOLUTION

Astoria (Oregon) 7 August: Every train and boat for the south carries large numbers of Hindus from this city and if the exodus keeps up much longer, Astoria will be entirely deserted by the East Indians. The majority of the Hindus employed at Hammond Hills have gone and the balance are preparing to depart in the immediate future. It is alleged that the men are returning to India by way of San Francisco, where it is said, a vessel had been chartered to aid in a revolution which is expected to break out in India as a result of England being occupied in the general European war. It is said that a Japanese steamer will carry the Hindus to their native land.

The Ghadar party was leaderless at that time. Secretary General Hardayal had escaped to Switzerland after having been denounced an 'anarchist' in San Francisco. Sohan Singh Bhakna and Kartar Singh, two other leaders, had reached India. Ram Chandra, a nominee of Hardayal, headed the Ghadar party. He told all the Indians to assemble at Moga in Punjab. 'Your duty is clear. Go to India. Stir up rebellion in every corner of the country. Rob the wealthy and show mercy to the poor. In this way gain universal sympathy. Arms will be provided to you on arrival in India. Failing this, you must ransack the police stations for rifles. Obey without hesitation the commands of your leaders.'

Another ship, the *Korea,* carried some Indians, who were arrested as soon as the boat reached Calcutta. A few who could evade the police reached Moga. But they did not get arms, although they waited for days. They had no recourse except to disperse to their villages.

People coming from Hong Kong, China, Japan, Borneo and the Philippines, made contacts with the Indian troops serving in those areas. None of them responded except the 26th Punjabi Regiment at Singapore. The British crushed the rebellion ruthlessly.

On the other hand, most Ghadarites coming through the northern ports, were arrested but many, travelling through the southern parts reached Punjab – nearly 1,000 of them. On 19 March, 1915 the government passed the Defence of India Act, which authorized the administration 'to empower any civil or military authority to prohibit the entry or residence in any area, of a person, suspected to be acting in a manner prejudicial to the public safety, or to direct the residence of such person in any specified area'.

Eventually the Ghadarites suffered because there was no real programme, no strategy. Alas, there was no revolutionary leader, Bhagat Singh said, to make use of the Ghadarites. They found the people in Punjab uncooperative. There was no agitation against the British, although World War I, which had started, provided an ideal opportunity for revolt. Gandhi had, instead, volunteered for medical service in the military. Radicals like Tilak too did not want to stall the war efforts. The Ghadarites were treated as unwanted people. The police, arrested and harassed them brazenly. Some of them were even killed.

The judicial report on the Budge Budge Harbour shooting confirmed the cold reception that the Ghadarites got there. 'The peasantry saw nothing justifiable in their acts, from whatever patriotic motive they might have been committed. To them, the revolutionaries became murderers and plunderers of honest men ... to be resisted by all means possible and captured.'

Still, the Ghadarites did not give up. They contacted Rash Behari Bose, a Bengal revolutionary, who had shifted base from Calcutta to Lahore. His men approached Indian soldiers in several cantonments, hoping to incite them to rebel. The Ferozepur cantonment was considered the best bet; Bose believed that the soldiers there would rebel and that would spark off a popular uprising. He expected Afghanistan to recognize to the revolutionary government which they would establish.

Bose fixed 21 February, 1915 as the date for the uprising. The 23rd Cavalry at Lahore and subsequently troops in other cantonments were to shoot British officers, capture arsenal and distribute rifles among the revolutionaries. The Ghadarites had established factories in Amritsar and Jhabal, near Ludhiana, to manufacture bombs. They were trained to derail trains and cut telegraph lines. Posters proclaiming the Ilan-e-]ung (declaration of war) were cyclostyled and readied for distribution.

But then one of the Ghadarites, Mula Singh, was incidentally arrested and he told the police everything. Bose advanced the date of the uprising to 19 February but the regiments he had chosen were disarmed. Many Ghadarites were picked up and executed. Bose managed to escape.

As many as 249 Ghadarites were tried. Forty-two were sentenced to death, 114 sent to the Andamans and 93 sentenced to varying terms of imprisonment. The 23rd Cavalry was transferred to Assam but the bombs that exploded from their luggage gave them away. Twelve of them were hanged and six sentenced to life imprisonment.

Thus the Ghadar movement was crushed. But it gave birth to the radical Akali movement. The Babbars, Akali extremists, were born out of the Ghadar movement. They killed many Britons to avenge the death of the Ghadarites. Some of the Ghadarites returned to Punjab after serving their sentences to revive the rebellion against the British. A few left-wing political movements took shape. *Kirti* was one of them.

Bhagat Singh traced the history of the Ghadar party for his comrades to impress upon them that for those involved in revolution death was something routine.

There was no doubt about the bravery of the Ghadarites, or the sacrifices they had made, but the question was how far had they succeeded?

Increasingly, Bhagat Singh and his comrades asked themselves the same questions: Were they achieving what they had left their homes for? Was the country closer to revolution because of their efforts? Should they change their tactics or compromise?

They had no answers but they were sure that however limited their success, there was no doubting their goal. Subjection to foreign rule was one of the most potent reasons for the decay of the nation. Any country that rose against its oppressors was bound to fail in the beginning. It could gain partial reforms during its struggle. But it was only in the last stage – having organized all the forces and resources of the nation – that it could strike the final blow to shatter the foreign government.

Nonetheless, Bhagat Singh and his comrades wondered whether their tactics had yielded the results they had envisaged. Bombs might be necessary at times to arouse attention, but the revolutionaries also had to convince people through argument and personal example, that theirs was the best way to release the common man from the bondage of foreigners and the shackles of poverty.

The government machinery was a weapon in the hands of the ruling class to safeguard its interests. 'We want to snatch and handle it to utilize it for the consummation of our ideal, that is, social reconstruction.' But then, Bhagat Singh said: 'We have to educate the masses to create a favourable atmosphere for our social programmes.'

The revolutionaries believed that the mood of the country was becoming more liberal. Nehru too noted the gentle breeze of socialism that was blowing across the country. Congress workers were borrowing books by Bryce on democracy and Mazzini on revolution. The British found from intelligence reports that the influence of the revolutionaries was spreading among workers, students and the youth. Trade union activities had gathered strength. Even some Indian officials were suspected of sympathizing with the revolutionaries.

Bhagat Singh and his comrades discussed the fall-out of Saunders' killing at the Agra house. They realized that it had not produced the desired results. There had been no exodus of the British as they had imagined. Only a few men had sent their wives back to England. The initial panic had given place to the belief among the British that stricter reprisals would teach the rebellious a lesson. Neither the Congress nor Gandhi posed any problem to them, only the revolutionaries did. So the British decided to introduce two new Bills before the Central Assembly to curb political and labour activities and cut the revolutionaries' appeal.

Even nine-and-a-half months after Saunders' murder the police had failed to trace his killers. The viceroy's telegram to the secretary of state at that time said, 'The investigation in the Saunders' murder case is not making much progress.' London's reply was that 'it is very disappointing to hear that the progress of investigation is not so satisfactory.

Viceroy Irwin scheduled the two Bills for discussion on 8 April, 1929. The revolutionaries chose the same day to register their protest. They knew that the British judicial system would never be fair to them after their arrest. The British would only stage a farce of justice.

Both the Bills were meant to smother resistance to British rule. The first Bill, the Public Safety Bill, was designed to empower the government to detain anyone without trial. The second, the Trade Disputes Bill, was meant to deter labour unions from organizing strikes, particularly in Bombay, where mill-owners had been forced to increase wages.

The revolutionaries sat for hours in their headquarters at Agra, debating the effect of the two Bills on the country and how they would restrict their movement. They considered the Assembly a worthless institution because it demonstrated the humiliation and helplessness of Indians to the world and gave credibility to the domination of an irresponsible and autocratic rule. Still the Assembly mattered because it put an official stamp on the illegitimate governance.

That is when the revolutionaries began to wonder if the Assembly could be made a forum to make the point that the Bills only served to make British tyranny more reprehensible. Was the Assembly the right place to raise their protest? The Bills were, in fact, a clear message to the revolutionaries to prepare themselves for more suppression and punishment. Should they respond to the challenge? It meant coming out in the open to test their own popularity and that of the HSRA.

Although the revolutionaries thought they were making some headway, they felt handicapped because their work, by its very nature, was secretive. The Bills would only throttle it further. How their message should reach the public was what they had to discuss. Saunders' killing had brought them into national prominence, but a year had lapsed since then. What should they do to re-focus the spotlight on themselves and their message? Another killing of a British official? Would that help? Already, there was a strong belief that mobilizing public opinion and making people believe in their ideology was the real necessity, not random bombs and killing.

They were conscious that any protest outside the Assembly would land them in trouble. They would be arrested and jailed straightaway. They then thought they could instead use the Assembly Hall for the propagation of their message. Some peaceful way to register their presence and protest was necessary. It would also defeat the malicious propaganda by the British that they were 'a bunch of killers'. The government had deliberately given them a bad name. They had to repudiate it.

A formal meeting of the HSRA was called to decide on the next step. Bhagat Singh, as usual, was the first to speak. He said: 'The British are out to loot and kill us, without even allowing us to raise our voice. More repressive laws will follow. Slaves as we are, we will have no scope even to protest.' He had already consulted Sukhdev in Lahore on the best method for voicing their opposition. Tara Chand, a comrade from UP, saw Bhagat Singh's point. He said: 'There is no other way except to open the eyes and ears of the Assembly members, particularly the Indians.' Azad intervened to ask: 'How?'

They all agreed that the central idea was to express loud resentment against the Bills.

The revolutionaries finally decided that two comrades from among them would hurl bombs from the public gallery at the treasury benches in the Central Assembly Hall, taking care not to hurt anyone. The explosion, in broad daylight in a public place, was sure to start a debate on why the revolutionaries had chosen the high-security environs of the Assembly to risk their lives. It would make people think. People would realize that the revolutionaries were courting arrest only to register their protest against the ' jungle raj' that the British had come to stand for in the country.

Two people, B.K. Dutt and Ram Saran Das, were nominated for the task. B.K. Dutt brought back memories of their Kanpur days. Bhagat Singh recalled how the two of them would discuss the changes they wanted to bring about in India through revolution. It was Dutt who introduced Bhagat Singh to a song, which they often hummed together:

Ek halora idhar se aaye
ek halora udhar se aaye
sara ulat pulat ho jaaye
dhuan dhar jagat mein chaye
nash aur satyanash ki dhul
udd chale dayein bayein.

(A gust of wind from here/ another from there/ Everything is upturned/Smoke engulfs the world/The dust of destruction spreads/ Right and left.)

Das, convicted in 1915, had recently returned from the Andamans after serving a sentence. Following his release, he had contacted Bhagat Singh and had become an activist in the HSRA. They were poles apart in their views. Still they were close. Das later authored a book, *Dreamland,* to which Bhagat Singh wrote the introduction:

His interpretation of the universe is ideological and metaphysical, while I am a materialist and my interpretation of the phenomenon would be casual. Nevertheless, it is by no means out of place or out of date. The general ideas that are prevailing in our country are more in accordance with those expressed by him. To fight that depressing mood, he resorted to prayers.

The whole of the beginning of the book is devoted to God. His praise, His definition, belief in God is the outcome of mysticism which is the natural consequence of depression. That this world is *maya* or *mithya,* dream or fiction, is clear mysticism which has been originated and developed by Hindu sages, such as Sankaracharya and others. But in the materialist philosophy this mode of thinking has got absolutely no place. This mysticism of the author is by no means ignoble or deplorable. It has its own beauty and charm.

Bhagat Singh wished he had been picked to throw the bomb. He would have used the courtroom to declare that the purpose of the explosion was to warn the British that the unrest of the people was increasing and that things could take a serious turn if they were not tackled in time. Bhagat Singh's suggestion that he replace Das was met with a condition: he would be considered only if he escaped after throwing the bomb, as he had done after killing Saunders.

Bhagat Singh rejected the idea. He said that it was time that words were spoken. Nothing had ever remained of any revolution but what was rife in the conscience of the masses. Words alone could do that. The rulers must be put in the dock. The court should be used as a forum to propagate revolutionary patriotic ideas and to awaken the people's fervour for freedom. The public must clearly understand and appreciate the motives of the revolutionaries.

If motive was not considered, said Bhagat Singh, then, 'Jesus Christ would appear to be a man responsible for creating disturbances, violating peace and preaching revolt and would be considered a dangerous personality in the language of the law. But we worship him.'

R.H. Tawney's *The Acquisitive Society* was the most recent book Bhagat Singh had read. *The Acquisitive Society,* he said, 'was a reality'. The reason people from the Tawney period adopted the socialist creed was the degrading economic and moral conditions under which so many people lived at that time. He underlined the contradiction between political freedom and economic dependence and underscored the necessity of freedom for economic improvement. The history of all societies, Bhagat Singh said, was the history of class struggles. It was a fight between those 'who do not work' and 'those who do'. It had been caused not by subversion or conspiracies and astute political leaders, but by the same inexorable social laws that destroyed previous systems like feudalism in Europe.

What Bhagat Singh was trying to convey was that he would be the best exponent of their philosophy. But Azad, who was presiding over the meeting, ruled over him. He did not want to expose him to the danger that loomed large. Azad was aware that Bhagat Singh was wanted by the Punjab police. Once they laid their hands on him, they would take him to court. The trial was sure to end with his conviction and hanging.

One point that had generated heated debate following the selection of the team was whether Dutt and Ram Saran should be rescued after they had thrown the bombs. Azad recalled how he had led his comrades to safety after Saunders' murder. But then the aim had been different. This time the idea was to surrender so that people could see that the revolutionaries had sacrificed themselves to register their protest against the oppressive measures the British were determined to enact. Dutt and Ram Saran would not try to escape but would use the forum of the court to explain themselves and their concept of revolution.

When Sukhdev learned that Bhagat Singh was not in the team, he was greatly upset. He took up the matter with Azad. If anyone among them could put across the party's point of view cogently and lucidly and defend the use of violence, it was Bhagat Singh, Sukhdev argued. 'We are sick of the stigma of violence attached to us. We are neither killers, nor terrorists. We want the country and the world to know about our faith in revolution.' Bhagat Singh had the name, the background and the commitment to explain their aspirations, Sukhdev said. Bhagat Singh too was tired of violence being associated with them. Gandhi's description of them as 'irresponsible young men' irritated him.

Had Gandhi ever tried to sit around an evening fire with a peasant and tried to gauge what he thought? Had he spent a single evening in the company of a factory labourer and shared his views with him? The revolutionaries knew what the masses thought. The day was not far off when they would attract thousands 'to work the will of the revolution'. He recalled that Lenin had once said to Maxim Gorky:

> I know nothing which is greater than the Appassionata; I would like to listen to it every day. It is marvelous, superhuman music. I always think with pride – perhaps it is naïve of me – what marvelous things human beings can do! … But I can't listen to music too often. It affects your nerves, makes you want to say stupid nice things, and stroke the heads of people who could create such beauty while living in this vile hell. And now you mustn't stroke anyone's head – you might get your hand bitten off. You have to hit them on the head, without any mercy, although our ideal is not to use force against anyone. *H'm, h'm,* our duty is infernally hard!

This was how the revolutionaries felt when they had to use guns or bombs. It was a necessity when the action was justified. When they were building their movement through the Naujawan Bharat Sabha in Punjab and the HSRA, they were aiming at two things. One was to frighten or eliminate the oppressive British officials. The second, more important aim, was to organize a mass movement of workers, peasants, students and the youth. However limited in extent their two-pronged strategy was, they believed they had accelerated the pace of the freedom struggle and drawn people closer to idealism and ideology.

Sukhdev chided Bhagat Singh for not joining the team for fear he would be jailed. This was unfair. Sukhdev was comparing Bhagat Singh with Bhai Parmanand, a revolutionary who later became a staunch Hindu leader. The reference was to an observation made by the Lahore High Court in Parmanand's case: 'Although the brain and spirit behind the party, he (Parmanand) was a coward at heart. He sent others to the stake, himself managing to remain in the background.'

'You are insulting me,' Bhagat Singh told Sukhdev.

'I am doing my duty towards a friend,' said Sukhdev.

Sukhdev did not stop at that. He hit him where it hurt most – in matters of the heart. He said: 'You would be of no use to revolution because you are now ensnared in the tresses (zulf) of a woman.' His reference was to Durga Devi who had travelled with Bhagat Singh in the train from Lahore to Calcutta to elude the police and escape after Saunders' murder.

Bhagat Singh was pained by what Sukhdev said but kept quiet at that time. Subsequently, he replied to Sukhdev through an emotional letter. He did not say whether he was in love with Durga Devi or not, but he did say that love was not incompatible with the life of a revolutionary. He reassured Sukhdev that he could renounce all at the time of need and, 'that is the real sacrifice'.

He gave the example of Mazzini who wrote that after the utter failure and crushing defeat of his first attempt at insurrection, the thought of his dead comrades haunted him and he could not bear the misery. One letter from the girl he loved saved him from going mad or committing suicide.

'As regards the moral status of love,' Bhagat Singh wrote in a letter to Sukhdev on 5 April, 1929:

> I may say that it in itself is nothing but passion, not an animal passion but a human one, and very sweet too. Love in itself can never be an animal passion. Love always elevates the character of man. It never lowers him, provided love be love... And I may tell you that a young man and a young girl can love each other, and with the aid of their love they can overcome the passions themselves and can maintain their purity.

Bhagat Singh sounded like Gandhi on celibacy. The tone of Bhagat Singh's letter suggested he had once been consumed by the feelings of love. He admitted:

> I rebuked the love of one individual...and that too in the idealistic stage. And even then, man must have the strongest feelings of love which he may not confine to one individual and may make it universal.

Bhagat Singh made a dig at Sukhdev:

> One thing I may tell you to mark, we, in spite of all radical ideas that we cherish, have not been able to do away with the over-idealistic Arya Samajist conception of morality. We may talk glibly about all the radical things that can possibly be conceived, but in practical life, we begin to tremble at the very outset.

The letter revealed Bhagat Singh's softer side. He was a revolutionary but that did not make him devoid of feelings. So long as his feelings did not come in the way of his revolutionary work in any manner, how did it matter whether he was up at night to gaze at the stars or whether he strained his ears to hear the refrain of a sad song in the distance?

Durga Devi, intelligent and articulate, had helped him escape the police. He had posed as her husband. True, she was married and had a son. But they had worked together. They had shared moments of triumph and despondency. Was there anything more to it? Bhagat Singh did not say.

What Sukhdev alleged was not hinted at by anybody else, not even by Azad, who was a father figure to Bhagat Singh. Perhaps Azad too felt that love was not such a sordid affair, to be run down and ridiculed, even though one was considered 'a dangerous revolutionary' and carried a price of 30,000 rupees on his head.

He was aware of what Bhagat Singh was going through. But Azad also knew that the Assembly Hall was going to be the end of Bhagat Singh's journey. He would be arrested, tried for the murder of Saunders and hanged. Azad and Bhagat Singh were not mere comrades. They had travelled a long way together to give shape to the revolutionary movement. They had dreamt together of an India that would be independent and would then lead the fight to free the enslaved countries of the world. That world would have a socialist order: from each according to his ability, to each according to his need.

At Bhagat Singh's request, the central committee meeting was reconvened. Bhagat Singh was able to prevail upon the members to nominate him in place of Ram Saran Das. He also put an end to the debate on surrender by saying that nobody would be rescued. He and Dutt would throw bombs from the public gallery and do so in such a manner that nobody got hurt. Since their act was meant to draw attention to their ideological goal, they would give themselves up after completing their job. Sukhdev did not say anything but his eyes were red, as if he had been crying all night. But duty to the country came first.

After Bhagat Singh's nomination to the team, Azad knew that Bhagat Singh's days were numbered. He could not bring himself to say goodbye to him. But he had no doubt that he would not meet Bhagat Singh as a free man again. Would his sacrifice be the foundation-stone for the edifice of the revolution? Would people realize that he could not put up any longer with the lack of respect for India?

Even when Lenin triumphed in Russia, it was the humiliation at their defeat in the war that gave the Russian forces the motivation to rise again. Lenin only articulated that purpose. Without their support, his revolutionary work was of little help. Azad told Shiv Verma, another comrade:

> In a few days, history will claim them (Bhagat Singh and Dutt) and only the legend will survive the corridors of time...

4

Usay yeh fikr hai hardam naya tarz-e-jafa kya hai,
Hamen yeh shauq hai dekhen sitam ki intiha kya hai

AWAY FROM THE SOUNDS AND SMELLS OF OLD DELHI, THE CITY of New Delhi had risen, imposing and impersonal, with high buildings and vaulted chambers. It was characterized by the distinctive columns and red stone buildings that a British architect from London, Edwin Lutyens, had envisioned. One of these buildings was the Council House, the Central Legislative Assembly, built by Herbert Baker, a colleague of Lutyens'. It was a monumental edifice with extravagant proportions of corridor space, dubbed by some critics as a 'dreary-go-round'.

Both Bhagat Singh and B.K. Dutt visited the Assembly Hall on 6 April, 1929, two days before the Bills were to be introduced, to see the public gallery overlooking the Hall and plan how to throw the bombs. They wanted to ensure that the bombs they threw did not hurt anyone. Though the Trade Disputes Bill, which sought to ban general strikes by industrial workers, had been passed by the Imperial Legislative Assembly, the president, Vithalbhai Patel, had not yet given his ruling on the Public Safety Bill that empowered the government to detain suspects without trial.

A few minutes before the session began on 8 April at 11 a.m. Bhagat Singh and B.K. Dutt sneaked in unnoticed, wearing khaki shirts and shorts, to the public gallery. An Indian member of the Assembly gave them passes at the entrance and then disappeared.

The gallery was overflowing with visitors. In the gallery they spied Sir John Simon whom they had demonstrated against outside the Lahore railway station. Inside the House, they recognized some national leaders – Motilal Nehru, Mohammad Ali Jinnah, N.C. Kelkar and M.R. Jayakar.

Their bombs, Bhagat Singh knew, would not stop the Bills from becoming Acts. The British had their 'yes-men' who were bound to put the legal stamp on them. Even otherwise, the viceroy had extraordinary powers. But at least the bombs would be symbolic of the simmering lava of resentment against the British government and its methods, and it would be a forewarning of the hatred that would spew out one day and burn foreign rule. Bhagat Singh recalled the words of Auguste Vaillant, a French anarchist: 'It takes a loud voice to make the deaf hear.' The bombs would create enough noise in the ears of inattentive rulers and indifferent people.

Bhagat Singh chose his moment carefully. He aimed the bomb carefully, to land away from the seated members, on the floor. It exploded with a bang. The hall plunged into darkness. There was confusion in the visitors' gallery. The screams of the ladies rose above the din all around. Then a second bomb was thrown by Dutt. The people in the public gallery ran towards the exit, jamming the passage in panic.

The first bang confused the members in the House. The second one scared them. Many, including the home member, ran for shelter. Some hid behind the wooden benches in the House. The bombs, deliberately of low intensity, had been thrown in such a way that no one was hurt. Then a sheaf of leaflets came fluttering down from the gallery like a shower of leaves and the members heard the sound of, 'Inquilab Zindabad!' and 'Long Live Proletariat!' rent the air. Bhagat Singh himself had written the text on the leaflets and had typed thirty to forty copies on a party letterhead on a machine that Jaidev

Kapur, a party member, had bought from a Marwari school drill-master.

The members picked up the leaflets and began to read them:

HINDUSTAN SOCIALIST REPUBLICAN ASSOCIATION

NOTICE

'It takes a loud voice to make the deaf hear.' With these immortal words uttered on a similar occasion by Vaillant, a French anarchist martyr, do we strongly justify this action of ours.

Without repeating the humiliating history of the past ten years of the working of the reforms (Montague-Chelmsford Reforms) and without mentioning the insults hurled at the Indian nation through this House – the so-called Indian Parliament – we see this time again, while the people, expecting some more crumbs of reforms from the Simon Commission, are ever quarrelling over the distribution of the expected bones, the Government is thrusting upon us new repressive measures like those of the Public Safety Bill and the Trade Disputes Bill, while reserving the Press Sedition Bill for the next session. The indiscriminate arrests of labour leaders working in the open field clearly indicate whither the wind blows.

In these provocative circumstances, the Hindustan Socialist Republican Association, in all seriousness, realizing their full responsibility, had decided and ordered its army to do this particular action so that a stop be put to this humiliating farce and to let the alien bureaucratic exploiters do what they wish but to make to come before the public eye in their naked form.

Let the representatives of the people return to their constituencies and prepare the masses for the coming revolution. And let the government know that, while protesting against the Public Safety Bill and the Trade Disputes Bill and the callous murder of Lala Lajpat Rai on behalf of the helpless Indian masses, we want to emphasize the lesson often repeated by history that it is easy to kill individuals but you cannot kill the ideas. Great empires crumbled but the ideas survived. Bourbons and Czars fell while the revolution marched ahead triumphantly.'

We are sorry to admit that we who attach so great a sanctity to human life, we who dream of a glorious future when man will be enjoying perfect peace and full liberty, have been forced to shed human blood. But the sacrifice of individuals at the altar of the great revolution that will bring freedom to all, rendering the exploitation of man by man impossible, is inevitable.

Long Live Revolution!
Balraj
Commander-In-Chief.

As the members began slowly returning to their seats, they saw two young men standing in the public gallery. Bhagat Singh and Dutt did not try to escape in the confusion that prevailed after they threw the bombs. Instead they stood steadfast as decided by their party. They chose to be arrested to use the occasion to explain the reasons for their actions. They looked forward to the opportunity they would get to speak in court.

The policemen on duty in the Central Assembly Hall stayed away from them, fearing the two were armed. They were not and said as much to the policemen. Their purpose was merely to create a disturbance to catch the attention of the government, and they had succeeded in doing that.

Bhagat Singh surrendered his automatic pistol, the same one he had used to pump bullets into Saunders' body, knowing fully well that the pistol would be the highest proof of his involvement in the Saunders' case. Although he and Dutt assured the authorities that they carried no arms on their person the policemen approached them hesitantly. The two were then handcuffed and searched. A British officer, who had run away on hearing the explosion, hurriedly came back and supervised the arrest. Both were taken to different police stations; Bhagat Singh to the main one and Dutt to the one in Chandni Chowk. The purpose was to question them separately. Both were kept in solitary confinement.

The authorities suspected that the bombings were only the tip of the iceberg. They feared a series of violent incidents would follow the explosion in the Assembly Hall. The press was asked to play down the Assembly incident. Though most versions that appeared in print were abridged, *The Hindustan Times,* New Delhi, managed to give the story a three-deck headline:

> *Bombs and Pistols Create Chaos in Assembly; Two Bombs Explode, Pistol Shots Fired.*
> *Screaming Women from Ladies' Gallery; Sir Fomanji Dalal Seriously Injured, Two Arrested.*
> *Sir George Schuster, Mr. S.C. Gupta and Other Officials Receive Minor Injuries.*

The viceroy issued a special statement where he conceded that the 'two assailants' had taken care not to kill anyone. He admitted that they could have caused havoc if they had so desired. But he said that their target was the 'institution' of the Central Assembly. Congress member Chaman Lall, reputed to be progressive in his leanings, was the first to denounce the revolutionaries. He said that the bomb-throwing was an act of madness. The revolutionaries rejected his observation with contempt.

The authorities believed that in Bhagat Singh they had caught a big fish and that he was the mastermind behind all revolutionary activity in India. The government was, however, intrigued by the two revolutionaries giving themselves up so easily. Did they intend to escape from jail? Was their surrender meant to fool the rulers? The British did not want to take any chances, so even the summons to the two revolutionaries were delivered to them in jail.

The style and format of the writing in the handbills struck British intelligence as suspiciously familiar. A senior police officer was sent to Lahore to scrutinize the posters announcing the murder of Saunders that had been plastered on the city's walls. The typed handbills and handwritten posters had certain common features. Both were written on pink paper. Both were issued by the Hindustan Socialist Republican Association, and both had the party's name on top. Both were signed by Balraj, commander-in-chief. And both began with the word 'Notice' and ended with the slogan, 'Long Live Revolution!'. Even the language used was similar. The concluding paragraph of the handbills thrown in the Assembly was: 'We are sorry to admit that we, who attach so great a sanctity to human life, we, who dream of a glorious future when man will be enjoying perfect peace and full liberty, have been forced to shed human blood. But the sacrifice of individuals at the altar of the great revolution that will bring freedom to all rendering the exploitation of man by man impossible, is inevitable.' The last paragraph of the poster in Lahore read: 'Sorry for the bloodshed of a human being; but the sacrifice of individuals at the altar of the Revolution that will bring freedom to all and make the exploitation of man by man impossible, is inevitable.'

The British began to suspect that Bhagat Singh was one of Saunders' killers. Suspicion against him deepened as the inquiry proceeded. He was singled out as the author of the text on the leaflets as well as the poster. Indeed, he was. He had written both in his own hand.

That the case was directed more against him did not worry Bhagat Singh. He had anticipated the direction the case would take from the day he replaced Das to throw the bomb. He had been preparing for a public appearance in court since then. He wanted to use the court as a platform to advocate the revolutionaries' point of view and in the process rekindle patriotic sentiments in the hearts of the people. If there was no struggle, there was no progress. People who said they favoured freedom and yet deprecated agitations were like men who wanted the final crop without ploughing the ground.

Bhagat Singh was charged with attempt to murder under Section 307 of the Indian Penal Code. Young Asaf Ali, a member of the Congress party, was his lawyer. At his first meeting with him, Bhagat Singh requested Asaf Ali to tell Chaman Lall that they were not lunatics. 'We humbly claim to be merely serious students of history and the conditions of our country and her aspirations.'

The British saw in Bhagat Singh's action a re-enactment of what Madan Lal Dhingra had done in 1909. Dhingra too had not put up any defence for killing Sir William Curzon Wyllie, aide-de-camp to the secretary of state of India at the Institute of Imperial Studies in London. Dhingra had refused to appear in court to vent his feelings against the British. Instead he had issued a statement through *The Daily News* in London:

> I admit the other day I attempted to shed English blood as a humble revenge for the inhuman hangings and deportations of patriotic Indian youths. In this attempt I have consulted none but my own conscience. I have, conspired with none but my own duty.

I believe that a nation held down by a foreign bayonet is in a perpetual state of war, since open battle is rendered impossible to a disarmed race. I attacked by surprise since guns were denied to me. I drew forth my pistol and fired. As a Hindoo I felt that wrong to my country is an insult to my God. Her cause is the cause of Ram, her service is in the service of Krishna. Poor in wealth and intellect, a son like myself has nothing else to offer to the mother but his own blood and so I have sacrificed the same on her altar. The only lesson required in India at present is to learn how to die and the only way to teach it is by dying ourselves. Therefore, I die and glory in my martyrdom. My only prayer of God is may I be reborn of the same mother and may I re-die in the same sacred cause till the cause is successful and she stands free for the good of humanity and the glory of God – *Bande Mataram.*

Dhingra was hanged on 17 August, 1909. The British compared Bhagat Singh and Dutt to the scores of revolutionaries who had ended up in the gallows.

Though Gandhi was a deeply respected leader, the Indian youth related more to the revolutionaries than to him. People like Bhagat Singh and Dutt were their heroes. So enthusiastic was their support that the British decided to hold court in Delhi Jail itself (now Maulana Azad Medical College). On 7 May, 1929, all roads leading to the jail were heavily guarded. CID men in plainclothes were posted at various points. Everybody entering the court was searched. Even pressmen were not spared.

The crown was represented by public prosecutor Rai Bahadur Suryanarayan. The trial magistrate was a British judge, P. B. Pool. Bhagat Singh's parents were also present in the court. When Bhagat Singh and Dutt were brought to the court, they raised clenched fists and shouted: 'Inquilab Zindabad!' and 'Samrajya Murdabad!' (Down with Imperialism!). The court recorded the slogans. The magistrate ordered the police to handcuff both the defendants. Neither of them offered resistance and sat down on a bench behind an iron railing, a makeshift arrangement.

The manner in which the prosecution presented its case left Bhagat Singh in no doubt that the British were out to nail him. He conveyed as much to his father and mother when he met them during a lunch-break, in the presence of police officials.

The prosecution's star witness was Sergeant Terry who said that a pistol had been found on Bhagat Singh's person when he was arrested in the Assembly. This was not factually correct because Bhagat Singh had himself surrendered the pistol while asking the police to arrest him. Even the eleven witnesses who said they had seen the two throwing the bombs seemed to have been tutored.

The entire operation had been so sudden that nobody could have either anticipated or noticed it. Indeed, both Bhagat Singh and Dutt had been very circumspect. They had carried the bombs in one pocket and the detonator in the other, walking slowly to make sure that there was no accidental explosion. It was an arduous task: staying apart, and at the same time ensuring that they aroused no suspicion.

When Bhagat Singh was finally allowed to speak he requested the court to allow them newspapers in prison, as was the practice for political undertrials. The court turned down his request saying it was not bound to follow any precedent. Already the court was treating them like petty criminals.

When Bhagat Singh and B.K. Dutt were brought to the court on the following day, 8 May, 1929, they wondered how they would get justice with such a hostile magistrate. As usual they shouted, 'Long Live Revolution!' and 'Down with Imperialism!' as they entered the court.

Bhagat Singh gave his name and said 'none' when questioned about his profession. Asked about his place of residence, he said: 'We are always moving from one place to another.'

The questioning went something like this:

Judge: 'Were you present in the Assembly on the 8th of April, 1929?'
Bhagat Singh: 'As far as this case is concerned, I feel no necessity to make a statement at this stage. When I do, I will make the statement.'
Judge: 'When you arrived in the court, you shouted, "Long Live Revolution!". What do you mean by it?'

Bhagat Singh's lawyer, Asaf Ali, objected to the question. The court sustained the objection. Bhagat Singh and Dutt vehemently denied an allegation that they had fired shots in the Assembly. The court then asked Dutt some questions but he refused to answer any one of them; he believed that, as leader, Bhagat Singh would attend to all queries.

As if it had already made up its mind, the court framed charges under Section 307 of the Indian Penal Code and Section 3 of the Explosive Substances Act. Bhagat Singh and Dutt were accused of throwing bombs 'to kill or cause injuries to the King Majesty's subjects'. The court once again asked them to make a statement, but they refused. The magistrate committed both of them to the sessions court, presided over by Judge Leonard Middleton.

The trial started in the first week of June, 1929. The public prosecutor produced some more witnesses, who too said that they had seen Bhagat Singh and Dutt throwing the bomb in the Assembly Hall. The same allegations of firing shots were repeated. The accused once again denied the charge.

Both Bhagat Singh and Dutt were especially irked by the allegation that they had fired shots from a gun. It was apparent that the government was not limiting the case to the bombs thrown in the Assembly. It was introducing extraneous elements to ferret out more information about the revolutionary party and its agenda. This was the stage when they decided to make their statement, that both of them had prepared in jail. The statement did not deny the throwing of the bomb. Asaf Ali read it out:

It was necessary to awaken England from her dreams... We dropped the bomb on the floor of the Assembly Chamber to register our protests on behalf of those who had no other means left to give expression to their heartrending agony. Our sole purpose was to make the deaf hear and give the heedless a timely warning.

Bhagat Singh also had a dig at Gandhi:

We have only marked the end of an era of Utopian non-violence of whose futility the rising generation has been convinced beyond the shadow of doubt.

Explaining the concept of violence which the revolutionaries had adopted, Bhagat Singh said:

It was the only effective method of solving the great social problems of the times – the problem of bringing economic and political independence to the workers and peasants, constituting the mass of people.

He justified their action after the Trade Disputes Bill was passed:

None whose heart bleeds for them, who have given their life-blood in silence to the building up of the economic structure, could repress the cry which this ruthless blow had wrung out of our hearts.

We are next to none in our love for humanity. Far from having any malice against any individuals, we hold human life sacred beyond words… The elimination of force at all costs is Utopian, and the new movement which has arisen in the country, and of that dawn we have given a warning, is inspired by the ideals which guided Guru Govind Singh, Shivaji, Kamal Pasha, Riza Khan, Washington, Garibaldi, Lafayette and Lenin. Both the alien government and the Indian public leaders appeared to have shut their eyes to this movement, we felt it is our duty to sound a warning where it could not go unheard… We repeat that we hold human life sacred beyond words, and would sooner lay down our own lives in the service of humanity than injure anyone else… And still we admit having deliberately thrown the bombs into the Assembly Hall. Facts speak for themselves and our intention would be judged from the result of the action without bringing in Utopian, hypothetical circumstances and presumptions…

'By revolution,' the statement said,

we mean the ultimate establishment of an order of society, which may not be threatened by such breakdown, and in which the sovereignty of the proletariat should be recognized and a world federation should redeem humanity from the bondage of capitalism and misery of imperial wars…

They said the viceroy was right when he said that they wanted to hit out at the institution,

Our practical protest was against the institution, which since its birth, has eminently helped to display not only its worthlessness but its far-reaching power for mischief.

Judge Leonard Middleton was no better than P. B. Pool. He too swallowed the prosecution story. Or was the outcome of the case a foregone conclusion? The judge accepted as proof the verbal testimony that Bhagat Singh and Dutt had thrown the bombs into the Assembly Chamber. Middleton even said that Bhagat Singh fired from his pistol while scattering the leaflets there.

The court held both Bhagat Singh and Dutt guilty of 'causing explosions of a nature likely to endanger life, unlawfully and maliciously, which constitute an offence punishable under Section 3 of the Explosive Substances Act, 1988'. They were sentenced to life imprisonment.

In his judgement, Judge Middleton ruled that he had no doubt that the defendants' acts were 'deliberate' and that they had made preparations for 'those acts of a complicated nature'. He rejected the plea that the bombs were deliberately low-intensity explosives since the impact of the explosion had shattered wood of one and a half inch thickness in the Assembly.

Nor did the judge accept the defence of the accused that they held human life sacred. He said their acts were not justified. 'It is probable that what they have done once they will do twice.' Still he did not want to hang them, the judge said.

Although both Bhagat Singh and Dutt were reluctant to file an appeal, they were persuaded to do so. If the purpose was to use the court as a forum to propagate the message of revolution, then why not exploit every opportunity to do so? The greater the noise, the greater their chance of awakening the masses from slumber and slavery. The appeal by Bhagat Singh and Dutt was rejected. They were sent to jail for fourteen years, the normal span for life imprisonment.

It was not Bhagat Singh's first introduction to jail. He had once been summarily arrested before on 29 May, 1927 from a public garden in Lahore. He was taken to the railway police lock-up and was kept there for a month before the police told him that he was 'responsible' for throwing a bomb at a crowd during Dussehra, which had been celebrated a few weeks earlier. He simply laughed when they wanted him to turn approver. People with views like his did not throw bombs on the innocent, he replied. One morning, Superintendent of CID Newman came to Bhagat Singh and gave him a long lecture on how the young were being led astray by bad elements in society. Bhagat Singh was struck by the sympathetic words he expressed. Newman asked him to confess; otherwise, he said, he would be forced to send Bhagat Singh for trial not only for the 'murders' at Dussehra, but also for the conspiracy to wage war in connection with the Kakori Case. The Englishman warned Bhagat Singh that the government had enough evidence to get him convicted and hanged. But this was not true. They did not have even a shred of evidence against him. Still the judge imposed a hefty bail of 50,000 rupees before releasing him. Since there was nothing to implicate him, the remand for bail had also been withdrawn later.

This incident had brought Bhagat Singh face to face with reality. The British would go to any extent to curb a revolt against their rule. They would frame false cases against those who raised their voices against them. They would imprison them for life or even hang them. The time had come for him to shoulder the responsibility.

5

Ham rukhe tukade khayenge. Bharat par ware jayenge
Ham sukhe channe chabayenge, Bharat ki baat banayenge.

SWAMI RAMTIRTHA

DURING HIS BRIEF IMPRISONMENT IN 1927 – WHEN HE WAS FIRST arrested on charges of association with the Kakori Case accused for an article written under the pseudonym *Vidrohi* and of supposedly being responsible for a bomb explosion at Lahore during the Dussehra fair – Bhagat Singh had protested against the conditions in jail. He could not bear the animal-like treatment meted out to prisoners and had tried in vain to draw the attention of the authorities to the torturous conditions in prison.

Back in jail, two-and-a-half years later, he found things worse than before. So Bhagat Singh decided to take up the issue again. He was, however, convinced that the government would not respond until he organized a prisoners' agitation. He also wanted to prove to Gandhi that the revolutionaries could endure the rigours of fasting and the torture of approaching death. But before he could plan anything, he was re-arrested for the murder of Saunders. The life imprisonment sentence given in the Assembly bomb case was kept in abeyance until the outcome of the murder trial.

Bhagat Singh knew something ominous was going to happen when the Assembly bomb trial was nearing an end. The judge was in a hurry to close the case. He even claimed that Bhagat Singh had been found guilty in connection with another case.

The police had gathered 'substantial evidence' against Bhagat Singh. Police raids in Saharanpur and Lahore had recovered bombs, pistols and cartridges. From Macleod Road in Lahore alone, where Bhagwati Charan lived, twenty-two bombs were said to have been recovered. Bombs were also found at Jhansi. It was apparent that one of their revolutionary comrades had informed the police about the exact location of the bomb factories. All the work they had done over the years stood revealed. Still worse, his colleagues, Jai Gopal and Hans Raj Vohra, had turned government approvers. Those who had fought against the government now became their tools.

The authorities had collected nearly 600 witnesses to establish their charges against Bhagat Singh. He was charged with involvement in the killings of Saunders and Head Constable Chanan Singh. Some twenty-one other cases, a few of a serious nature, were registered against him. The authorities knew that Bhagat Singh was not alone in this movement. Who were the others? Could they establish a conspiracy and show that the revolutionaries were all in it together, scheming, planning and executing the killings? How could the government string together their individual acts of violence to establish a well-hatched plot to kill the British?

Bhagat Singh was sent to Mianwali Jail and Dutt to Borstal Jail in Lahore. Both were put on the same train on 12 March, 1930 but in different compartments. Whatever the government did, it was conscious of the fact that its image had been tarnished by the one-sided trial in the Assembly Case, first before the magistrate and later before the sessions judge. The people of India, particularly the youth in the country, were convinced that the trial was a farce and that the British had conspired to execute these young radicals whatever the outcome.

Bhagat Singh wondered if the message of the revolution had been understood at all. It was not the romance of the pistol but a self-inflicted ordeal of suffering. Even though fully trapped by the society that suppressed him, a revolutionary was capable of changing it. He too was bound by rights and values but he had to find roads of his own, sometimes through force and sometimes through persuasion. Going on hunger strike was one road too. Demanding an improvement in living conditions in jail was one way of drawing the attention of the authorities.

Bhagat Singh decided that he and Dutt should go on a hunger strike on 15 June, as soon as they reached their respective jails. But he wondered how to convey the date of the fast to Dutt.

A British officer, specially deputed to keep an eye on Bhagat Singh, told him more than once on the journey to jail that a young man like himself should not waste his life. Bhagat Singh felt that the officer was tractable. He requested the officer to allow him to travel with Dutt for a short distance since it might well be their last journey together. They were old friends and their parting was going to be final; a few farewell moments would in no way violate any rule. Nor, Bhagat Singh pointed out, could they run away because they were handcuffed. The officer relented and transferred Bhagat Singh to Dutt's compartment up to the next station. Bhagat Singh told Dutt to go on a hunger strike in Borstal Jail on 15 June and that he would do the same in Mianwali Jail.

After reaching Mianwali, Bhagat Singh told his co-prisoners that though the Kakori revolutionaries fought long to improve jail conditions and even extracted a promise from the authorities on concessions, nothing tangible had materialized. (The same manual for prisoners was in operation when I was detained during the Emergency – Author's note). The British had reneged on their word. The first thing he did when he arrived at Mianwali Jail was to get hold of a list of the amenities provided to prisoners, both Indian and European. He found that the Europeans got better accommodation, food and daily-use items. Maltreatment at the hands of the jail authorities was difficult to quantify, but rations were not.

The Indian prisoners, although detained for political reasons, appeared to have reconciled themselves to the adverse conditions. Bhagat Singh found the members of the Babbar Akali being treated like criminals. Even bare necessities were denied to them. He identified the main problems as (a) getting sufficient rations (b) the creation of a bearable environment and (c) ensuring human treatment for the prisoners. Often bread was simply thrown at them in the way it is flung at animals in cages. The authorities were also very abusive in their language.

Bhagat Singh took up the cause of bettering jail conditions and proposed a hunger strike in protest – a completely Gandhian way. He wanted to prove that the revolutionaries were willing to employ any method to fight the British. A few days after the hunger strike, he wrote a letter to the home member, Government of India, on 24 June, 1929 :

> We, as political prisoners, should be given better diet and the standard of our diet should at least be the same as that of European prisoners. (It is not the sameness of dietary material that we demand, but the sameness of standard of diet). We shall not be forced to do any hard and undignified labour at all. All books, other than those proscribed, along with writing materials, should be allowed to us without any restriction. Toilet necessities should be supplied. Better clothing. At least one standard daily paper should be supplied to every political prisoner. Political prisoners should have a special ward of their own in every jail, provided with the necessities as those of the Europeans. And all the political prisoners in one jail must be kept together in that ward.

Until his letter reached the jail authorities, they had taken no notice of the hunger strike. Bhagat Singh had underlined in his letter that, when a European broke an ordinary law in order to fulfil a selfish motive he got all kinds of privileges in jail. He got a well-ventilated room with electrical fittings, the best food, such as milk, butter, toast, meat, etc. and good clothing, while they, the political prisoners, were deprived of such things.

Earlier, on 17 June, he had sent a letter to the inspector-general (jails), Punjab:

Despite the fact that I will be prosecuted along with other young men arrested in the Saunders' shooting case, I have been shifted to Mianwali Jail from Delhi. The hearing of the case is to start from 26 June, 1929. I am totally unable to understand the logic behind this kind of shifting. Whatever it be, justice demands that every undertrial should be given all those facilities which help him to prepare and contest the case. How can I appoint any lawyer while I am here? It is difficult to keep contact with my father and other relatives. This place is quite isolated, the route is troublesome and it is far from Lahore.

The letter had its effect. Bhagat Singh was shifted to Lahore Central Jail. Little did he realize then that the transfer would be used for an ulterior motive.

Before sending him to jail, the authorities took him to the cantonment police station in Lahore. The witnesses, already assembled there by the investigating staff, were allowed to see Bhagat Singh at close quarters so that they would have little difficulty spotting him during the identification parade.

Bhagat Singh continued the hunger strike in Lahore Central Jail. Here he met Udham Singh who told him that he would one day go to London and kill Michael O'Dwyer, who had been lieutenant-governor of Punjab when the Jallianwala Bagh massacre was committed. Udham singh was true to his word. He shot O'Dwyer dead at Coxton Hall in London on 13 March, 1940, nine years after Bhagat Singh was hanged. When sentenced to death, Udham Singh said: 'I do not care about dying. I am dying for a purpose,' more or less the same words that Bhagat Singh had uttered at the scaffold.

The hunger strike initiated by Bhagat Singh spread to other jails. Baba Sohan Singh, after serving a sentence of fifteen years, was awaiting his release when Bhagat Singh gave the call for the hunger strike. He too went on fast. The authorities punished him by extending his term by another three years.

When the country came to know of the hunger strike that the political prisoners had undertaken to protest their inhuman treatment in jail, there were wide protests. The Congress took serious note of this and Motilal Nehru condemned the government saying: 'The hunger strike is for a general cause and not for themselves.'

As the fast continued indefinitely with no solution in sight, Jawaharlal Nehru met Bhagat Singh and the other hunger strikers. He expressed his concern and issued a statement: 'I was very much pained to see the distress of the heroes. They have staked their lives in this struggle. They want that political prisoners should be treated as political prisoners. I am quite hopeful that their sacrifice would be crowned with success.'

Mohammad Ali Jinnah, who had by then distanced himself from the Congress because of differences over its functioning, raised the matter of the hunger strike in the Central Legislative Assembly. In his speech, on 12 September, 1929, he said:

They (Bhagat Singh and Dutt) were not given the treatment – not on racial grounds – but according to the standard and the scale which is laid down for Europeans in the matter of diet and bare necessities of life. It is not a mere question that they want to be treated as Europeans. [Jinnah had a dig at the British.] So far as I know, Bhagat Singh and Dutt wore *topees* and their figures appeared in shorts [when they appeared in the public gallery in the Assembly Hall]. Therefore, they ought to have been treated as European.

Jinnah criticized the government for discriminating between Indian and European prisoners:

You ask me, who is a political prisoner? It is very difficult to lay down any particular definition. But if you use your commonsense, if you use your intelligence, surely you can come to the conclusion with regard to the particular case and say, here are these men who are political prisoners and we do not wish to give them proper treatment. We want to give them treatment as undertrial prisoners. If you had said that, the question would have been solved long ago. Do you wish to prosecute them or persecute them?…

…I regret that, rightly or wrongly, youth today in India is stirred up, and you cannot, when you have three hundred and odd million of people, prevent such crimes being committed, however much you may deplore them and however much you may say that they are misguided. It is the system … of government which is resented by the people… But, remember, there are thousands of young men outside. This is not only the country where these actions are resorted to. It has happened in other countries, not youths, but grey bearded men have committed serious offences, moved by patriotic impulses…

There was no response from the government to all these protests. After many days, it reacted but only to express concern over the health of the hunger strikers, not to concede any demand. This observation made the prisoners more furious and they decided to ignore it. There was no let-up in the hunger strike. The disgusted prisoners lifted their spirits by breaking into song: *Kabhi woh din bhi ayega, ke jab azad hum honge…*

At times, Bhagat Singh engaged the attention of the hunger strikers by urging them to focus on the ideals of the movement. The moderates agitated to get sixteen annas but pocketed one anna and fought for the rest, he said. The revolutionaries must always keep in mind that they were striving for complete revolution, for a complete mastery of power. British Labour leaders had betrayed their real struggle and been reduced to mere hypocritical imperialists. Diehard conservatives were better than the polished imperialist Labour leaders. Revolution, he said, was not a philosophy of despair or the creed of desperadoes. It was a vital living force that was indicative of eternal conflict between the old and the new; between life and living death, between light and darkness. There was no concord, no symphony, no rhythm without revolution. Revolution was law, revolution was order and revolution was the truth. Without it, there could be no progress either in nature or in human affairs.

Talk of the hunger strike was now on everybody's lips. There was a spontaneous outburst of sympathy for the imprisoned men. Many from the public registered their support by going on fast themselves. Some newspapers began publishing a daily health bulletin chronicling the status of the hunger strikers. Many meetings were held to voice outrage against the British. At a meeting held at Jallianwala Bagh in Amritsar a warning was administered to the bureaucracy saying that it would be held responsible if any harm came to the prisoners. At another meeting in Lahore, more than 10,000 people raised their hands to express solidarity with the hunger strikers. So wide was the sympathy that 21 June, 1929 was celebrated as Bhagat Singh Day throughout the country. Still the government did not relent. More and more political prisoners in jail wanted to take up the challenge and join the hunger strike.

Jatindra Nath Das, a young but tough revolutionary, was opposed to the emotional approach. He advised caution. It would be a long struggle, he warned. 'Inching toward death in a hunger strike is far more difficult than death in a gunfight or on the gallows,' he felt. It would be against revolutionary traditions to withdraw a strike without attaining the objective, the hunger strikers replied. 'It is better not to join the strike than to suffer a premature withdrawal,' Jatindra rejoined. They did not listen to him. Jatindra Nath Das was not against the hunger strike. He just wanted his comrades to understand the full import of the mission they had undertaken. In fact it was he who led the fast and sustained it till the very end.

When the authorities realized that the hunger strikers were adamant they tried several tricks to break the strike. Delicacies of different types were placed in their cells and then removed to test the resolve of the hunger strikers. But nobody faltered. Water pitchers in cells were filled with milk so that either the prisoners remained thirsty or were forced to break their fast.

When the government realized that it was making no headway with this approach it tried to use the same tricks it had used to dupe the Kakori railway prisoners – agreeing to concessions but not implementing them. The government announced that it would give better facilities and adequate food to the political prisoners. Some of the hunger strikers were promised special treatment on medical grounds. But nobody was taken in. Bhagat Singh told the authorities that the promises were all too familiar. The hunger strikers rejected the offer.

The authorities resorted to force-feeding. The hunger strikers resisted these attempts. One of the prisoners, Kasuri, swallowed red pepper and drank boiling water to clog the passage of the feeding tube. The government saw no course other than compromise. The Governor came down from Shimla to meet jail officials but no agreement could be reached.

The British were forced to appoint the Punjab Jail Enquiry Committee to look into the matter. The committee gave an undertaking on behalf of the government that a special diet and other facilities would be provided to the political prisoners. Some of the hunger strikers broke their fast. However, they sent the committee's chairman, Duni Chand, a note that the strike had only been suspended, not abandoned. The prisoners did not have to wait long to find that, as expected, the government had gone back on its word.

6

Meri hawa mein rahegi khayal ki khushboo,
Yeh musht-e-khaq hai, fani rahe na rahe.

WHEN THE GOVERNMENT REALIZED THAT THE FAST HAD RIVETED the attention of the people throughout the country, it hurried up the trial, which came to be known as the Lahore Conspiracy Case. The trial started in Borstal Jail, Lahore, on 10 July, 1929. Rai Sahib Pandit Sri Kishen, a first-class magistrate, was the judge. He had earned the title of Rai Sahib for loyal service to the British. Bhagat Singh and twenty-seven others were charged with murder, conspiracy and waging war against the king. Ironically, the average age of the revolutionaries was twenty-two.

On the day the trial was scheduled to commence the police barricaded the magistrate's court. The general public was not admitted inside. Even the counsels for the accused were stopped from entering the court and were allowed to enter only after they insisted on being let in. Bhagat Singh's parents were among the few visitors.

On their part, the revolutionaries' strategy was to boycott the proceedings; they showed no interest in the trial and adopted an attitude of total indifference. They had neither faith nor respect for the court constituted by the British. Still they wanted to go through the motions of the court. They thought they would also show the public that the mind of the court was already made up. The people respected their stance. They said the English loved liberty for themselves and hated all acts of injustice, except those which they committed themselves. A handcuffed Bhagat Singh, still on hunger strike, was brought to the court on a stretcher. His weight had fallen by 14 pounds, from 133 to 119.

Jatindra Nath Das's condition was deteriorating rapidly. The Jail Committee recommended that he be unconditionally released. The government rejected the suggestion, making it a matter of prestige. It offered to release him on bail but he did not agree. Someone deposited the bail money for him but Jatin refused to accept it. He was so weak that he could not even turn in bed. The government claimed that he was demanding that all the hunger strikers, including the ones chargesheeted, be released unconditionally. This was not true. Jatindra had scrupulously kept the issue of jail facilities separate from the case.

Jatindra was sinking fast; the end could come any day. Bhagat Singh and his comrades were helpless. The entire country was outraged. Jatin did not give up the fast even though most of his other comrades had relented after the Jail Committee's assurance that they would improve conditions.

At Bhagat Singh's personal request, he agreed to an enema to clear the toxins from his bowels. 'Who can say no to Bhagat Singh,' he told the jailor. However, Jatin refused to touch any food. Nor did he allow himself to be force-fed. He was a Bengal revolutionary. And though they had relinquished the cult of the bomb they had resolved to set themselves up as examples of sacrifice, hoping to tug at the conscience of people. Jatin followed his resolve to the very end. His fast lasted sixty-three days. His last words were: 'I do not want any obsequies to be performed at Kali Bari in the orthodox Bengali fashion. I am an Indian.'

Jatin died on 13 September, 1929. Subhash Chandra Bose, sent 600 rupees to transport his body from Lahore to Calcutta. Bombay and Punjab too offered money. After his death, the viceroy informed London:

Jatin Das of the Conspiracy Case who was on the hunger strike, died this afternoon at 1 p.m. Last night, five of the hunger strikers gave up their hunger strike. So, there are only Bhagat Singh and Dutt who are on strike...

The official announcement on the death was cold and businesslike:

J.N. Das died yesterday at about 1.10 p.m. His brother K.C. Das received Rs. 600 from Subhash Chandra Bose from Calcutta to pay for the carriage of the body by car.

The country fell silent. People felt as if they had lost a family member. They had followed Jatindra Nath's long hunger strike with bated breath. Now it was all over. They were sad and angry but felt proud of him for resolutely keeping his word till the very end. The entire nation felt a vicarious pride in the uncompromising Jatin and viewed him as one unvanquished by the mighty British empire.

His funeral procession started from Borstal Jail at about four in the afternoon, with eighty eminent Punjab Congress leaders and volunteers in attendance. As the procession wended its way to the railway station, hundreds more joined it. Shops downed their shutters in silent homage.

The news of Jatin's death spread all over India in no time. There was a sense of loss, but also a feeling of helplessness. People expressed their grief by standing in silence with their heads covered at every railway station that the train carrying the body passed through.

In Calcutta, some six lakh people waited at Howrah station platform and outside it. Many more joined in as the funeral cortege moved through the crowds that lined both sides of the streets. It took many hours to reach the banks of the Hooghly where the cremation took place. All along the way his body was showered with flowers. The walls were plastered with posters saying in Bengali: 'Let my son be like Jatin Das.' As the pyre was lit by his brother, cries rose into the sky.

The viceroy informed the secretary of state in London about the procession through a telegram, saying:

> The procession in Calcutta is stated to have been of a record size and to have consisted of five lakhs of people...The crowd was undoubtedly enormous... Meetings of sympathy with Das and of condemnation of the Government have been held in many places, but no report has yet been received of any clash with the authorities.

Highest tributes were paid to Jatindra by practically every leader in the land. Two Punjabi leaders, Mohammad Alam and Gopichand Bhargava, resigned from the Punjab Legislative Council in protest. Motilal Nehru proposed the adjournment of the House at the Central Assembly as a censure against the government's policy on the treatment of the Lahore prisoners. He accused the government of 'inhumanity' and blamed it for adopting an attitude that had 'resulted in the death of Jatindra Nath Das and endangered the lives of others.' Another member, Neogy, described the home member as belonging to 'the race of Dyer and O'Dwyer'. The censure motion was carried by 55 against 47 votes.

Gandhi did not share the enthusiasm the hunger strike had generated. He disapproved of the publication of Bhagat Singh and Dutt's joint statement – handbills bearing which had been thrown in the Assembly Hall – in the Congress bulletin. Gandhi expressed his unhappiness in a letter to Nehru, then the Congress general secretary.

Gandhi's disapproval forced Nehru to issue a clarification:

As a matter of fact, I am not in favour of the hunger strike. I told this to many young men who came to see me on this subject but I did not think it worthwhile to condemn the fast publicly.

Bhagat Singh felt the loss of Jatin acutely. Highly emotional as he was, he wept openly. Taking out the notebook in which he regularly penned lines from his favourite books he recited a verse by U.N. Figner, a relatively unknown poet, whose verse he had copied in his book and captioned: 'The Noblest Fallen.'

The noblest have fallen. They were buried obscurely
In a deserted place.
No tears fell over them,
Strange hands carried them to the grave.
No cross, no enclosure, and no tombstone tell their glorious names.
Grass grows over them,
A feeble blade bending low keeps the secret.
The sole witnesses were the surging waves which furiously beat
Against the shore.
But even they, the mighty waves,
Could not carry farewell greetings to the distant home.

Jatindra's death only steeled the determination of the revolutionaries. They now readied themselves for the next ordeal. They believed that the conspiracy case was being staged by the British to hang Bhagat Singh and his comrades. They decided to treat the court proceedings as the farce that it was.

Bhagat Singh, Sukhdev and Bijoy Kumar Sinha constituted the brain trust for the case. They decided that their strategy would be to simply not attend the court on some days, to make it clear that they did not recognize the right of a foreign-power-appointed magistrate to try the freedom fighters. They also decided that on some days they would attend the court only to raise slogans like 'Long Live Revolution!' and 'Down with Imperialism!' The slogans would be followed the singing of a patriotic song. On other days, they decided, they would attend court solely to repeat their resolve in public that the deliverance of their country could only come through freedom and revolution.

The court proceedings were often disturbed by the students from nearby schools and colleges who assembled outside to wait for Bhagat Singh and his associates. The moment they spotted their heroes they would join them in singing: '*Kabhi woh din bhi ayega…*'

On other days the beautiful song, '*Sarfaroshi ki tamanna ab hamare dil mein hai*' filled the skies.

The revolutionaries often used the court as a place to expound the ideology of revolution. First they wanted to liberate India from foreign rule and then they would transform it into a socialist society. Revolution, as their party's manifesto said 'may be anti-God but is certainly not anti-man'. They were clear that the struggle in India would not end so long as 'a handful of exploiters go on exploiting the labour of the common people for their own ends'. It mattered little whether the exploiters were British capitalist or Indians. Their class, as one, must go.

The Jail Committee requested Bhagat Singh and B.K. Dutt to give up their hunger strike but it failed to persuade them to do so. Finally, it was Bhagat Singh's father who had his way. He came armed with a resolution by the Congress urging them to give up the hunger strike. The revolutionaries respected the Congress party because they were knew of its struggle for India's freedom. They called Gandhi 'an impossible visionary' but they saluted him for the awakening he had brought about in the country.

Both Bhagat Singh and Dutt agreed to suspend the hunger strike at the Congress party's request. It was on the 116th day of the fast, on 5 October, 1929 that the hunger strike ended. Bhagat Singh had surpassed the 97-day world record for hunger strikes, set by an Irish revolutionary.

After agreeing to break the fast, Bhagat Singh and B.K. Dutt sent a message to the Congress:

In obedience to the resolution of the All India Congress Committee, we have today decided to suspend the hunger strike till the final decision by the government in regard to the question of treatment of political prisoners in Indian jails. We are very anxious that all those who went on the hunger strike in sympathy with us should also discontinue it forthwith…

7

Jis dhaj se koi maqtal mein gaya woh shaan salaamat rehti hai
Yeh jaan to aani jaani hai, is jaan ki koi baat nahin

FAIZ AHMED FAIZ

AFTER THE HUNGER STRIKE, BHAGAT SINGH REFOCUSED HIS attention on the trial. The crown was represented by the government advocate C.H. Carden-Noad, assisted by Kalandar Ali Khan, Gopal Lal, and Bakshi Dina Nath, prosecuting inspector. The accused were defended by Duni Chand, Barkat Ali, Mehta Amin Chand, Bishan Nath, Amolak Ram Kapur, W. Chandra Dutt and Mehta Puran Chand, all lawyers.

The court recorded an order prohibiting slogans in the courtroom. But Duni Chand, the defence counsel sitting nearest to the magistrate, pointed out that the text of the order had been dictated by Kalandar Ali Khan, the public prosecutor. Duni Chand asked if it was part of the duty of the crown counsel to frame the orders of the court. Did the police dictate the court, Duni Chand asked. Khan, however, denied the charge.

The government advocate filed the orders by the government sanctioning the prosecution under the Explosive Substances Act and Sections 121,121 A, 122 and 123 of the Penal Code relating to sedition.

Hamilton Harding, the senior superintendent of police, Lahore, filed the formal complaint under the orders of the government. He first read out the names of the accused, then the complaint, which alleged the hatching of a conspiracy to wage war against the king. The accused were also charged with collecting men, arms and ammunition for overthrowing the government. The complaint referred to the Hindustan Socialist Republican Association and their meetings at Lahore and other places in India 'with a view to establish a federal republican government in its stead'. The revolutionaries gave their reply by raising the slogan, 'Inquilab Zindabad!'. The court remarked, 'Every sane person would object to such shouts (slogans).'

Duni Chand stood up to object to the court holding its sessions in jail. He said the so-called courtroom was small and it was surrounded on all sides by the police. He also pointed out that the relatives and friends of the accused were waiting out on the road and were not being allowed into the courtroom.

Court: 'Should the whole city come here?'
Counsel: 'Everybody who wants to come should be admitted provided there is room. And there should be no preference for persons from the prosecution.'

Carden-Noad said that no discrimination was made between members of the bar and others or between the prosecuting counsel and the defence counsel. There was not enough room in the hall for all who desired to attend the proceedings.

Counsel Barkat Ali challenged the statement. He pointed out that while he was stopped at the gate, the government advocate and another European walked straight in without anyone questioning them or asking them to produce a permit. Ali asked the sub-inspector on duty the reason for the discrimination and was informed that the government advocate and Europeans did not require a pass.

Carden-Noad at this stage drew the attention of the magistrate to the distribution of flowers among the accused. He said he wanted his objection to be recorded. The court took notice of Carden-Noad's objection but overruled the protest by the defence counsel regarding the restrictions on admission. The magistrate held that to control the congestion it was necessary to regulate admission by passes, but every facility would be given to the relatives of the accused.

The government's decision not to allow many visitors was defeating the purpose of the revolutionaries. They were not getting enough opportunity to disseminate their message – which was their primary purpose. They too took up the matter of entry to the court strongly with the magistrate. The restrictions were relaxed. Visitors were allowed in but only in restricted numbers.

At the very beginning of the trial a whisper went around that the British and the Congress would reach some sort of compromise. Bhagat Singh cautioned young political workers against these rumours. He asked them to concentrate on working with farmers and peasants. The real revolutionary armies were in villages and factories. He advised them to adopt Marxism as their ideology.

One day, Durga Das Khanna, a close friend of the revolutionaries, managed to attend court. Seeing him in the visitors' gallery, Bhagat Singh pulled him aside and said, 'What a fool you are! Why are you here? You must leave immediately and should not be seen around here at all.' A Sikh deputy superintendent of police, an admirer of the revolutionaries, overheard what Bhagat Singh was saying to Khanna. The police officer turned to Khanna quietly and said: 'Your leader is giving you very sound advice. I am not going to take any action. I too advise you to leave at once.' Indeed, some in the police establishment were sympathetic to the revolutionaries.

As the trial progressed the government was satisfied that the case, despite interruptions, was on track again. But Bhagat Singh and his comrades thought differently. One day they recalled the Kakori prisoners' bravery and narrated the whole incident despite the court's repeatedly asking them not to. On Lenin Day, 21 January, 1930, the accused appeared in court wearing red scarves. As soon as the magistrate sat in his chair, they shouted, 'Long Live Socialist Revolution!', 'Long Live People!', 'Lenin's Name Will Never Die!' and 'Down with Imperialism!'. Bhagat Singh then read out the telegram that he wanted to be sent to the Third International. The telegram said:

> On Lenin Day we send hearty greetings to all those who are doing something for carrying forward the ideas of the Great Lenin. We wish success to the great experiment Russia is carrying out.

(Little did they realize then that their God would fail sixty years later.)

Soon the case settled into a predictable routine. The magistrate would listen to complaints and reject them, almost as if he had been instructed to do so. A typical example was that of Prem Dutt Verma, one of the accused. Verma complained to the court that a police constable, who was on guard duty had used abusive language with him. He requested the removal of the constable. Otherwise, he said, he would be compelled to take the law into his own hands. Mehta Puran Chand, counsel for Verma, argued that in view of the complaint, the constable should be removed from his present duty. The court asked how it could be established that the constable had abused the accused. Amolak Ram Kapur, the defence counsel, submitted that the incident had happened only a few minutes ago in the open court and that there were several witnesses. The matter had been immediately brought to the notice of the court and it was the magistrate's duty to conduct an inquiry into it. It was a serious matter and if the court refused to look into it, the accused might have to lodge a formal complaint. The court refused to take notice of the matter and continued with the proceedings.

Matters came to a head one day when Jai Gopal, who had turned approver, swaggered up to the witness box twirling his moustache and showered abuse on Bhagat Singh and his comrades. Cries of 'Shame! Shame!' were heard from the gallery. Verma, the youngest of the accused, hurled a slipper at Jai Gopal. The proceedings were stopped. The magistrate passed an order stating that the undertrials would henceforth be handcuffed in court. Immediately Bhagat Singh declared that they would not attend court until the order was withdrawn.

After the slipper incident, the prisoners were subjected to untold savagery. The *Young Liberator*, Bombay, wrote:

There is no limit to official brutality and lawlessness. The treatment meted out to the Lahore prisoners may not have been accorded even to medieval brutes and uncivilized barbarians.

The following day the police used force to take the revolutionaries to court. Of the sixteen undertrials, five were physically lifted and forcibly put into the prison van but they too held on to their seats and refused to step out when the van reached the court. Finally the jail superintendent made a deal with them, promising that the handcuffs would be removed in court. The five relented, only to discover that it was a ruse. Their handcuffs were not removed in court. So they paid the authorities back in the same coin. They requested the police to remove their handcuffs during lunch and when the police tried to slip them back on after the meal, they resisted their attempts to do so. This led to a scuffle and the policemen beat the undertrials in court before the visitors.

Bhagat Singh was singled out by the police and set upon with particular savagery. He angrily asked the magistrate: 'Have you ordered the police to kick us? Can't you control them?' Verma complained that the policemen had even inserted their fingers into the prisoners' rectums and kicked them in their testicles. 'You call this civilized behaviour?' he asked indignantly.

The magistrate did precious little then but he was forced to rescind the order on the handcuffing when the press, including some newspapers in London, reported the 'brutal beating of prisoners'.

As time passed, the Lahore Conspiracy Case got publicity beyond the shores of India. This is precisely what Bhagat Singh and his comrades had wished for but had been uncertain about accomplishing. Contributions to the HSRA began to pour in from all over the world. Indians living in Canada, Japan and America sent donations. One lady sent money all the way from Poland and wanted to know all about the proceedings. Photographs of Bhagat Singh and Dutt were displayed all over the country in homes and shops. Calendars bearing their pictures did roaring business. The people of India felt great pride in what the revolutionaries were doing in the court. Many eminent people including Motilal Nehru, Rafi Ahmed Kidwai and the raja of a small state in UP, Kalakarkar, visited the court to express their solidarity with the revolutionaries.

During one of his visits, Motilal Nehru praised Bhagat Singh for the admirable work the revolutionaries had done. He said their bravery had brought the dream of independence closer to India. Bhagat Singh used his services to publicize the case and to warn the British that they would continue to be targeted by the youth till they withdrew from the country.

While in prison, Bhagat Singh had learnt of two things: that the revolutionaries still at large had planned to gun down Khan Bahadur Abdul Aziz, the superintendent in charge of the investigation into the Lahore Conspiracy Case, who had concocted his evidence, and two, that they had planned the electrically-controlled detonation of a bomb on the viceroy's train. As it turned out, both the intended victims escaped narrowly. The bullet fired at Aziz went astray. A rear carriage of the viceroy's train was destroyed but the compartment in which he travelled suffered no damage. It was Azad's doing. Bhagat Singh was sure of this.

The attack on the viceroy came at a time when the hearings in the magistrate's court had tarnished the image of the government. The stock of the revolutionaries rose. One, they were able to expose the rampant fabrication of evidence in the case. Two, the impression got around that their reach was long enough to take on anyone in the government.

The case built by the prosecution was that a revolutionary conspiracy had been hatched as far back as September, 1928, two years before the murder of Saunders. The government alleged that various revolutionary parties had joined together to forge one organization in 1928 itself to operate in the north and the north-east of India, from Lahore to Calcutta.

The amalgamation part was correct. The HSRA had come into existence by coalescing revolutionary groups from different states. But to draw a line between revolutionary activities before 1928 and after was like dividing water. All the revolutionaries, wherever they were, had been working for many years for the same purpose: to change society and rid the country of foreign rule.

The case proceeded at a snail's pace. The government got so exasperated that it approached the Lahore High Court for directions to the magistrate: he should have the right to refuse the examination of further witnesses whenever he considered that a prima facie case had been established.

A division bench of the Lahore High Court, headed by chief justice Sir Shadi Lal, dismissed the application of Carden-Noad. In his judgement, Shadi Lal said:

This is an application under Section 561 of the Criminal Procedure Code, made by the government advocate on behalf of the Crown in a case which is pending before a magistrate. The circumstances under which the application has been made do not admit of any dispute.

For reasons known only to the authorities, Duni Chand, Bhagat Singh's legal adviser, was not allowed to take his seat in the court one day – neither among the defence counsel, nor as a member of the bar or in the press gallery. Duni Chand walked out of the court in protest saying, 'In no part of the world are the members of the bar treated in the manner in which they are treated in this court.'

The day Duni Chand was insulted, Bhagat Singh and his comrades decided to stay away from court. They also resumed their hunger strike. They told the magistrate that they had no alternative because the government had gone back on its commitment to provide better treatment, better facilities and better diet for the prisoners. The *Civil and Military Gazette,* an English daily from Lahore, assailed the prisoners for boycotting court. Bhagat Singh defended his stance and explained his reasons for not attending the proceedings in a letter to the magistrate.

Bhagat Singh said that after going through the *Civil and Military Gazette,* he considered it necessary to explain the reasons for resuming the hunger strike. He complained of the harassment to which their supporters had been subjected. Their closest well-wishers were not allowed to meet them. He said,

I myself cannot keep a whole-time lawyer; therefore I wanted that my trusted friends should observe the court proceedings by being present there, but they were denied permission without any explicit reason...

Bhagat Singh ended his letter with the observation:

We can never like this drama acted in the name of justice,
because we do not get any facility or benefit for defending
ourselves. One more serious complaint is against the
non-availability of newspapers. Undertrial prisoners
cannot be treated like convicted prisoners. We should
be given at least one newspaper regularly. We want one
newspaper also for those who do not know English...
We will rejoin the proceedings when these
inconveniences are removed.

Ten days after the second hunger strike, on 19 February, 1930
the government issued a press communique on the classification
of convicted and undertrial prisoners. The accused gave up their
hunger strike the next day. But the government again went back
on its word. All the accused were placed in the 'C' class and
treated with 'vindictive brutality'.

First announcing facilities and then withdrawing them was
in keeping with the government's track record for perfidy. It
wanted to trick the revolutionaries into a situation where they
would give up the hunger strike before getting the facilities.
The government broke its promise so many times and so
brazenly that even the revolutionaries felt embarrassed for it.

Through March, 1930, the proceedings were relatively smooth.
Both sides, the authorities and the revolutionaries, had come to
realize that they were at the end of the road. The magistrate felt
he could not make any headway without the cooperation of the
undertrials. The undertrials, in turn, were convinced that the
proceedings were a sham. It was a charade for both of them.

The farce ended on 1 May, 1930 when the viceroy, Lord Irwin,
promulgated an Ordinance to set up a tribunal to try what was

already known as the Lahore Conspiracy Case. The Ordinance, LCC Ordinance No. 3 of 1930, put an end to the proceedings pending in the magistrate's court. The case was transferred to a tribunal of three high court judges without any right to appeal, except to the privy council. The tribunal was similar to the one which tried the Ghadarites during the First World War. It was also given powers to deal with wilful obstruction and to dispense with the presence of the accused.

The statement of objectives, issued along with the ordinance, were:

1. The offences were of an unusually serious character.
2. The conduct of the accused rendered it impossible to count upon obtaining a conclusion by the normal methods of procedure within any calculable period.

The viceroy also blamed the revolutionaries on trial for stalling the proceedings through their hunger strike. Bhagat Singh refuted the charge in a letter to the viceroy written on 2 May, 1930 in which he pointed out that the hunger strike had nothing to do with the trial:

It was not the hunger strike that had forced you to promulgate the ordinance. There is something else, the consideration of which confused the heads of your government. It is neither the protection of the case nor any other emergency which forces you to sign this lawless law. It is certainly something different. But let us declare once and for all that our spirits cannot be cowed down by ordinances. You may crush certain individuals but you cannot crush this nation. As far as this ordinance is concerned, we consider it to be our victory.

The appointment of the tribunal signalled a clear message that the British were prepared to go to any extent to crush any challenge to their rule or the system. Even if it meant desecrating every canon of justice.

The tribunal was viewed by the people as a mere formality, an exercise whose sole purpose was to hang the leaders of the revolution, particularly Bhagat Singh. The youth had come to idolize him. The Lahore Conspiracy Case had put new life in the freedom movement which had been wallowing in depression after the failure of the non-cooperation movement. In fact, the people were so fired up that Gandhi found the atmosphere opportune for initiating the Dandi March, challenging the government's dictum disallowing the local people from making salt from sea water.

When the appointment of the tribunal was announced in court, Bhagat Singh thanked the magistrate on behalf of the accused. He told him that they had nothing personal against him, the revolutionaries were devoid of hate and fear, the prolongation of their harassment, Bhagat Singh assured him, had not made them bitter.

The revolutionaries, who had embarked on the path of 'propaganda by action' – a phrase coined by Sukhdev – felt confident that they were finally getting somewhere. Both the Assembly Case and the magistrate's court had helped get them attention. They had been able to put across to the people not only the idea of the need for independence but also for the establishment of a classless society, a concept different from that of Gandhi's – who wanted the rich to stay as the trustees of the wealth they produced. The revolutionaries believed that unfair conditions would continue even after the attainment of freedom, if the wealthy went on exploiting the common people.

The tribunal was a formality to silence the voice of the revolutionaries once and for all.

Life or death? What did it matter?

They had known from the outset of the trial that they were fated to hang.

Bhagat Singh and his comrades were laying down their lives to shake off the fetters of slavery. They were fighting for the freedom of people in bondage – economic, social, political– all over the world.

8

Ek halora idhar se aaye, ek halora udhar se aaye
sara ulat pulat ho jaaye…

MAY IN NORTHERN INDIA IS AN OPPRESSIVE MONTH. THE
monsoon does not break until two months later. Any lingering
touch of spring is well over by this time. Lahore, in fact, swelters
in the sun without any respite.

5 May, 1930, when the case opened in the stately Poonch
House, was a hot day, the temperature touching 106.3°
Fahrenheit. But it was not so much the heat as the terror that
had deterred people from attending court. Many had preferred
to stay away because they had heard that those who went would
be harassed. For many days, the authorities had been picking up
people at random. More than 200 had been detained on the
suspicion that they were sympathetic to the cause of the
revolutionaries. The city swarmed with turbaned policemen and
white officers in sola-topis. Poonch House was like a small
cantonment area, heavily guarded by armed police because the
intelligence department had warned the government about a plot
to rescue Bhagat Singh. Entry was through passes which were
issued selectively.

A large oblong room with a high ceiling of corrugated
asbestos sheets served as the courtroom. Placed on a wooden
platform was a table. Fans with wooden blades hung from the
ceiling. Even at full speed, they were ineffective. Not even forty
chairs were occupied when the three tribunal members – Justice

Coldstream, followed by Justice Agha Haider and Justice J. C. Hilton – entered the courtroom at two minutes after ten. The judges sat behind the table in high-backed chairs. Behind their heads was a photograph of King George V which had been hastily put up on the wall.

In the audience was Bhagat Singh's father, Kishen Singh, who had constituted a defence committee despite his son's opposition. Bhagat Singh had told his father in vain that political workers must ignore the courts and should be ready to pay the heaviest price with a smile on their face, but he did not listen. Most of the forty-odd visitors used a photograph of Bhagat Singh's – distributed widely in the city – to fan themselves. Their eyes were fixed not on the dais but on the side-door from where Bhagat Singh and his comrades were expected to enter. When they heard the screeching of vans, the shuffling of feet and the raising of slogans, they stood up in respect. Their heroes, eighteen of them accused in the Lahore Conspiracy Case, burst into the room, and the hall resounded with shouts of 'Inquilab Zindabad!' and 'Gora ja! ja!' (white man go, go).

Bhagat Singh and his associates entered the court singing:

Sarfaroshi ki tamanna ab hamare dil mein hai
Dekhna hai zor kitna bazua-i-katil mein hai…
Waqt ane de bata deinge tujhe eh asman
Ham abhi se kya batain, kya hamare dil mein hai.

While the judges sat stonily impassive, the visitors in the courtroom tapped their feet and clapped in time with the song. Both the revolutionaries and the visitors were in total harmony – as if the two had become one. Coldstream, in the chair, lost his temper and summoned Gopal Lal, the public prosecutor, and asked him to provide the tribunal with an authoritative translation of the song. Agha Haider tried to translate the words, but his voice was drowned by the song. Coldstream looked towards the police, who awaited his orders. All of a sudden the song stopped. Rajguru broke away from his comrades and positioned himself opposite the judges. He challenged the very constitution of the tribunal. He said it was illegal, *ultra vires*. The viceroy, he said, did not have the power to cut short normal legal procedure. The Government of India Act, 1915, authorized him to promulgate an Ordinance to set up a tribunal but only when the situation so demanded. No such conditions obtained for his step. There was no breakdown in the law and order situation. Nor had there been any uprising. He had to prove before the court that an emergency-like situation prevailed in the country.

Rajguru asked the tribunal to defer the hearing till it was decided whether the viceroy had the authority to use extraordinary powers in normal times. He was not alone to question the validity of the Ordinance. Several other revolutionaries in the dock also backed him. Five of them also demanded a fortnight's adjournment to enable them to make necessary arrangements for their defence.

The tribunal ruled that the petition was 'premature'. Coldstream also rejected Rajguru's objection, and refused to adjourn the proceedings. He believed all this was part of the 'tactics' that had been used earlier to disturb the hearings before Magistrate Sri Kishen.

Coldstream was determined to reject any objection to proceed further. Equally determined were Bhagat Singh and his comrades not to let the tribunal proceed. It was as if both were trying to stonewall each other. The revolutionaries once again raised the slogan 'Long Live Revolution!' to disrupt proceedings. Once again Rajguru got up from his seat, this time delivering a speech in Urdu. He lamented that British rule had sucked India's blood and had reduced it to destitution and helplessness. He said there was only one form of government, whatever it might be called, where the ultimate control was in the hands of the people. He was still speaking when Coldstream interrupted him to say that the tribunal did not follow the language in which he addressed it. Rajguru shot back that he too did not understand English, the court language. He wanted an interpreter. Coldstream acceded to his request.

It was a little after 11 a.m. that the case was started. Carden-Noad, the government advocate, asked for leave of the court to state the facts of the case in his capacity as complainant. Malik Barkat Ali, Duni Chand, Mehta Amin Chand and other counsel objected to this. They argued that Carden-Noad was not a complainant because he had not taken oath to enjoy that status. Since there was no evidence before the court, it would not be possible to stop the crown counsel if he strayed into irrelevant arguments. This was bound to prejudice the defence. The tribunal left the matter at that, without giving any decision on whether Carden-Noad could make a statement without taking oath.

Carden-Noad made the opening speech on behalf of the prosecution and charged Bhagat Singh and his comrades with conspiracy to murder and wage war against the king. He accused them of initiating the cult of the gun which he said had spread throughout the country. Carden-Noad alleged that the revolutionaries had an organization called the Hindustan Socialist Republican Association, which used arms, bombs and explosives. He charged them with getting money from abroad for their activities. Carden-Noad referred to the murder of Saunders and said it was part of a much wider conspiracy. He mentioned various fictitious names used by the undertrials.

Carden-Noad then elaborated on the charges which included dacoities, robbing money from banks and treasuries and the collection of arms, men and ammunition. He spoke of the manufacture of explosives, the murdering of police and other officials, the blowing up of trains, throwing bombs in the

Assembly, circulating seditious literature, rescuing convicts and inducting educated youth into the revolution movement.

Carden-Noad said that there were twenty-eight accused in all. Eighteen were present, five had absconded and five had turned approver. He read out the names of the eighteen accused in the Lahore Conspiracy Case in the order given below:

1. Bhagat Singh
2. Sukhdev *alias* Dayal *alias* Swami *alias* Villager
3. Kishori Lal Rattan *alias* Dee Dutt Rattan, *alias* Mast Ram Shastri
4. Agya Ram
5. Des Raj
6. Prem Dutt *alias* Master *alias* Amrit Lal
7. Jai Dev *alias* Harish Chandar
8. Shiv Verma, *alias* Parbhat *alias* Hamarain *alias* Ram Narain Kapur
9. Gaya Prashad, *alias* Dr. B. S. Nigham, *alias* Ram Lal, *alias* Ram Nath, *alias* Desh Bhagat
10. B.K. Dutt
11. Kanwal Nath Trivedi, *alias* Kanwal Nath Tewari
12. Ajoy Kumar Ghosh *alias* Negro General
13. Jatinder Nath Sanyal
14. Surrinder Nath Pandey
15. Mahabir Singh
16. Bijoy Kumar Sinha *alias* Bachu
17. Kundan Lal *alias* Partap *alias* No1
18. Shiv Ram *alias* Rajguru

The evidence of G. T. Hamilton Harding, senior superintendent of police, took the court by surprise. He said that he had filed the First Information Report (FIR) against the accused 'under the instructions of the chief secretary to the government of

Punjab. 'I do not know the facts of the case, nor did I make the statements. I am acting only as a formal complainant under the instructions of the government.'

The judges were shaken by Hamilton's statement. Carden-Noad tried to lessen the shock over Hamilton's evidence by talking about the dangers posed to him by the accused who were still absconding. He said that there was no immediate prospect of arresting Bhagwati Charan, Azad, Kalicharan and Yash Pal. Hardly had Carden-Noad finished his observations when Jatinder Nath Sanyal, one of the accused, rose and said that he proposed to address the court on behalf of the accused – Mahabir Singh, Prem Dutt, Gaya Prashad Nigam, Kundan Lal and himself.

Without waiting for the court's permission, he made a virulent attack on the British government. Sanyal said, reading from a statement prepared by Bhagat Singh and also signed by four other signatories, that the British had committed so many murders that it was not possible for Indians to avenge them even if they wanted to do so. Subjugating people was the biggest crime in the world and the British were guilty of it. With their brute force, he said, they had sought to suppress the struggle for what is man's birthright – freedom.

Raising his voice, Sanyal said that they were not the accused, but the defenders of India's honour and dignity. The accused were those who represented the British raj. He was reading from a paper which he was trying to finish as quickly as possible. Coldstream stopped him from doing so, observing that reading a paper in an open court was highly improper. He ruled what Sanyal had already read out as being entirely irrelevant to the guilt or innocence of the accused and smacking of 'seditious propaganda'. However, he ordered the paper to be placed on record.

When Sanyal was abruptly stopped, there was pandemonium in the court. The hall once again resounded with slogans. The sounds of 'Inquilab Zindabad!' and 'Down with Imperialism!' reverberated through the court. Sanyal, who was still on his feet, said that trial was 'a sham'. 'We decline to be party to this farcical show,' he said in disgust. 'We shall not take part in the proceedings.' All the accused joined Sanyal in voicing their protests and announcing that they would boycott the proceedings. Before withdrawing from the court all the accused repeated Sanyal's words: 'We decline to be party to this farcical show,' and they said that henceforth, 'we shall not take any part in the proceedings of the court'.

As they were leaving, a diminutive man walked in and said he was the interpreter. He knew Hindi, English and Marathi. It was an anticlimax. The case was adjourned to the following day.

Bhagat Singh found the court's attitude towards him and his comrades reminiscent of the earlier time he had been in court. Then, too, he had sensed that the judge had already made up his mind about his guilt.

Bhagat Singh was sure that the attitude of the tribunal would have convinced his colleagues about the mockery of the trial. There was no sense in pursuing the case. He was convinced that their earlier decision to treat the court proceedings as a farce was the correct approach. They should expose the British sense of justice more openly and more persistently. He told his colleagues after the earlier trial that they should take no cognizance of the tribunal. But some among them said that they should participate in the proceedings so that they might make a statement like the one Bhagat Singh had made in the Assembly Case.

Bhagat Singh was, however, happy that the visitors in the courtroom had wholeheartedly supported the revolutionaries, both in the case of Saunders' murder in Lahore and of throwing bombs in the Assembly Hall in Delhi. He recalled how once when an overzealous approver had made a statement against the revolutionaries, the people in the magistrate's court had shouted 'Shame!' Since the British had already made up their minds to hang them, why should they give credibility to the court by their presence? It was better to boycott the proceedings. Such was the thinking of the revolutionaries. To whatever extent possible, they would expose the shallowness of British justice. They did not believe even for a second that they would be able to stall their execution. Their death was only a question of time and they were prepared for it.

Any defence was pointless; this was Bhagat Singh's argument to his comrades. He sent a message to his father to wind up the defence committee he had constituted in an attempt to save his son's life – which had never had his approval in the first place. When he and his colleagues were not sorry for what they had done, then why have a defence committee? Theirs was an ideological stand, deliberate and open. The issue was not whether a Britisher had been killed but whether the assassination would make London understand that there was a group of determined Indians who would stop at nothing to unfetter not only their own country but also people in shackles all over the world. The tribunal searched for members of the defence committee who had submitted a petition to intervene but there was no trace of them; Bhagat Singh's father had finally complied with his son's wishes and dissolved the committee.

Even though they knew full well that the trial was a sham, Bhagat Singh and his comrades wanted to see how the tribunal would go about its business of sentencing them when there was no evidence, no witness, no proof. Even Inspector W.J.C. Fern, a British officer who had been present at the scene of Saunders' murder, had not recognized Bhagat Singh at the identification parade held in jail.

True, there were five approvers. Three of them – Jai Gopal, Hans Raj Vohra and Phonindro Nath Ghosh – had been associated with them for a long time. But Jai Gopal had only been used as a messenger and did not know much about the movement. Vohra was associated more with students and Ghosh had not done any important revolutionary work. How could the corroboration of what one approver said by another approver be sufficient ground for conviction? Their statements could not be regarded as evidence.

The following day, on 6 May, 1930 when the tribunal reassembled, Bhagat Singh put up an application that he wanted a legal adviser to watch the proceedings and advise him from time to time. He named Duni Chand – who had intervened during the hunger strike case – as his legal adviser. To make sure that it was only a formality, Bhagat Singh said that the legal adviser would not cross-examine witnesses, or address the court. Carden-Noad did not object to the arrangement. The tribunal readily gave its sanction.

The tribunal formally asked the accused whether they wished to be represented at the expense of the crown. Nine said 'no'. Five did not care to reply to the question and four of them agreed to the suggestion. The tribunal recorded their wishes as given below.

1.	Bhagat Singh	*No.*
2.	Sukhdev	*No.*
3.	Kishori Lal	*Yes, but wants to consult Kishan Singh, a member of the Defence Committee.*
4.	Agya Ram	*No.*
5.	Des Raj	*Yes, cannot at present say whom he wants.*
6.	Prem Dutt	*Yes, cannot at present say whom he wants.*
7.	Jai Dev	*Wants to consult Kishan Singh.*

8.	Shiv Verma	*No.*
9.	Gaya Prasad	*No.*
10.	B.K. Dutt	*States he will give no reply.*
		I refuse to answer any question by this court.
11.	Kanwal Nath Trivedi	*No.*
12.	Ajoy Kumar Ghosh	*Yes, cannot say whom until he sees the Defence Committee.*
13.	Jatindar Nath Sanyal	*States 'I give no reply'.*
14.	Surrinder Nath Panday	*No help from this court.*
15.	Mahabir Singh	*Says he will take not part in the proceedings.*
16.	Shiv Ram *alias* Rajguru	*No help.*

[In his cell, Sukhdev commented in the margins of the case proceedings: No one but we ourselves through our own failures proved to be the worst enemies of ourselves, hence of the cause. At every step you can find a confession... Sukhdev wrote 'False witness (FW) and Tutored witness (TW) against the names of many witnesses in the margins of his copy of the proceedings.]

For the next few days, the accused came to court, shouted 'Inquilab Zindabad!', or sang '*Sarfaroshi ki tamanna ab hamare dil mein hain*', and sat down on the benches. The trials began to follow a pattern: when the slogans stopped, the judges appeared and when the slogans began, they walked out of the room. Once in a while, when the slogans were raised, the judges stayed on to watch the scene.

One week after the opening of the case, on 12 May, 1930, Coldstream reached the court before Bhagat Singh and his colleagues. When they entered the dock shouting 'Inquilab Zindabad!' Coldstream ordered them to stop. They refused to obey him and raised their voices higher. At this point, Coldstream asked the police to handcuff them and clear the court. Even the press correspondents were asked to leave. This did not deter the revolutionaries from shouting slogans. Bhagat Singh protested against being handcuffed. Coldstream then recorded an order, which Hilton signed, to handcuff the prisoners and remove them from court.

The police entered the box where the accused were sitting on benches and began showering lathi blows on them. They retaliated with their hands. A serious fight followed. Coldstream sat back and watched as the police dragged the accused on the floor and forcibly pushed them into a van. Bhagat Singh and his comrades were injured in the fight and announced a boycott of the proceedings in protest. Coldstream contended that the slogans and revolutionary songs amounted to contempt of court. The accused maintained that until Coldstream offered an apology for the beating, they would not recognize the court.

Agha Haider, the only Indian member of the tribunal, was not happy about the beating. He recorded a note:

I was not party to the order of the removal of the accused from the court to jail and I was not responsible for it in any way. I dissociate myself from all that took place today in consequence of that (Coldstream's) order.

(Sukhdev characterized his stance as 'praiseworthy' in the comments he had scribbled in the margins of his copy of the proceedings).

When the proceedings resumed the next day, Agha Haider made a statement that he dissociated himself from all that had taken place the earlier day in consequence of the order.

The viceroy received a daily report about the proceedings in the court. He knew about the boycott and he knew about the slogans. But he did not know that things would come to such a pass that the only Indian judge on the tribunal would record his protest. The suspicion of the accused that the trial was only a public exercise was confirmed. Still they were shocked when the tribunal did away with the formality of the identification of the accused. The identification that had taken place in the magistrate's court was taken as evidence for the tribunal's proceedings as well.

For most of the others, the identification was held in the jail itself. The accused were paraded in front of the witnesses and they were asked to identify them by name or otherwise. If a witness claimed that he had identified the accused in jail in the presence of officials, that identification was considered bonafide.

After the beating incident, none of the accused, except Sukhdev from the Borstal Jail, were produced in court because they had refused to come unless brought by force. Each of the accused was asked individually to come to court and each of them refused. From then on, the jail authorities reported in each hearing that the accused had resisted coming before the tribunal. The tribunal, in turn, recorded the statement of the jail authorities and totally dispensed with the attendance of the accused.

For example, a typical order issued by Coldstream on 18 June, 1930, said: 'Both Bhagat Singh and B.K. Dutt today refused to attend court. Both were brought to the main gate where the police inspector took each of them by the arm and ordered them to come to court, whereupon they each refused to move.'

It was the same on every day.

The tribunal did not suspend proceedings despite the boycott by Bhagat Singh and his associates. Most Indian lawyers dissociated themselves from the case. The press too walked out. The tribunal went ahead and recorded the statements of the approvers.

The prosecution case was based mainly on the story that the three approvers – Phonindro Nath Ghosh, Jai Gopal and Hans

Raj Vohra – had reconstructed. They were associates of Bhagat Singh and his comrades. The last two had inside information on what went on at the Mozang Road house. Both had made confessions and both knew all because they were members of the Central Committee of the HSRA. The government's case was based on their disclosures, because apart from their revelations, they had no other source of information about what the revolutionaries had planned and how they had executed it.

Ghosh concentrated on the amalgamation of provincial revolutionary parties into a single revolutionary party, the Hindustan Socialist Revolutionary Army. Jai Gopal spoke about the murder of Saunders, and Vohra disclosed details about sundry other activities that Bhagat Singh and his comrades had planned. All the three approvers moulded their facts to fit the framework of the 'conspiracy', which the government was trying to prove had been hatched by the revolutionaries to overthrow it.

The government's prize witnesses were Jai Gopal and Hans Raj Vohra. Jai Gopal was the first to give his confessional testimony. Bhagat Singh felt personally disappointed by him because he had once described Jai Gopal as 'a jewel' of the party. Jai Gopal's was a long and tedious testimony spread over ten days. He told the tribunal how, in the middle of September, 1928, when he was at the revolutionary party headquarters at Ferozepur, Bhagat Singh and Sukhdev had come in at night. Bhagat Singh cut off his long hair (kesh), shaved off his beard and dressed himself in a dhoti and kurta – the attire that men in UP traditionally wear. This was all meant to help him escape detection.

At another point in his testimony Jai Gopal narrated an instance of their efforts to collect funds. The revolutionaries had decided to raid the Punjab National Bank in the city. Bhagat Singh was to hang out on the street, ostensibly practising motor driving, on the day picked for the heist. Kalicharan was to cut the telephone wires. Sukhdev was to snatch the gun from the sentry at the entrance of the bank and Kishori Lal and Jai Gopal were to stash the money in bags. 'When I reached the bank I saw Chandra Shekhar Azad, Sukhdev and Hans Raj Vohra,' Jai Gopal said. 'But even by 3 o'clock, Bhagat Singh and Pratap Singh did not arrive with the taxi. They came in a tonga since no arrangements for a taxi could be made and the dacoity was postponed.' (After robbing the bank the revolutionaries would leave a receipt of the amount stolen with the remark: 'You can encash it after Independence!')

'Many days later,' Jai Gopal said, 'we decided at the Mozang Road house that Scott, senior superintendent of police, should be murdered because he had struck Lala Lajpat Rai with a lathi. I was deputed to identify Scott's car, No. 6728. I watched his movements for three to four days. Finally 17 December was fixed for the murder.'

Jai Gopal revealed that Bhagat Singh had made a number of posters on thin paper and printed them in red ink. The posters were printed on behalf of the Hindustan Socialist Republican Association. The original typed version said: 'Scott is dead; Lalaji is avenged.'

Jai Gopal recalled how Sukhdev had asked him whether he wanted to serve the country. When the defence counsel asked him to identify Sukhdev, he pointed his finger straight at him. 'I will wear khaddar and join the Congress,' he told him. His purpose was to underline the differences between Gandhi's non-violent approach and the revolutionaries' faith in the cult of the bomb. Jai Gopal said he wanted to change his revolutionary views and disown the past. He said he knew what the party stood for when he joined it. Its manifesto opened with the sentence, 'The food on which the tender plant of liberty thrives is the blood of the martyr.'

Sukhdev, Jai Gopal said, had persuaded him to become a member of the secret society, the object of which was to overthrow the government . 'I stole a book entitled *Manufacture and Use of Explosives* for Sukhdev from the school library.'

Another incident that Jai Gopal revealed was that three or four days after Saunders' murder, he, Sukhdev and Kishori Lal had gone towards the Canal bridge on Ferozepur Road and found Scott and his wife driving past. Jai Gopal said that he suggested to Sukhdev that, if he desired, he could 'shoot down Scott'. But Sukhdev had replied that there was no use killing him now as Fate had saved him once.

[Writing in the margins of his copy of the trial proceedings in his cell Sukhdev refuted this charge. 'Nonsense,' he wrote. 'As a member of a body, I could not do so.' Sukhdev added: 'I believed him too much. Many a time I disclosed before him what I should not have.' All the three – Bhagat Singh, Sukhdev and Rajguru – were given a copy each of the trial proceedings after the hearings were over. Sukhdev was the only one of the three who wrote as many as 241 comments in the margins.]

After Jai Gopal, it was Hans Raj Vohra, who chose to talk. The blue-eyed boy of the revolutionaries, Bhagat Singh could not believe that Vohra would turn approver and betray the cause in which he once had so passionately believed. Vohra too had been pardoned by the magistrate.

Hans Raj Vohra gave evidence towards the end of May, 1930. His testimony was crucial to the government's case. During his testimony, the public prosecutor asked him: 'Previously when you were arrested on 17 December, 1928 (the Dusshera bomb blast), in spite of the fact that you were in police custody for seventeen days, you did not divulge any secrets of the party. This time you made a statement shortly after you were arrested. What are your reasons?'

Vohra replied: 'I should like to submit before this tribunal a statement giving my reasons by which I was guided to give a statement before the police and accept a pardon.'

Agha Haider said: 'It is not open to the prosecution to put this question to the witness. The question is disallowed.'

Hilton remarked at this point: 'The question is one, the object of which is to test the veracity of the witness, and it should not be allowed to be put in by the examination-in-chief.'

In his testimony Vohra said he would be able to express himself better in English than in Urdu. He was allowed to do so.

Vohra said Sukhdev was the brother of his wife's uncle. 'In our meetings, we began to discuss the futility of the Congress programme and the necessity under the special circumstances and the justification, both moral and political, of the creation of revolutionary parties. Sukhdev told me that inasmuch as India had no constitutional means by which to determine her progress, we must necessarily resort to unconstitutional means.'

Sukhdev had already been identified by Vohra in the magistrate's court. Vohra said Sukhdev enlisted him as a member of the party and had entrusted him with the task of propagating revolutionary ideas by circulating revolutionary literature amongst the students.

While describing the view of the revolutionaries, Vohra clarified at one stage that when he said 'my clothes', he meant they were being temporarily used by him. 'Those clothes were the common property of the party, the members of whom did not believe in "right of property".'

When it came to Saunders' killing, Vohra said that Sukhdev called him on the evening of 1 December, 1928 to the Lawrence Gardens, Lahore, and from there he took him to the Mozang Road house. 'I was present at the house for twenty or twenty-five minutes. Bhagat Singh told me there that the party wanted to resort to some action and for that purpose, they had even summoned some members from UP. That is all I was told that day,' Vohra said. At this stage Jai Gopal was brought into the court. Vohra identified him. Vohra said that on 15 December:

'Bhagat Singh showed me some typed pink-coloured posters, the heading of which was in pink print. Their bottom corners were printed on one side with the date and the other with the word, "commander-in-chief". The heading of the typed part of the poster was "Scott is dead. Lalaji is avenged".'

Vohra admitted that Bhagat Singh had told him that the party had decided to murder Scott for showering lathi blows on Lajpat Rai 'which was a sort of challenge to the revolutionary party'. Vohra said he agreed to the proposal to shoot Scott dead. He, however, said that he was never informed where the murder would take place. He passed the spot, where the killing had taken place, purely by chance.

The tribunal, even after Vohra had turned approver, questioned him closely, trying to show how independent it was. The questions it asked Vohra were:

Q. 'Did the keeping away from you of the details of Saunders' murder come to your knowledge after the murder or before the murder?'

A. 'Before the murder.'

Q. 'Did you protest that you were not being let into the secrets?'

A. 'I was not expected to protest, nor was I expected to ask any such searching questions from them according to the discipline of the party.'

Q. 'What was the occasion for Sukhdev to let you into the secret of the places to which the various alleged murderers were sent by the party?'

A. 'There was no particular occasion that I can allude to.'

Q. 'Was it a case of pure and simple outburst of confidence?'

A. 'Yes.'

Vohra was too callow to understand the police's tactics. He told them everything when they informed him that his guru, Sukhdev, had made a full confession about Saunders' killing. Vohra divulged details about the working of the revolutionaries, their hideouts and their arsenals.

After the testimony of Vohra and the other two approvers, Khan Bahadur Abdul Aziz was called upon as witness. He was superintendent of police, Montgomery, when he had been put in charge of investigations into the Dussehra bombing. He had been specially entrusted with the investigation of the Lahore Conspiracy Case. He testified before the court that during his investigation of the Dussehra bombing he became aware of Bhagat Singh and also of Babu Singh, a member of the Naujawan Bharat Sabha. Babu Singh offered to give him information if he paid him one thousand rupees. It was Babu Singh who told him that Bhagat Singh was one of Saunders' killers and also gave him information about the formation of their society. Aziz said he ordered the arrest of Bhagat Singh there itself but Bhagat Singh had disappeared by then, only to surface on 8 April, 1929 in Delhi. Abdul Aziz then disclosed how he had discovered the secret bomb factory in Lahore at a house in Kashmiri Building and raided it on 12 April, 1929. He said that Sukhdev, Kishori Lal and Jai Gopal were arrested from the Kashmiri building from where a lot of incriminating evidence was unearthed.

On 30 May, 1930 Ram Saran Das, the author of *Dreamland*, who briefly turned approver, retracted his statement and said that it had been made at the instance of the police. (He had made a statement before the magistrate on 11 June, 1929. It was later changed by the police and he was made to sign the amended statement.)

Even with all these revelations, because the accused had boycotted the trial, the proceedings were perfunctory and farcical.

The British wanted the revolutionaries to attend court. Bhagat Singh and his comrades said they would attend court only if Coldstream was removed. So Coldstream was sent on long leave but the dissenting member, Agha Haider, was also dropped from the reconstituted tribunal. Two new members, J.K. Tapp and Abdul Qadir, were appointed in their place and Justice J.C. Hilton took over as chairman. The accused said that Hilton should not be made the tribunal president since he had concurred with Coldstream on the beating of the revolutionaries.

The objection to Hilton was rejected. Proceedings started without the presence of the accused and their lawyers. However, when the new tribunal met one day after its constitution, almost all the accused voluntarily came to court. This was after a lapse of six weeks. Agya Ram alone refused to attend. He did not recognize the tribunal or the court.

Again, on 23 June, all the accused, except Agya Ram, appeared before the tribunal. He had resisted being forcibly produced in court. The tribunal passed an order dispensing with his attendance. However, the proceedings of two days convinced the revolutionaries that there was no difference between the tribunal headed by Coldstream and the one headed by Hilton. They resumed their boycott.

The following day, thirteen of them did not attend. The tribunal again passed orders condoning their absence. On 25 June none of the accused was present. The tribunal followed a similar procedure and proceeded with the case in their absence. In a joint letter written on the same day to the commissioner of the tribunal, Bhagat Singh and Dutt protested that the judge who was party to the order of beating had been appointed president:

> In these circumstances we want to emphasize one thing
> that we had absolutely no grudge against the person of
> Justice Coldstream. We had protested against the order

passed by the president on behalf of the majority and
the subsequent maltreatment meted out to us...
On 10 July charges were framed against fifteen of them
and three were discharged.

The tribunal's proceedings were now a bigger farce than before.
It was like *Hamlet* without the Prince of Denmark. What
legitimacy could the case have when even the presence of Bhagat
Singh, Sukhdev and Rajguru was not considered necessary?

The tribunal realized that the conspiracy story was weak in
the absence of corroborators. True, Jai Gopal and Hans Raj Vohra,
from different backgrounds, said more or less the same thing.
But both were approvers. Their evidence was not sufficient to
justify the conviction of any accused present without
corroboration from an outside source. The tribunal knew that
corroboration from the same source was necessary for credibility.
But since the tribunal could not get any such evidence, it said
that there was no ostensible ground to disbelieve the facts stated
by the two approvers.

The tribunal depended on Section 9 (1) of the Ordinance
dispensing with the attendance of the accused. On 10 July, 1930,
the tribunal issued an order, and copies of the framed charges
were served on the fifteen accused in jail, together with copies
of an order intimating them that their pleas would be taken on
the charges the following day. That day, on 11 July, the accused
again resisted being produced in court.

On the same day, an order was passed assigning the case to
the following day with the direction that all the accused would
be required at the commencement of the next hearing. They
would then state whether they intended to cross-examine any
of the witnesses whose evidence had already been recorded. None
of the accused came to court. All of them resisted forcible
attendance and the tribunal passed an order recording the fact

that none of the accused had appeared in court or expressed any wish for cross-examining any witness.

There were practically no proceedings between 12 July and 4 August. On 4 August the evidence of medical officers was recorded who said that all the accused, except Prem Dutt and Kundan Lal, were on a hunger strike and were too weak to appear before the tribunal. Once again their presence was dispensed with. On 11 August the tribunal recorded that Bhagat Singh, Sukhdev and Bijoy Kumar Sinha were fit to attend proceedings but they had refused to do so.

On 26 August – by which time 457 witnesses had been examined – the public prosecutor said he would not produce any more witnesses and closed the case from his side. The tribunal then adjourned the case to 27 August, asking the accused if they wanted to put any questions to the court.

The tribunal passed a separate order under Section 256 of the Criminal Procedure Code calling upon all accused to attend the proceedings in person on the following day. A copy of the order was served to each one of the accused in jail. On 28 August, as before, all the accused resisted being made to appear before the tribunal. No defence witness appeared, and no list was put up for any defence witness to be summoned on their behalf. The tribunal was adjourned. On 29 and 30 August it was similarly adjourned, without transacting any business.

On 1 September all the accused again resisted being produced before the tribunal. Their attendance was dispensed with till 5 September. On 5 September Amolak Ram Kapur, a lawyer sympathethetic to the revolutionaries, appeared for two of the accused, Bijoy Kumar Sinha and Ajoy Kumar Ghosh, and made an ordinary application before the tribunal for recalling forty-five prosecution witnesses for cross-examination. The five approvers – Jai Gopal, P.N. Ghosh, Man Mohan Bannerjee, H.R. Vohra and Lalit Mukherjee – in the custody of the court

should also be summoned for cross-examination, Kapur
demanded.

Jai Gopal was actually put into the witness box, but Kapur,
the defence lawyer, declined to cross-examine him and stated
that he had no instructions to cross-examine the approvers. Later,
Kapur reappeared before the tribunal and brought an application
signed by Bijoy Kumar Sinha and Ajoy Kumar Ghosh asking for
a week's adjournment before beginning the cross-examination
of any of the Prosecution's witnesses. The request for adjournment
was refused as 'dilatory'. Kapur then withdrew from the court.

The trial had been a long and protracted one, beginning on 5
May, 1930, and ending on 10 September, 1930. It was a one-
sided affair which threw all rules and regulations out of the
window. It was a kangaroo court. The new tribunal simply went
through the same rigamarole of justice again.When the tribunal
was told that the accused had boycotted the proceedings, it
ordered that they be brought in by force. This had been tried
earlier. No amount of violence could bring them to court. More
thrashing had no effect. The tribunal ultimately decided that the
presence of the accused was not necessary and proceeded with
the case. Even then the case took nearly four months to complete.
The accused did not attend most of the hearings. Nor did they
defend themselves. The tribunal passed orders that paid scant
attention to decency much less to justice. The mighty British
had already made up their minds to hang those who dared
challenge them and their rule. Seldom before in history had there
been such a farce of a trial where the judges, the prosecution and
the police bent every law in the book to pronounce a death
sentence, a verdict they had already decided on, before the onset
of the trial.

The prosecution presented the statements of seven approvers
and confessions by three unknown accused. There were 450-

odd witnesses who claimed to have identified the various accused at different times. There were handwriting experts, printing experts and arms and ammunition specialists. As the prosecution continued to produce more fake witnesses, indulging more in fantasy than fact, it became evident that the government was only tightening *the* noose around Bhagat Singh's neck. Bhagat Singh refused to offer any defence. His father became so nervous that he submitted on 20 September, 1930 a petition to the tribunal, with a copy to the viceroy, to establish that Bhagat Singh was not in Lahore on the day of Saunders' killing. The petition stated that Bhagat Singh was in Calcutta on the day of Saunders' murder. Bhagat Singh was deeply angry with his father's doing and disowned the petition.

Finally the tribunal framed charges against fifteen of the accused. Agya Ram and Surendra Pandey were discharged, while the case against B.K. Dutt was withdrawn as he had already been sentenced to transportation for life in the Assembly Bomb Case.

In a letter to Dutt, Bhagat Singh wrote:

…You will live and, while living, you will have to show to the world that the revolutionaries not only die for their ideals but can face every calamity. Death should not be a means to escape the worldly difficulties. Those revolutionaries who have by chance escaped the gallows, should live and show to the world that they can not only embrace the gallows for the ideal but also bear the worst type of tortures in the dark dingy prison cells.

Finally, on 7 October, 1930, about three weeks before the expiry of its term, the tribunal delivered its judgement, convicting all the accused except three. The three – Ajoy Ghosh, Jatinder Nath Sanyal and Des Raj – were acquitted.

Bhagat Singh, Sukhdev and Rajguru were sentenced to death by hanging. Kishori Lal, Mahabir Singh, Bijoy Kumar Sinha, Shiv Verma, Gaya Prashad, Jai Dev and Kamalnath Tewari were sentenced to transportation for life. Kundan Lal was sentenced to seven years' rigorous imprisonment and Prem Dutt to five.

The 300-page judgement went into the details of the evidence and said that, 'Bhagat Singh's participation in Saunders' murder is the most serious and important fact proved against him and it is fully established by ample evidence…'

The evidence that Bhagat Singh took part in Saunders' murder was assumed to be supported by three points: one, the evidence of various eyewitnesses, who claimed to have identified Bhagat Singh; two, the statements by the two approvers, Jai Gopal and Hans Raj Vohra, 'who were with him as participants in the murder', and, three, the posters (Scott is Dead) 'were written by him and proved to be so by the handwriting experts'.

Since the accused had boycotted the proceedings, they learned of the sentences from a special messenger who brought the tribunal's order to the jail. The warrants for the execution of Bhagat Singh, Sukhdev and Rajguru were marked with a black border.

For some reason, Sukhdev expected life transportation. This meant staying in jail for another fourteen years. Sukhdev wrote to Bhagat Singh that he would commit suicide if convicted for life. Sukhdev wanted either unconditional release or death, no middle course. It is strange, that he could even think he would not be hanged.

In a letter to Sukhdev Bhagat Singh replied that life in prison had made them not care about things that they were once passionate about and vice versa. 'For example,' he said, 'I believed in personal life, but now this feeling has ceased to occupy any particular position in my heart and mind. While, outside, you were strongly opposed to it.'

Bhagat Singh reminded Sukhdev that he once abhorred the idea of suicide but he had now made an about-face. 'May I ask you whether the situation outside the jail was any more favourable to our ideas? Even then, could we have left it because of our failures? Do you mean to imply that had we not entered the field, no revolutionary work would have taken place at all?' He advised Sukhdev: 'Serve, serve and live to struggle for the cause.'

Bhagat Singh, now spent most of his time in his cell. He did not bother even with the formality of making an appearance in court. He read a lot, devouring one book after another. Even the Dwarka Das library could not satiate his hunger. All his visitors were instructed to only bring him books because he sniffed at any other gifts they offered. And as usual he copied in his diary his favourite extracts and quotes from the books. One day he copied the following passage from a book by Charles Fourier (1772-1837) into his notebook:

> The present social order is a ridiculous mechanism, in which portions of the whole are in conflict and acting against the whole. We see each class in society desire, from interest, the misfortune of the other classes, placing in every way, individual interest in opposition to public good. The lawyer wishes litigation and suits, particularly among the rich; the physician desires sickness. (The latter would be ruined if everybody died without disease as would the former if all quarrels were settled by arbitration.) The soldier wants a war, which will carry off half of his comrades and secure him promotion; the undertaker wants burials; monopolist and forestallers want famine, to double or treble the prices of grain; the architect, the carpenter, the mason, want conflagration that will burn down a hundred houses to give activity to their branches of business.

The news of the death sentence came as a shock to the people. There were spontaneous hartals and processions in protest all over the country. Meetings were held in all major towns to condemn the ex-parte death sentence. Despite the imposition of Section 144 of the Criminal Procedure Code, there were hundreds of gatherings of people who made virulent attacks against the British. Even the women in several places were lathi-charged by the police. A DAV College professor and eighty students were assaulted by a sergeant when they were protesting.

At Lahore, the students took the lead. All colleges were closed, except the government college where the sons of the elite studied. There was picketing at the government college. At Bradlaugh Hall, where Bhagat Singh had addressed many meetings, students and young men and women passed a resolution praising him and the others for their 'brave sacrifice'. The Mori Gate meeting beat all previous crowd records. It was presided over by the daughter of the late Lala Lajpat Rai.

The undertrials of the Chittagong Armoury Raid Case sent an appeal to Gandhi to intervene. So did Surendra Mohan Ghosh, who presided over a mammoth meeting in Calcutta. At the Buxa Camp, where leading revolutionaries of Bengal were detained, a resolution was passed requesting the viceroy to commute the death sentence. A public petition signed by thousands of people was sent to him making the same request.

A defence committee was constituted in Punjab to file an appeal to the privy council against the sentence. Bhagat Singh and his comrades were not in favour of it but they were persuaded on the plea that it would expose the British before the world and show what humiliation the political prisoners in India had to face. Bhagat Singh's only satisfaction was that the appeal would draw the attention of people in England to the existence of the HSRA.

The proceedings before the five-judge bench of the privy council in London were surprisingly short. In the case of Bhagat Singh v The King Emperor, the point raised by the appellants was that the ordinance promulgated to constitute a special tribunal for the trial was invalid. It deprived the accused of his right of appeal to the high court which they otherwise would have had. The government argued that Section 72 of the Government of India Act, 1915, gave the governor-general unlimited powers to set up a tribunal.

The trial had evoked a formidable opinion among the liberals in the UK. It saw how farcical the proceedings in the tribunal were. Legal luminaries like D.N. Pritt volunteered to argue in favour of appeal for Bhagat Singh and his comrades at the privy council in London.

D.N. Pritt, who appeared on behalf of Bhagat Singh, said that the legislative power of the governor-general was subject to three conditions: one, there must be an emergency; two, the ordinance must be for the peace and good government of British India; and three, the ordinance must be within the legislative power of the Indian legislature. 'None of these conditions existed,' said Pritt.

The prosecution, Pritt said, was supposed to prove that an emergency existed, but it had failed to do so. There was no emergency within the meaning of Section 72. The statement by the governor-general, which accompanied the ordinance, did not show any emergency.

Pritt said that what the government had done was to deprive the accused the right to have a *prima facie* case made against them and thus denied them access to a sessions judge and a jury of assessors; it had denied them the right to appeal to the high court in Lahore. They had been tried before a special tribunal without having any idea what the case against them was, except as and how it developed and emerged from the mouths of approvers and independent witnesses.

The privy council dismissed Pritt's appeal. Judge Viscount Dunedin, who read the judgement, said that the only case made was that Section 72 of the Act did not authorize the governor-general to constitute a special tribunal. The judge said that a state of emergency did not permit any exact definition. It connoted a state of matters calling for drastic action which had to be judged as such by someone.

'It is more than obvious that that someone must be the governor-general and he alone. Any other view would render utterly inept the whole provision. Emergency demands immediate action and that action is prescribed to be taken by the governor-general.'

As regarded the argument that the ordinance was not conducive to 'peace and good government of British India' the judge said that 'the governor-general is also the judge of that. The power given by Section 72 is an absolute power without any limits prescribed, except only that it cannot do what the Indian Legislature would be unable to do...'

Judge Viscount Dunedin, who had Lord Thankerton, Lord Russel of Killowen, Sir George Lowndes and Sir Dinshah Mulla on the bench, added that the governor-general was not in any way bound under the law to expound the reasons which induced him to promulgate the ordinance.

From the the lower court to the tribunal to the privy council—it was a preordained judgement. The people of India had known this all along.

The privy council's verdict did not surprise them.

9

Khush raho ahle watan hum to safar karte hain...

THE APPEAL TO THE PRIVY COUNCIL HAD AROUSED SOME HOPE. A few thought that the highest court of justice in England might change the sentence from death to life imprisonment. Once the death penalty was confirmed, the hanging of Bhagat Singh, Sukhdev and Rajguru was only a matter of time. There was despondency and outrage all over the country. A procession of some two lakh people marched through the streets of Lahore to stage demonstrations. There were hartals in Lahore and in many other cities. Once again, there were demonstrations held everywhere. The bazaars reverberated with slogans of 'Bhagat Singh, Sukhdev, Rajguru Zindabad!'. A song specially composed for the occasion was on everybody's lips:

> *Bhagat Singh ke khoon ka asar dekh lena*
> *Mitadenge zaalim ka ghar dekh lena.*

(Wait and see, the effect of Bhagat Singh's execution;
The tyrant's home will be destroyed, wait and see...)

Bhagat Singh's comrades outside the jail did not give up. They proposed a daring scheme to rescue Bhagat Singh, Sukhdev and Rajguru. A plan to blast their way through the stone walls of the prison and shoot their way out, was hatched by the revolutionaries. Vishwanath Baishampayan, Sukh Desraj and

Bhagwati Charan were to be the members of the advance guard. Tragically, the scheme never took off. A bomb with a loose pin exploded in Bhagwati Charan's hands during the dry run that he held across the Ravi. He was killed on the spot.

Be that as it may, what the would-be rescuers did not realize was that Bhagat Singh did not want to be rescued in this manner. He did not want to let down the deputy superintendent of the jail, Khan Bhadur, to whom he had grown very close during the 400 days he had spent there. Khan Bhadur had even arranged a farewell dinner for Bhagat Singh and his two comrades with the jail functionaries.

All eyes were now on Gandhi. Only he had the influence to do something. His pact with Viceroy Irwin was on the anvil. Although people realized that Gandhi was opposed to the cult of the bomb, they believed that the situation had taken a different turn. It had passed the stage of wrong or right, moral or immoral. Bhagat Singh and his comrades had to be saved.

None denied the fact that the revolutionaries represented a different philosophy. Non-violence was the antithesis of violence. If Gandhi was the sun on the political sky of India, Bhagat Singh was the star that had risen from the depths of darkness. Why should Gandhi hesitate to support those who were in no way less committed than him in the struggle for freedom? At stake were three lives, not a philosophical treatise.

Gandhi looked inclined to agree to a settlement with the government under which the Congress would cooperate with the British in its scheme towards limited participation in governance. The viceroy was indebted to Gandhi because he was not disturbing the stability in any way and helping him establish a peaceful rule. One word from Gandhi to the viceroy would be enough to get the sentences commuted, the people thought.

Bhagat Singh was keen to be hanged because of the fillip his death would give their ideology. Inspired by their bravery, other young men would join the struggle to make India free and just. Earlier he had wanted the sentence to be postponed for some time so that the reasons for their sacrifice would be clearly established in people's minds. But now the time was ripe. The country was rife with agitations and lathi-charges; the hangings would agitate them further. Bhagat Singh was also confident that Gandhi's pact with the viceroy would outrage the people. Signing it would arouse more anger. Bhagat Singh wanted the hangings to take place at a time when the Congress lay exposed, thus further strengthening the revolutionaries' stand. Their three corpses would lie between the people and Gandhi's settlement with the viceroy.

Bhagat Singh was confident that the concept of social justice had won many supporters in the country. Stretching from the last quarter of the nineteenth century to the early part of the twentieth, there were two broad phases of the freedom struggle: the pre-Gandhian and the Gandhian phase. The revolutionary movement, though smouldering in both these phases, was not central to either, although it had provided the engine-power.

The failure of the 1857 revolt dealt a major blow to the Indian hopes to oust foreign rule. It also marked the last time that the Indians went to the battlefield in medieval fashion – with soldiers on horseback, flashing swords, rampaging elephants and individual acts of bravery but little concerted action. The revolt made the Indians realize that, for the time being at least, British might could not be challenged effectively on the battlefield.

Developments of a completely different kind began to transform important aspects of Indian life. There were factors like the revivalism of the Hindus, the spread of English education, the rise of the middle class, slow industrialization, the emergence of the Indian press and the integration of the area called India.

Some of these developments took the form of protests against the British. This gave birth to a national consciousness. A sense of togetherness began to emerge among the Indians who were unified by their desire to oust the British. In the beginning, protests took the shape of political associations led by the middle class. Their demands were prayers and petititons, articulated by speeches and strong newspaper articles. Some of them began a militant religious revivalism, which was hostile to the western presence. Many of these religious leaders propagated a return to the ideals of the pure Hindu culture, inspired by the Gita and the Vedic texts.

It was not one event which marked the beginning of another. There were many small incidents. Coming as they did at a time when the economic condition of the country was rapidly worsening, they only served to inflame passions. Many Indian leaders of the period pointed out the pitfalls of the rapid commercialization of agriculture, destruction of cottage industries, de-industrialization and then industrialization only up to a certain point which only served to further the impoverishment of India. In spite of the country's abject poverty, the British regularly presented surplus budgets. This gross callousness of the British towards the living conditions of the people, especially during times of famine – there were ten major famines between 1860 and 1910 – made the people extremely angry and ready to take up arms.

Newspapers too played an important role in awakening the anger of the people. They strongly advocated independence, demanding rights for the Indians and urging the nation to wake up and participate in the struggle. Among the prominent newspapers were *Sandhya* (edited by Brahmomadhab Upadhayaya), *Bande Matram* (Bipin Chandra Pal), *Karma Yogin* (Aurobindo Ghosh), *Sanjibani* (Krishna Kumar Mitra), *Bangadarshan*

(Bankim Chandra Chatterjee), *Amrita Bazaar Patrika* (Sisir Kumar Ghosh and Motilal Ghosh) and *Jugantar* (Barindra Kumar Ghosh).

The revolutionary phase started when the moderates were on the decline. But the revolutionaries were like flares that burnt out after lighting up the sky for a while. Reprisals by the government snuffed out their fire. The revolutionaries had made a remarkable comeback when the complacency and conservatism of the Congress caused widespread frustration among the people. The people had great expectations. When they were not fulfilled, the people revolted. Yet the revolutionaries had failed to find or provide anything that could create conditions like the ones that made the French and Russian revolution possible. They had a long way to go. They had to stress the need to do more than just propagate, agitate and make speeches – they needed self-sacrifice from the youth, a militant programme of resistance, the boycott of foreign goods, and the like. Would Bhagat Singh's hanging disseminate the ideals they cherished?

Lost in such thoughts and in the ferocious devouring of books, Bhagat Singh spent the last days of his life in prison. One day he was visited by Asaf Ali and his wife, Aruna. When they reached his cell they found him singing cheerfully, rapping his handcuffs on the bars to keep beat. They asked him if he wanted anything. He smiled in reply and showed them what he had just written in his notebook from *India Old and New*.

How many of the Western-educated Indians who have thrown themselves into political agitation against the tyranny of the British bureaucracy have ever raised a finger to free their own countrymen from the tyranny of those social evils? How many of them are entirely free from it themselves, or, if free, have the courage to act up to their opinion?

Asaf Ali told him that the Congress had almost negotiated a settlement with the British. This would create an atmosphere of conciliation. The hangings would not fit into that scenario.

After Asaf and Aruna left, Bhagat Singh sat down and composed a letter 'to young political workers' on 2 February, 1931. He warned them:

> The term revolution is too sacred, at least to us, to be so lightly used or misused. But if you say you are for the national revolution and the aim of your struggle is an Indian republic of the type of the United States of America, then I ask you to please let me know on what forces you rely that will help you bring about that revolution. The only forces on which you can rely to bring about any revolution, whether national or the socialist, are the peasantry and the labour. Congress leaders do not dare to organize those forces.
>
> ...If anybody has misunderstood me, let him amend his ideas. I do not mean that bombs and pistols are useless, rather the contrary. But I mean to say that mere bomb-throwing is not only useless but sometimes harmful. The military department of the party should always keep ready all the war-material it can command for any emergency. It should back the political work of the party. It cannot and should not work independently.

Bhagat Singh, Sukhdev and Rajguru were shocked when their relatives asked them to file a mercy petition. How could they even suggest such a thing? Apparently, they were oblivious of the trail they wanted to blaze, to inspire the youth of India to take up the cause for India's freedom.

The idea of a mercy petition made them write a joint letter to the governor of Punjab through the jail superintendent. The letter, his last petition, dated 20 March, 1931, three days before the execution, said:

> With due respect we beg to bring to your kind notice the following – That we were sentenced to death on 7 October, 1930 by a British court, L.C.C. tribunal, constituted under the Special L.C.C. Ordinance, promulgated by H.E. The viceroy, the head of the British Government in India, and the main charge against us was that of having waged war against H.M. King George, the King of England.
>
> The above mentioned findings of the court presupposed two things: First, that there exists a state of war between the British nation and the Indian nation and, secondly, that we had actually participated in that war and were, therefore, war prisoners. The second presupposition seems to be a little bit flattering, but nevertheless it is too tempting to resist the design acquiescing in it...
>
> Let us declare that the state of war does exist and shall exist so long as the Indian toiling masses and their natural resources are being exploited by a handful of parasites. They may be purely British capitalists or mixed British and Indian, or even purely Indian. They may be carrying on their insidious exploitation through mixed or even purely Indian bureaucratic apparatus. All these things made no difference...
>
> As to the question of our fate, please allow us to say that when you have decided to put us to death, you will certainly do it. You have got the power in your hands and the power is the greatest justification in the world We know the maxim 'Might is right' serves as your guiding motto. The whole of our trial was just a proof of that. What we wanted to point out was that according

to the verdict of your court we had waged war and we are therefore war prisoners. And we claim to be treated as such, i.e., we claim to be shot dead instead of being hanged. It rests with you to prove that you really meant what your court had said. We request and hope that you will very kindly order the military department to send its detachment to perform our execution.

Bhagat Singh, Sukhdev and Rajguru had come to the conclusion that the Congress leaders, although sympathetic to them during the trial, did not think of 'the homeless and penniless workers' when negotiating for more powers from the British. They realized that the revolution that they had led had not made much progress either.

Sitting in their cells they heard of the noble sacrifice of Bhagwati Charan Vohra. They learnt that Chandra Shekhar Azad had not surrendered to the police when they finally surrounded him in Allahabad but had fought them single-handed and died a hero's death. Their time, too, was almost up, they thought. Would it also be the end of the HSRA when the British had smashed all their underground factories and arrested their comrades, some of whom had joined the enemy? There was relentless repression. Was it all over – the revolutionaries' struggle of militant nationalists?

Bhagat Singh was confident that others would rise and evolve their own methods to free people from slavery and exploitation. The struggle would take different shapes at different times. It could be open, hidden, agitational or fierce. But the war would continue till the present social order was completely replaced by a new social order, devoid of exploitation.

He rummaged through his notebook and read a passage he had written some days earlier captioned *The Prisoner:*

It is suffocating under the low, dirty roof; my strength grows weaker year by year. They oppress me, this stony floor, this iron chained table, this bedstead, this chair, chained to the walls, like boards of the grave. In this eternal dump, deep silence one can only consider oneself a corpse.

The Indians still believed that some sort of agreement would be reached in the talks between Irwin and Gandhi. When the text of the pact was published, without any reference to Bhagat Singh or the others, there was outrage. And when the Congress Working Committee endorsed the Gandhi–Irwin Pact on 4 March, one day before it was signed, progressive forces termed the pact as a 'betrayal'.

Ever since the sentence was announced, efforts to at least commute the death sentence had been afoot. A petition under *habeas corpus* act that the accused had been 'illegally detained' by the government was rejected by the Lahore High Court. So was another petition to approach the privy council to reconsider its earlier decision.

Gandhi began to be blamed. When he came to attend a public meeting in Delhi on 7 March, 1931 a leaflet was distributed among the audience which read:

Where is peace today? Search the hearts of the mothers whose sons have fallen victims to the bullets, or are still awaiting the gallows. Ask the wives of those husbands who have left them widows or are serving life-long imprisonment in the dungeons of a foreign bureaucracy. Do you remember your duty to the martyrs? Will you be partners to such an ignoble pact?

Gandhi did not react to what was said.

Appeals from all over India, from all sections of people were pouring in, usually addressed to the viceroy, asking him to stay the execution. Madan Mohan Malviya sent a telegram to the viceroy which read:

> May I appeal to your excellency to exercise your prerogative of mercy in cases of Bhagat Singh, Rajguru and Sukhdev to commute sentences of death passed upon them into those of transportation for life... Execution of these young men whose action was prompted not by any personal or selfish consideration but by a patriotic impulse, however misguided, will give a great shock to the public feeling in the country...Such an act of mercy on your excellency's part will, at this juncture, produce a very beneficial effect on Indian public opinion.

Two petitions were sent by Vidyavati, Bhagat Singh's mother on February 17 and 19, 1931 :

> Pray stay execution death sentence passed on my son Bhagat Singh by special tribunal appointed under Ordinance three of 1930. 1 petition for mercy on grounds of youth of Bhagat Singh and special circumstances of the case. Detailed petition being submitted through post.

A public memorial was also sent to the viceroy:

> May it please your excellency, we the undersigned request that the death sentences passed by the tribunal at Lahore on Messrs Bhagat Singh, Sukhdev and Rajguru be commuted.'

Hundreds of people had signed the petition.

On 20 March, 1931 Subhash Chandra Bose, speaking at a meeting at Azad Maidan in Delhi, said:

The whole of India knows by this time that Bhagat Singh and his comrades, Rajguru and Sukhdev, are going to be executed before long. I must say that the news came as a terrible shock to me when I alighted at Delhi Station yesterday noon... We demand with one voice and one will that the death sentences on Bhagat Singh and his comrades be at once commuted. Bhagat Singh is today not a person but a symbol. He symbolizes the spirit of the revolt which is abroad in the country. We may condemn his methods, but we cannot ignore his selflessness...

It was apparent that Gandhi did not want to identity himself with the revolutionaries because that would negate his whole stand. But he did not want them to be hanged. His worry was that many people believed that he had taken no initiative to get the death sentence commuted to life imprisonment. Lord Irwin, after his talks with Gandhi, wrote:

In conclusion, not connected with above (talks on the pact), he (Gandhi) mentioned the case of Bhagat Singh. He did not plead for commutation. But he did ask for postponement in the present circumstances.

In greater detail, the viceroy wrote about his meeting with Gandhi on 19 March, four days before the execution:

As he (Gandhi) was leaving, he asked me if he might mention the case of Bhagat Singh, whose execution on March had been reported in the press. He said, 'This was an unfortunate day as it coincided with the arrival of the new President (of the Congress) in Karachi and there would be much popular excitement.'

The viceroy's note said:

I told him that I had considered the case with most anxious care, but could find no grounds on which I could justify to my conscience commuting the sentence… He appeared to appreciate the force of the argument and said no more.

Many years later Lord Irwin, in his autobiography *Fullness of Days* wrote:

If the young man was hanged, said Gandhi, there was a likelihood that he would become a national martyr and the general atmosphere would be seriously prejudiced… Gandhi said that he greatly feared, unless I could so something about it, the effect would be to destroy our pact. I said I should regret that no less than he, but it would be clear to him there were only three possible courses. The first was to do nothing and let the execution proceed, the second was to change the order and grant Bhagat Singh a reprieve, the third was to hold up any decision till after the Congress meeting was well over. I told him that I thought he would agree that it was impossible for me from my point of view to grant him his reprieve…

On the same day , Gandhi met Herbert Emerson, the viceroy's advisor, who recorded Gandhi's feelings thus:

Gandhi did not seem to be particularly concerned in the matter. I told him that we should be lucky if we got through without disorder and I asked all that he could to prevent meetings being held in Delhi during the next new days and to restrain violent speeches. He promised to do all he could.

Indeed, Gandhi was concerned. His letter to the viceroy on 23 March shows his anxiety:

Dear Friend,

It seems cruel to inflict this letter on you, but the interest of peace demands a final appeal. Though you were frank enough to tell me that there was little hope of your commuting the sentence of death on Bhagat Singh and two others, you said you would consider my submission of Saturday. Dr (Tej Bahadur) Sapru (a liberal leader) met me yesterday and said that you were troubled over the matter and taxing your brain as to the proper course to adopt. If there is any room left for reconsideration, I invite your attention to the following:

Popular opinion rightly or wrongly demands commutation. When there is no principle at stake, it is often a duty to respect it.

In the present case, the chances are that, if commutation is granted, internal peace is most likely to be promoted. In the event of execution, peace is undoubtedly in danger.

Seeing that I am unable to inform you that the revolutionary party has assured me that, in the event of these lives being spared, that party will stay its hands, suspension of sentence pending cessation of revolutionary murders becomes in my opinion a preemptory duty.

Political murders have been condoned before now. It is worthwhile saving these lives, if thereby many other innocent lives are likely to be saved, and maybe even revolutionary crime almost stamped out.

Since you seem to value my influence such as it is in favour of peace, do not please unnecessarily make my position, difficult as it is, almost too difficult for future work.

Execution is an irretrievable act. If you think there is the slightest chance of error of judgement, I would urge you to suspend for further review an act that is beyond recall.

If my presence is necessary, I can come. Though I may not speak, I may hear and write what I want to say (Being Monday, it was his silence day).
Charity never faileth.

I am,
Your sincere friend

On that very day the viceroy wrote back:

I have again thought very carefully over everything that you have said and the last thing I should wish to do would be to make your task, especially at this juncture, more difficult. But I am afraid, for the reason I sought to explain fully to you in conversation I cannot see any way to feel that I would be right to take the action you request...

If any proof of British resolve to execute Bhagat Singh and his two comrades from the very outset of the trial proceedings was needed, then the viceroy's letter was there for all to see. They could deal with Gandhi's non-violent revolution but not Bhagat Singh's violent one. The latter would duplicate many Saunders and unleash a wave that would uproot the British forever. Gandhi's revolution was predictable; Bhagat Singh's was not. He and his comrades were executed the same day.

10

Qurra-e-khalk hai gardish mein tapish se meri
Main woh Majnu hoon joh zindaan mein aazaad raha.

WAS THE MEETING WITH HIS RELATIVES ON 3 MARCH, 1931 TO BE his akhiri mulaqat, his last meeting, a legal obligation that the authorities had to allow before the hanging, or would there be another meeting, Bhagat Singh wanted to know, so as to prepare himself to say a final farewell to his loved ones. Head Jail Warden Charat Singh chose not to answer and Bhagat Singh did not push him. He understood the warden's compulsions.

Sukhdev and Rajguru stood behind the iron bars of their respective cells as Bhagat Singh walked by, following behind Charat Singh with measured steps. Neither of them had any visitors. Rajguru had told Bhagat Singh that he had no close relatives left and expected nobody but Sukhdev had said his uncle had promised to come. Apparently, he had not turned up either. Bhagat Singh felt sad for them; he could not imagine anyone's family members staying away when there was a chance – perhaps the last ever – to meet them before their death.

The family was Bhagat Singh's refuge. Though he had spent only a few early years at home he was extremely attached to his family. And they were all present that day. Bhagat Singh had sent them a message asking them not to bid him a tearful farewell. He wanted his last meeting to be full of happy moments; moments he could relive as he walked towards the scaffold. Finding his family unable to contain its sorrow, he was disturbed.

He knew only too well how hard his death would hit them. Still they should have known that death was inevitable on the path he had chosen. He implored them to stay together and bear his loss bravely.

Bhagat Singh found that his grandfather Arjun Singh – who had named him Bhagat and affectionately called him Bhagatu – was inconsolable. His father's long white beard glistened with tears. Kulbir, his younger brother, was wiping his cheeks. Kultar, the youngest, ten years old, was sobbing. His mother's dupatta was soaked. She was trying to stem her tears. His three sisters – Amar Kaur, Sumitra Kaur and Shakuntala Kaur – wept uncontrollably.

Bhagat Singh felt his mother's eyes fixed on him, as if she wanted to cherish and remember every last gesture of his; to fill her vision with him, to draw upon this last meeting in the long years ahead when he was no more. Her grief would be uncontrollable after he was hanged. He could see the tears streaming from her eyes. 'If you go on crying, Ma, I shall not be able to hold myself back,' he said. 'Let not people even be able to say there were tears in Bhagat Singh's mother's eyes when he was hanged. This does not become you or our family of freedom fighters.' Why should his mother cry? For that matter, why should anybody cry? He had committed no crime. He had taken up arms to drive out the foreign rulers from his country. Nobody had the right to enslave and rule over others. The British were as unwanted in India as were the French and the Portuguese. He wanted not only India but all the enslaved countries in the world to be free.

Bhagat Singh's mother touched his long hair which was pulled into a knot on the top of his head. She had been unhappy with him when he had cut it off. Now it had grown back. Caressing his head she said: 'Everyone has to die one day. But the best deaths are the ones that the entire world can cherish.' Smiling bravely through her tears she told him to shout 'Inquilab Zindabad!' when he stood at the gallows.

Gazing into his mother's face took Bhagat Singh back to his place of birth, to the the childhood he had spent in his village, Banga, roaming the dusty streets with boys of his age. He remembered how he endlessly argued with his father on every point. Whenever his father took him to task for baghawati (revolutionary) work, his mother stood by him. Though she never defied her husband, she always managed to pacify him. She was the one who resolved the differences between the two of them. Sometime father and son did not speak to each other for days on end. The differences arose when Bhagat Singh defied his father. It was his mother who persuaded him to return when he left home after his father insisted on his marriage. In a letter to his father, he had tried to explain to him that his life was committed to India's freedom. Though a revolutionary himself, his father had never wanted Bhagat Singh to follow him or his uncle Ajit Singh who had raised the standard of revolt against the British. But Bhagat Singh had always treasured his uncle's book, *Muhibb-e-Watan* (patriots) which he had personally gifted him. He vividly remembered the scars of the wounds inflicted by the British on his uncle's body.

When his father realized that Bhagat Singh would not be stopped from participating in revolutionary activities, all that he advised him was to be careful. It was not unnatural for a father to do so. Caution did not mean cowardice. But Bhagat Singh had thrown caution to the wind. Those who wanted the country to be released from British bondage would have to come out in the open and be counted, he believed.

'Gandhi is in touch with the viceroy to stop the hanging,' Kishen Singh said, trying to reassure his son. Bhagat Singh smiled. He had little faith in Gandhi or his non-violence. Bhagat Singh told his father that Gandhi's non-violence was an excuse for inaction. It was a cover for cowardice. He had no faith in his leadership, or his creed of non-violence. Gandhi was a kind-hearted person. But it was not philanthropy that was required at this point in the freedom struggle. He did not want to join issue with his father, at this, his last meeting with him, so he conceded that they would be ungrateful if they did not salute the Mahatma for the immense awakening he had generated through the non-cooperation movement but he also believed that the Mahatma was an impossible visionary. The revolutionaries respected him but did not want to follow him, he said. Bhagat Singh found his father relieved when he uttered the word 'respect' for Gandhi.

But the truth is he had not forgiven Gandhi for the withdrawal of the non-cooperation movement against the rulers some ten years ago. Every sequence of his surrender was etched in his mind. Gandhi gave a call for non-cooperation at a Congress meeting in November, 1920. Students renounced their studies, lawyers their practices, doctors their clinics, civil servants their jobs and they rallied behind him from all over the country. More than 30,000 people went to jail. Foreign goods were boycotted. Piles of textiles were burnt in public to protest against imported cloth from Lancashire and Birmingham. Gandhi had said that the love of foreign cloth had brought foreign domination. He wanted the British to 'declare in clear terms a policy of absolute non-interference with all non-violent activities in the country'. Indeed, non-cooperation was the biggest non-violent movement the Indians had ever launched against the British.

Yet Gandhi withdrew the movement suddenly. He did not approve of villagers from Chauri Chaura, near Gorakhpur in UP, turning violent. But what was their fault? On 12 February, 1921, they had taken out a procession past a local police station to protest against British rule. Towards the end, the procession was jeered at by the police, provoking the people to retaliate. The policemen, numbering twenty-three, ordered the processionists to disperse, but they stood their ground firmly and peacefully. The angry policemen then started firing on them and went on doing so till their ammunition was exhausted. Three men were killed and many injured. The infuriated crowd set the police station ablaze, twenty-one policemen were either gutted alive or hacked to pieces and thrown into the fire. Gandhi withdrew the movement but did not utter a word to condemn the police. No revolutionary, Bhagat Singh believed, would have retracted his stand because such incidents were the essence of all uprisings; they had their own logic, their own way of churning politics. Stopping them was like pouring cold water on the fire of defiance which would otherwise surely have engulfed the nation.

Bhagat Singh believed that India had lost a great opportunity to bring the enemy to its knees when Gandhi withdrew his non-cooperation movement. What was possible that day would not be possible the next day. The loss of even a single day, postponed not only the deliverance of the people but also defeated the psychological moment. Bhagat Singh could understand why the villagers had retaliated. They had been driven to the wall. They had to hit back. Bhagat Singh told his father that he could neither understand Gandhi's political strategy, nor his moral approach, which had crushed the movement with a single blow. Alien rule could not be defeated wearing kidgloves; an iron fist was required. At times, action was inevitable. Force when aggressively applied was nothing but violence and morally unjustifiable, but when it was used for a legitimate cause, it had moral justification.

Bhagat Singh did not favour terrorism. Killing was senseless; it often targeted the innocent. Acts of terrorism were meant to display power and win publicity. Revolution was an act of defiance, not of violence. It was an ideological war. Terrorism did not go beyond the limits of revenge. It was anger against an individual, not the establishment. It aggravated violence and sidetracked the issue of social transformation. It only instilled fear. True, courage was involved, but not idealism. Terrorism lowered society in its own eyes.

A revolutionary fought for the improvement of the society that oppressed him. He was part of it. At the same time, he tried to transcend it through his efforts for change. His struggle was against the system, the exploitation of man by man, nation by nation. His sacrifice purged ugliness. Revolutionary change was a qualitative alteration of existing social relations and created new human beings who were superior in moral and material terms. But revenge meant action, not just a passive vision. Bhagat Singh believed that oppression should evoke feelings of retaliation, not mere protest. Violence was a catharsis for the oppressed. It was a cleansing force. It freed the subjugated from their inferiority complex, their despair. It made them fearless and restored their self-respect. It was a phase, an inevitable phase of the revolution.

The cult of martyrdom was what Bhagat Singh liked most in Sikhism, the faith that he was born into. He would often recall the words of Gobind Singh, the tenth Sikh Guru. 'It is incumbent on people to sacrifice their life to strengthen the cause they uphold.' He derived inspiration from the Guru's words: *'Chidiyan noo baaz nall ladaoon, taan Guru Gobind Singh kahalson.'* (Only when I make sparrows fight with eagles, can I be called Guru Gobind Singh.) But Bhagat Singh did not believe in the cult of Sikhism or, for that matter, any other religion. He was an atheist. For him religion was a disease, born out of fear. It was the opium of the masses. He remembered the words of Marx: 'Man makes religion, religion does not make man.'

His father told Bhagat Singh that Mahatma Gandhi has said if these three young men were to be hanged, it should be done before the all India Congress session in Karachi. Bhagat Singh asked when the Karachi session was. His father said: 'Towards the end of this month (March).' Bhagat Singh said it was then a matter of great rejoicing. Summer was approaching. It was better to die than get roasted in one's cell. People said that after death one got a better life. 'I shall be reborn in India. Perhaps I may have to face the British once again. My country should win independence,' said Bhagat Singh.

Although he had not forgiven his father for making a written request to the tribunal saying that his son was innocent and that he had nothing to do with Saunders' murder, he knew his father was a sincere patriot who had devoted his life to the cause of independence. His father's filial affection at times had embarrassed Bhagat Singh the revolutionary. But he knew the harrowed look in his father's eyes was his way of saying sorry. Bhagat Singh had chided him through a letter:

I have not been able to understand how you could think it proper to submit such a petition at this stage and in these circumstances…You know that in the political field my views have always differed with those of yours. I have always been acting independently without having cared for your approval or disapproval.

Head Jail Warden Charat Singh indicated to him that the time allotted for the mulaqat (meeting) was over. But Bhagat Singh lingered. His family's love had overwhelmed him. He was pensive. Charat Singh told him to hurry up. His relatives embraced Bhagat Singh one by one. He touched his mother's feet. It was a gesture of reverence but it brought tears to everyone's eyes. His sisters sobbed openly. Bhagat Singh was greatly upset. 'Stay together,' were his last words to them. Then he folded his hands and left.

On his way back to his cell he saw Sukhdev and Rajguru still standing behind iron bars, forlorn and lonely. Despite Charat

Singh asking him not to, he stopped to chat with them. It will be any day now, he told them. The last meeting with his family was indicative of it. They nodded in assent.

Prisoners in nearby cells craned their necks for a glimpse of Bhagat Singh, the man they held in such high esteem. Word had got around, mostly from Barkat, the jail barber, who flitted from one ward to another, that Bhagat Singh had had his *akhri mulaqat*. The hanging was imminent.

Back in his cell Bhagat Singh touched his kurta which was damp with the tears of his family. Little Kultar had wept incessantly. As he clung to his older brother and said goodbye he had sobbed, 'Life will not be worth living without you.' His innocent, grief-stricken face haunted Bhagat Singh. As the cell door closed behind him, he reached for his pen and wrote him a letter in Urdu, the language he normally used in personal letters.

Dear Kultar, I was deeply grieved to see tears in your eyes. Your words today were full of pain. I cannot bear your tears. Darling, go on pursuing your studies with determination and take care of your health. Don't lose heart. What more can I say? Let me recite some couplets for you,

Usay yeh fikr hai hardam naya tarz-e-jafa kya hai,
Hamen yeh shauq hai dekhen sitam ki intiha kya hai

(Fresh avenues of fidelity are what my friend is seeking but I want to experience the limits of tyranny.)

Meri hawa mein rahegi khayal ki khushboo,
Yeh musht-e-khaq hai, fani rahe na rahe.

(Our faith and ideas will fill the air.
What harm if this handful of dust is destroyed?)

It was a strange, smouldering love that Bhagat Singh had for death. He often compared the death of a revolutionary to a tryst with one's beloved. Like a lover, a revolutionary too wanted to feel the embrace of death. He too burned in the fire of overpowering desire for sacrifice. Nothing could satiate him till he got what he cherished.

He believed that people like him must die to keep the torch of defiance burning. Revolutionaries were like tiny insects that hovered around a candle and threw themselves into the flame. He knew that his death was not far off. A couplet by Ghalib that Bhagat Singh used in the letter to Kultar was particularly poignant.

Koi din ka mehman hun ai ahle mehfi
Chiragh-e-sehar hun bujha chahta hun

(Like the last flicker of a lamp at dawn, I have but a few breaths of life left.)

Bhagat Singh had never considered himself anything special. He was just one of thousands of Indians who, unmindful of their religion and region, were engaged in the battle to free India. They had been thrown into the same crucible. Together they were struggling and suffering for the cause. He had no doubt that they would emerge victorious one day.

He believed that after a revolutionary's arrest, the political significance of his action did not diminish in comparison to the personal glory of the revolutionary. Those who were arrested did not become more important than what they did. He and his two comrades were relevant to the extent that they were the instruments used to relay the message to propagate and serve the cause of revolution. It was the revolution that was important, not they.

The letter to Kultar was done. He hoped his words would soothe his brother. But what about the millions of people who believed in him? They had given him more love than he deserved. They had been with him through his hunger strikes, through the trials before the magistrate and the special tribunal. They had supported him even when Gandhi had dismissed his party as a bunch of 'misled' people dictated by the cult of the bomb. He must reciprocate their love. He used the letter to Kultar to bid them goodbye. Once again he used an Urdu couplet to express himself.

Khush raho ahle watan hum to safar karte hain.

(Goodbye, dear countrymen, we proceed on a journey.)

After writing to his brother, Bhagat Singh reached for a notebook he maintained. It was neither a personal account nor a record of his reactions. He just jotted down his favourite passages from the books he was reading. They were passages, mostly in English, by thinkers like Aristotle, Plato, Descartes, Hobbes, Locke, Rousseau, Trotsky, Bertrand Russell, Karl Marx and Engels. Among the Indian authors he read were Rabindranath Tagore and Lajpat Rai. Bhagat Singh was also fond of poetry. He would recite even from Wordsworth, Byron and Omar Khayyam. But his favourite was Ghalib whom he quoted frequently.

The meeting with his family had shaken him emotionally but Bhagat Singh took it in his stride and immersed himself once again in his books. In his notebook he copied an extract from Rousseau's novel, *Emile,* which he had been reading before Charat Singh led him to the akhri mulaqat:

> People think only of preserving their child's life; this is
> not enough; he must be taught to preserve his own life
> when he is a man, to bear the bullets of fortune, to brave

wealth and poverty, to live at ease among the snows of
Iceland or on the scorching rocks of Malta.

Teach him to live, rather to avoid death. Life is not
breath, but action. The use of our senses, our mind, our
faculties, every part of ourselves which makes us
conscious of our being. Life consists less in length of
days than in a keen sense of living. A man may be buried
at a hundred but may never have lived at all; he would
have fared better had he died young.

Ramanand Chatterji, editor of *Modern Review,* Calcutta, had
ridiculed the slogan, 'Long Live Revolution!', and asked Bhagat
Singh its exact meaning. Chatterji had written in an article:

> When a desire is expressed for revolutions to live long, is it
> desired that the revolutionary process should be at work
> every hour, day, week, month and year of our lives? In
> other words, are we to have a revolution as often as
> possible?... No doubt, no revolution can produce a final
> state of improvement; there must be change even after a
> revolution. But these should be brought about by evolution.

Bhagat Singh's reply was they were not the originators of this
cry. The same cry had been used in the Russian revolutionary
movements. He said that the phrase did not mean that sanguinary
strife should ever continue, or that nothing should ever be
stationary even for a short while:

> By long usage this cry achieves a significance which may
> not be quite justifiable from the grammatical or the
> etymological point of view, but nevertheless we cannot
> abstract from that the association of ideas connected with
> that.

The sense in which the word revolution had been used in that phrase, argued Bhagat Singh,

...is the spirit, the longing for a change for the better. People generally get accustomed to the established order of things and begin to tremble at the very idea of a change. It is this lethargic spirit that needs to be replaced by the revolutionary spirit. Otherwise degeneration gains the upper hand and the whole humanity is led astray by the reactionary forces. Such a state of affairs leads to stagnation and paralysis in human progress. The spirit of revolution should always permeate the soul of humanity so that reactionary forces may not accumulate (strengthen) to check its eternal onward march. Old order should change, always and ever, yielding place to new, so that one 'good' order may not corrupt the world. It is in this sense that we raise the shout: Long Live Revolution!.

With Chatterji, Bhagat Singh's confrontation was only on paper. He sent the reply four years after the article. However, his confrontation with Baba Randhir Singh, a freedom fighter detained in the same jail, was face to face, almost on a daily basis. Randhir Singh came to his cell one day to try to convince him of the existence of God. Bhagat Singh told him:

If, as you believe, there is an almighty, omnipresent, omniscient and omnipotent God, who created the earth or the world, please let me know why he created it. This world of miseries, an eternal combination of numberless tragedies: not a single human being is perfectly satisfied. Why does He not first produce a certain sentiment in the mind of the British people to liberate India?

Randhir Singh was so angry that he nearly abused him. 'You are giddy with fame and have developed an ego which is standing like a black curtain between you and God.' Bhagat Singh was hurt. He wrote a long essay in reply, 'Why I am an Atheist'. He resented the accusation:

> I do not boast to be quite above these human traits. I am a man and nothing more. None can claim to be more. I have also this weakness in me. Vanity does form a part of my nature...

Bhagat Singh had once been a devout believer, an Arya Samajist although his father was a Sikh. His hair was long, unshorn and unclipped, till his teens. But he could never believe in the mythology and doctrine of Sikhism or any other religion. By the time he came to shoulder the responsibility of revolutionary work, he had undergone a change.

It was in the name of God, Bhagat Singh recalled, that Hindu-Muslim riots broke out after the non-cooperation movement. He had been horrified. How could two communities, who had sunk their religious differences years ago and fought side by side to oust the British , thirst for each other's blood to support the Caliphate in Turkey? Not that he believed it was a correct cause to take up. What disappointed him was the ferocity with which members of the two communities jumped at each other's throats after sharing the same ideals, the same campaigns and even the same jails. They had participated in the movement together yet remained strangers. They never fought as Indians, never as human beings on the grounds of humanity. Religious, political or personal considerations had brought them together. But at heart, they remained biased and bigoted, Hindus and Muslims till the very end.

In contrast, ideology bound the revolutionaries. Even a one-day agitation revealed their kinship. They were all on the same wavelength. They were against importing religion and its idioms to the struggle for independence. No more mysticism, no more blind faith. Realism became the cult. He studied Bakunin, the anarchist leader, much of Lenin, Trotsky, and others. They were all atheists. He read and was deeply influenced by *Common Sense* a book of mystic atheism by Nirlamba Swami.

Even Gandhi had a tendency to mix religion with popular movements. True, it aroused wide response but in the process it also sowed narrow religious feelings in the minds of people and destroyed the secular ethos of the land. Ram Rajya was a concept of an ideal state in Hindu religion. It was like Plato's Republic, not attainable. And terms like Ram Rajya sowed suspicion in the minds of minorities, making them feel that Hindu ideology was being imposed on them. A pluralistic society required a secular approach; even a bit of bias could contaminate the nation.

It seemed strange to him that the revolutionaries, who fought against prejudice all their lives, fell victim to it before dying. He was thinking in particular of the revolutionaries in the Kakori Case. That they funded revolutionary activities through dacoities was completely acceptable to him, as it was to Chandra Shekhar Azad and some of his other comrades. Ram Prasad Bismil and Ashfhaqullah Khan had entered a train carrying a government tajori (strong box) on 9 August, 1925, at Shahjahanpur, and pulled the chain at a wayside railway station, Kakori, between Hardoi and Shahjahanpur. They fired their revolvers to create confusion and then captured the tajori. So strongly was it built that the muscular Ashfhaqullah had to use a hammer to break it open. Bhagat Singh appreciated their bravery and believed there was no harm in looting the government treasury, which was, after all, filled by extracting hard-earned money from the Indians. But he could not understand why Bismil and Ashfhaqullah decided to highlight their religious identities, and not the revolutionaries' creed of secularism before they were hanged. Ashfhaqullah went to the gallows with the Koran dangling from his neck while Bismil held the Gita. Why did they have to do so? Before he was hanged Ashfhaqullah, an Urdu poet, recited one of his couplets, which was patriotic, not religious.

Kuchh arzoo nahi hai, hai arzoo to yeh
Rakhde koi zarasi khak-e-watan kafan mein.

(I have no desire; if at all there is one, it is this/ that with me in my coffin is placed a handful of my country's soil.)

Bhagat recalled how the first revolutionary he had come in contact with would not dare deny the existence of God. He would say: 'Pray whenever you want to.' This was like riding two horses at the same time. Why didn't people understand that religion made people accept the status-quo, making them believe fatalistically that 'God has ordained it this way'. How could the promoters of change believe in the inevitability of holy books?

Bhagat Singh had found to his dismay that in the early days revolutionaries in Bengal were recruited exclusively from the Hindu middle class. In fact, the revolutionary groups were recognizably anti-Muslim. Since the British government tended to use the Muslims to thwart the national struggle – and many Muslims played the establishment's game – they were suspect in the eyes of the revolutionaries. When East Bengal was sought to be made into a separate province, Barnfield Fuller, then the lieutenant-governor, openly said that the government looked upon the Muslim community as its 'favourite wife'. This remark had rubbed the Bengal revolutionaries the wrong way. They felt that the Muslims were an obstacle in the way of India's freedom and must, like other obstacles, be removed.

The Bengali revolutionaries had another reason to dislike the Muslims. The British felt that they could not trust Bengali employees fully in dealing with revolutionary activities because they were 'politically awake'. So Muslim government employees from UP were brought to man the intelligence branch of the Bengal police. The result was that the Hindus of Bengal began to feel that Muslims were against political freedom and against the Hindu community at large.

For Bhagat Singh, a revolutionary was not super human. He was conscious of his frailties. And he fought them relentlessly and tried to overcome them. But how could he fall prey to bigotry? Idealism bound him by conviction and commitment and gave him power to devise methods to attain his objective. While immersed in society, he transcended it. If he could not rise above bias or prejudice, he was not a revolutionary.

Bhagat Singh flipped the pages of his notebook and read a quotation from Bertrand Russell:

My own view of religion is that of Lucretin. I regard it as a disease born of fear and as a source of untold misery to the human race. I cannot, however, deny that it has made some contribution to civilisation. It helped in early days to fix the calendar and it caused the Egyptian priests to chronicle eclipses with such care that in time they became able to predict them. These two services, I am prepared to acknowledge but I do not know of any other.

Going through the pages of the notebook, Bhagat Singh's eyes rested on a sentence he had reproduced from the writings of Lajpat Rai. 'No rule over a foreign people is so exacting and so merciless in its operation as that of democracy.' True, if the democratic Great Britain could conduct fake trials with impunity to execute those who wanted freedom from its bondage, it was worse than an imperialist nation. It had no justification to hang them because swaraj was their birthright.

Again and again young Kultar's tear-streaked face came to Bhagat Singh's mind. How could he explain to his brother that life was not words, but action, the use of our senses, our mind, every part of ourselves? In his notebook he copied a verse by James Russell Lowell. He captioned it, 'Freedom'.

> ...*True Freedom is to share*
> *All the chains our brothers wear,*
> *And, with heart and hand, to be*
> *Earnest to make others free.*
>
> *They are slaves who fear to speak*
> *For the fallen and the weak;*
> *They are slaves who will not choose*
> *Hatred, scoffing and abuse,*
> *Rather than in silence shrink.*
> *From the truth they need must think;*
> *They are slaves who dare not be*
> *In the right with two or three.*

11

Sarfaroshi ki tamanna ab hamare dil mein hai
Dekhna hai zor kitna bazu-e-katil mein hai…
Waqt ane de bata deinge tujhe eh asman
Ham abhi se kya batain, kya hamare dil mein hai.

RAM PRASAD BISMIL

AS THE NEWS OF THE EXECUTION SPREAD, THE NATION WENT into mourning. There were processions throughout the country. Many went without food. People wore black badges and shut down their businesses to express their grief. The British stayed indoors. Among the Indian political leaders, Jawaharlal Nehru was the first to pay his tributes. He said that Bhagat Singh was a clean fighter who faced the enemy in an open field. He was a young boy full of passionate zeal for the country. He was like a spark that grew into a great flame in a short time and spread from one city of the country to the other, illumining the darkness everywhere.

Gandhi was profuse in his praise for the courage of the executed heroes. He said:

Bhagat Singh and his companions have been executed and have become martyrs. Their death seems to have been a personal loss to many. I join in the tributes paid to the memory of these young men. Bhagat Singh and his two associates have been hanged. Many attempts were made to save their lives, and even some hopes were entertained, but all was in vain. Bhagat Singh did not wish to live. He refused to apologize and declined to file an appeal. If at all he would agree to live, he would do so for the sake of others; if at all he would agree to it, it would be in order that his death might not provide anyone to indiscriminate murder...

But these words were lost on many people, who were angry with Gandhi for not having done enough to save Bhagat Singh and his comrades.

A pall of gloom hung over the Motilal Nehru pandal at the annual Congress party session in Karachi. When the session was scheduled for 29 March, 1931 nobody had an inkling that Bhagat Singh, Sukhdev and Rajguru would be hanged six days ahead of schedule. A procession to be led by president-elect Sardar Vallabhbhai Patel was abandoned in grief. Reception Committee Chairman Choithram P. Gidwani said in a welcome speech that the tragic news had 'plunged the whole country in sorrow and indignation'. The public was desolate. It had expected that the lives of its heroes would be spared. This was natural in the wake of the Gandhi–Irwin Pact and the reconciliation between the Government of India and the Congress.

At the Karachi session, Subhash Chandra Bose, representing the left wing of the Congress, could see disappointment in the eyes of the youth, all of whom wore black bands on their arms. They wanted to know what the Congress had done to save the lives of the three men. Their feeling was that Gandhi had not tried enough. Had he threatened to abrogate his pact with Irwin, the British would have commuted the death sentence to life imprisonment.

Bose had told Gandhi that they should, if necessary, break with the viceroy on the question of Bhagat Singh and his two comrades. 'Because the execution was against the spirit, if not the letter, of the Delhi pact.' Still, Bose added, 'It must be admitted that he (Gandhi) did try his very best.'

Gandhi's secretary Mahadev Desai also quoted the Mahatma as saying in Gujarati:

> I was not here to defend myself and hence I have not placed the facts as to what I have done to save Bhagat Singh and his comrades. I have tried to persuade the viceroy with all the methods of persuasion that I had. After my last meeting with the relatives of Bhagat Singh, on the appointed date, that is, 23rd morning, I wrote a personal letter to the viceroy, in which I had poured in my whole being – heart and soul – but it has all gone in vain… The attempt that a human mind with all its feelings and sentiments can do was not done by me alone. Pujya Pandit Malaviyaji and Dr Sapru also did their utmost.

Faced with the public's ugly mood, Congress leaders tried to come up with several explanations for their failure to rescind the sentence. But nothing worked to soothe the frayed tempers of the public. One explanation the Congress offered was that Irwin promised Gandhi he would commute the death sentence to life imprisonment but he went back on his word when senior British ICS officers threatened to resign *en bloc* if the three men were not hanged.

Another incredible story doing the rounds was that the viceroy had sent orders for commutation to Lahore Central Jail through a telegram but the bureaucrats conspired to delay its transmission and jail officials received the telegram after the hanging.

In an appeal to mollify the anger of the huge gathering Sardar Patel, who was to take over as Congress president, paid glowing tributes to Bhagat Singh and his comrades in his address and expressed the deep resentment in the country over the execution. But he spoke Gandhi's language when he said:

> I cannot identify myself with their methods. I have no doubt that political murder is no less reprehensible than any other; but the patriotism, the daring and the sacrifice of Bhagat Singh and his comrades command my admiration.

Cries of 'Bhagat Singh Amar Rahe!' and 'Inquilab Zindabad!' resounded through the air outside the pandal as Patel spoke. He said:

> The heartless and foreign nature of the government was never more strikingly demonstrated than in their carrying out the executions in the teeth of the all but universal demand for the commutation of the death sentence. Let us not, however, be deterred from our purpose in a fit of resentment. This insolent exhibition of their armed power adds to the heavy indictment against the soulless system and increases our capacity for vindicating our position if we would refuse to be deflected from the straight and narrow path we have chosen.

Gandhi's statement, after the execution, was distributed again:

> Bhagat Singh and his comrades have been executed and have become martyrs. Their death seems to have been a personal loss to many. I join in the tributes paid to the memory of these young men. And yet I must warn the youth of the country against following their example. We should not utilize our energy, our spirit of sacrifice, our labours and our indomitable courage in the way they

have utilized theirs. This country must not be liberated through bloodshed.

About the government I cannot help feeling that it has missed a golden opportunity to win over the rebels to its side. At least from the point of view of the settlement, it was its duty to postpone indefinitely the carrying out of the death sentence. The government has by its own act dealt a severe blow to the settlement and has shown its capacity to disregard public opinion once again and to exhibit the enormous strength it possesses.

The reliance on violence is perhaps ominous and suggests that in spite of high sounding and pious proclamations, it does not want to part with power. But the people's duty is clear.

The Congress must not swerve from the path it chalked out for itself. According to my view, notwithstanding the gravest provocation the Congress should endorse the settlement and test its capacity to secure the results hoped for...

...Hence though we praise the courage of these brave young men we should never countenance their activities. By hanging these men the government has demonstrated its own brute nature, it has provided fresh proof of its arrogance resulting from its power by ignoring public opinion. From this hanging it may be concluded that it is not the intention of the Government to part with any real power to the people. The Government certainly had the right to hang those young men. However, there are some rights that do credit to those who possess them if they are enjoyed in name only. If a person exercises all his rights on all occasions, in the end they are destroyed. On this occasion, the Government would have brought credit to itself if it had not exercised its rights and this would have been highly useful in maintaining peace.

However, it is obvious that the Government has not to date developed such discretion. It was given a clear reason for the public to get enraged. If the latter shows anger, it will lose the games which it is bound to win. Some officials may even hope that the public will give vent to its anger. Whether they do so or not, ours is a straightforward path. While negotiating the settlement, Bhagat Singh's hanging was weighing upon us. We had hoped that the Government would be cautious enough to pardon Bhagat Singh and his associates to the extent of remitting the sentence of hanging. We should not break the pledge we have taken just because our hopes have not been fulfilled, but should bear this blow which has fallen upon us and honour our pledge. By doing so under even such trying circumstances, our strength to get what we desire will increase rather than decrease, while, if we break our pledge or violate the truce, we shall suffer loss of vigour, loss of strength and it will add to our present difficulties in reaching our objective. Hence our *dharma* is to swallow our anger, abide by the settlement and carry out our duty.

In an interview to the press in Karachi, three days before the Congress session, Gandhi said:

I failed in my efforts to bring about the commutation of the death sentences on Bhagat Singh and his friends and that is why the young men vented their wrath against me. I was quite prepared for it. Although they were incensed against me, they gave vent to their wrath in what I would call a most dignified manner. It was open to them to do physical injury but they refrained from doing so. It was open to them to insult me in many other ways, but they confined their resentment and insult to handing me black cloth flowers representing, I imagine, the ashes of the three patriots. These also they could have showered on me or thrown at me instead of which they gave the option of receiving the flowers from their hands which I did gratefully. Of course they shouted 'Down with Gandhism', 'Go back Gandhi'.

This I consider to be a legitimate expression of their anger. Having been used to such an exhibition and that in a much worse and serious form, I was unruffled and took these insults as only a mild expression of their deep grief and anger. I am only hoping that they will exercise the restraint that they did yesterday throughout the INC (Indian National Congress) session for they know I am trying to reach the same goal with them. Only I am following a method wholly different from theirs. I have not a shadow of doubt that as time goes they will discover the error of their ways. Whatever may be true of other countries, in this country which is teeming with famished millions, the cult of violence can have no meaning. In this country of self suppression and timidity almost bordering on cowardice we cannot have too much bravery, too much self-sacrifice. One's head bends before Bhagat Singh's bravery and sacrifice. But I want the greater bravery, if I might say so without offending my young friends, of the meek, the gentle and the non-violent, the bravery that will mount the gallows without injuring, or harbouring any thought of injury to a single soul.

Later, journalists asked Gandhi two questions: The first question was: did the execution of Bhagat Singh and his friends alter his perspective on the settlement? He answered,

> My own personal position remains absolutely the same, though the provocation has been of the most intense character. I must confess that the staying of these executions was no part of the truce, and so far as I am concerned, no provocation offered outside the term will deflect me from the path I had mapped out when I agreed to the settlement.

The second question was: Did he think it impolitic to forgive a government which was guilty of a thousand murders?

> I do not know a single instance where forgiveness has been found so wanting as to be impolitic.
> But no country has ever shown such forgiveness as India is showing to Britain.
> That does not affect my reply. What is true of individuals is true of nations. One cannot forgive too much. The weak can never forgive. Forgiveness is the attribute of the strong.

Sensing that there was a pronounced anti-Gandhi feeling at the session, Nehru hailed Gandhi as 'the greatest apostle of non-violence in the world'. But Nehru also warned,

> Our way is not Bhagat Singh's way. We have always declared that we cannot free our country by the use of arms... only by the method of Gandhi will the country gain freedom. If we leave the path of non-violence, we shall not be free for years to come.

Nehru sponsored a resolution which was seconded by Madan Mohan Malviya. The resolution said:

This Congress while dissociating itself from and disapproving of political violence in any shape or form, places on record its admiration of the bravery and sacrifice of the late Sardar Bhagat Singh and his comrades, Sukhdev and Rajguru, and mourns with the bereaved families the loss of these lives. This Congress is of the opinion that this triple execution is an act of wanton vengeance and is a deliberate flouting of the unanimous demand of the nation for commutation. This Congress is further of the opinion that the government has lost the golden opportunity of promoting goodwill essential at this juncture and of winning over to the method of peace the party, which being driven to despair, resorts to political violence.

Gandhi chose Nehru to pilot the resolution because he was popular among the youth. Patel was heckled. What acted as a catharsis was a speech by Bhagat Singh's father, Kishen Singh. Delegates wept loudly and openly as Kishen Singh recalled Bhagat Singh's words:

Ham se Bhagat ne kaha tha, ke tum pareshan na ho. Mujhe phansi lagne do, yehi thik hai. Hamein phansi lagi to ek hafte main hi swaraj mil jayega. Woh kehta tha ke privy council mein jane se koi faida nahin chunki ghulamon ka haq nahin hai ke shikayat karein.

(Bhagat Singh told me not to worry. Let me be hanged. One week after the execution, the country will get independence. He warned me against going to the privy council because he said slaves had no right to complain.)

Kishen Singh spoke about how he and other members of his family were not permitted by the jail authorities to meet Bhagat Singh a day before the execution.

> He was there, we could see him. But the police did not allow us to meet him. We just waved hands. How could they do this to a father whose son was being snatched away before his eyes?

But he made a fervent appeal:

> You must support your general (Gandhi). You must support all Congress leaders. Only then will you be able to win independence for the country.

Despite its vocal appreciation of Bhagat Singh and his comrades, the resolution was not appreciated by many members. One delegate moved an amendment for the deletion of the words, 'Whilst disassociating itself from and disapproving of political violence in any form or shape'. He said that the honour to Bhagat Singh, Sukhdev and Rajguru should be given without being qualified.

'Having actually lived the life of a non-violent follower of Gandhiji, I (still) claim that it is now derogatory to the sense of dignity and nobility of the house to say that we all stand against any form or shape of violence,' said Lal Bahadur Shastri.

Another delegate supported Shastri and seconded the amendment: 'Prominent leaders have praised the bravery of Bhagat Singh and his comrades. But I do not understand why their action has been assessed in a contemptuous way. Whatever they have done, they have done for the sake of the country.'

Before any other delegate rose to speak on the amendment, there was a move for closure. Many hands went up in Shastri's support but it was obvious that Gandhi did not approve of the amendment. The resolution Nehru moved had been drafted with Gandhi's approval. Gandhi wanted the amendment to be withdrawn. A vote was cast. The amendment was lost.

The support of the Congress was too crucial for Gandhi to be majorly affected by the hangings. Gandhi had already agreed in principle at the Round Table Conference in London to a 'settlement'. He had to have the full and unfettered support of the Congress. Jamnadas Bajaj, the Congress party's treasurer, made a telling remark when he told Gandhi: 'You cannot go to the Round Table Conference hedged in by conditions and tell the world that you are still sticking to independence.'

In the *Young India* of 11 June, 1931, Gandhi said, 'I had interested myself in the movement for the commutation of the death sentence on Bhagat Singh and his comrades. I had put my whole being into the task.' In another public utterance, he said: 'I would gladly have surrendered my life to the viceroy to save Bhagat Singh and others.'

Still, Gandhi refused to associate himself with the move to raise a memorial to Bhagat Singh.

The annual conference was still in session when Mathura Das, Sukhdev's brother, delivered a letter written by Sukhdev to Gandhi's private secretary, Mahadev Desai. The letter had been written just a couple of days before the hanging. Sukhdev had heard that Gandhi was negotiating with the government for the release of prisoners not convicted of violence. At the same time, Gandhi was also appealing to the revolutionaries to stop their movement. In the letter, which was later published in *Young India* on 21 April, 1931 Sukhdev addressed Gandhi as 'Most Gracious Mahatmaji':

Since your compromise you have called off your movement and consequently all of your prisoners have been released. But what about the revolutionary prisoners? Dozens of Ghadar party prisoners imprisoned since 1915 are still rotting in jails; in spite of having undergone the full terms of their imprisonment scores of martial law prisoners are still buried in these living tombs and so are dozens of Babbar Akali prisoners. Deogarh, Kakori, Machhua Bazar and Lahore Conspiracy Case prisoners are amongst those numerous still locked behind bars. More than half a dozen conspiracy trials are going on at Lahore, Delhi, Chittagong, Bombay, Calcutta and elsewhere. Dozens of revolutionaries are absconding and amongst them are many females. More than half a dozen prisoners are actually waiting for their executions. What about all of these people? The three Lahore Conspiracy Case condemned prisoners, who have luckily come into prominence and who have acquired enormous public sympathy, do not form the bulk of the revolutionary party. Their fate is not the only consideration before the party. As a matter of fact their executions are expected to do greater good than the commutation of their sentences.

But, in spite of all this, you are making public appeals, asking them to call off their movement. Why should they do so? You have not mentioned any very definite things. In these circumstances your appeal means you are joining hands with bureaucracy to crush the movement. And your appeals amount to preaching treachery, desertion and betrayal amongst them. If that were not the case, the best thing for you would have been to approach some of the prominent revolutionaries and talk over the whole thing with them. You ought to have tried to convince them to call off their movement. I do not think you also share the general conservative notion that the revolutionaries are devoid of reason, rejoicing in destruction and devastation. Let us inform you that in reality the case is quite contrary. They always consider the pros and cons of every step they take and they fully realize the responsibility which they thus incur and they attach greater importance to the constructive phase of the revolutionary programme than to any other, though in the present circumstances, they cannot but occupy themselves with the destructive part of their programme.

The present policy of the government towards them is to deprive them of the sympathy and support of the masses which they have won in their movement, and then crush them. In isolation they can be easily hunted down. In face of that fact any sentimental appeal to cause demoralisation amongst their ranks would be utterly unwise and counter-revolutionary. It would be rendering direct assistance to the government to crush them.

Therefore we request you either to talk to some revolutionary leaders – they are so many in jails – and come to terms with them or to stop these appeals. Please, for goodness sake, pursue one of these two alternative courses and pursue it wholeheartedly. If you cannot help them, then please have mercy on them. Let them alone; they can better take care of themselves, they know that the hegemony of the revolutionary party in the future political struggle is assured. Masses are rallying around them and the day is not far off when they will be leading the masses under their banner towards their noble and lofty ideal – the socialist republic.

Or, if you seriously mean to help them, then have a talk with them to understand their point of view, and discuss the problem in details.

Hope you will kindly consider the above request and let your view be known publicly.

Sukhdev ended the letter thus: 'Yours, One of the many'.

Since Sukhdev had asked Gandhi to react to his letter publicly, the Mahatma did so. He wrote:

The writer is not 'one of the many.' Many do not seek the gallows for political freedom. However condemnable political murder may be, it is not possible to withhold recognition of the love of the country and the courage which inspires such awful deeds. And let us hope that the cult of political assassination is not growing if the Indian experiment succeeds, as it is bound to, the occupation of the political assassin will be gone for ever. At any rate, I am working in that faith.

The writer does one less than justice when he says that I have made no more than sentimental appeals to the revolutionaries to call off their movement, and I claim on the contrary that I have given them hard facts which, though they have been often repeated in these columns, will bear recapitulation:

1. The revolutionary activity has not brought us near our goal.
2. It has added to the military expenditure in the country.
3. It has given rise to reprisals on the part of the government without doing any good.
4. Whenever a revolutionary murder has taken place, it has for a time and in that place demoralised the people.
5. It has in no way contributed to mass awakening.
6. Its effect on the masses has been doubly bad in that they tend to bear the burden ultimately of additional

expense and the indirect effect of government wrath.

7. Revolutionary murder cannot thrive in the Indian soil, Indian tradition, as history teaches us, being unfavourable to the growth of political violence.

8. If the revolutionaries seek to convert the masses to their method, we would have to wait for an indefinitely long time for it to permeate the masses and then to gain freedom.

9. If the method of violence ever becomes popular, he is bound to recoil, as it has done in other countries, on our own heads.

10. The revolutionaries have an ocular demonstration of the efficacy of the opposite method, i.e., non-violence, which has gone on in spite of sporadic cases of violence on their part and in spite even of violence, occasionally dared by the so-called votaries of non-violence.

11. Revolutionaries should accept only testimony which tells them that their activity has not only not done any good to the movement of non-violence, but it has, on the contrary, harmed the cause. In other words, if I had a completely peaceful atmosphere, we would have gained our end already.

These, I claim, are hard facts and no appeal to (sentence). But the writer further objects to my making public appeals to the party and suggests that thereby helping the bureaucracy to crush the movement. Surely, the bureaucracy is in no need of my help to deal with the movement. It fights for life both against the revolutionary and me. One scents more danger from the non-violent movement than from the violent. It knows how to deal with the latter. It is baffled by the former which has already shaken it to its foundations.

Moreover, authors of political murder count the cost before they enter upon their awful career. No action of mine can possibly worsen their fate. And seeing that the revolutionary party must work in secret, I have no other way open to me but that of making public appeals to its unknown members. I count many past revolutionaries among my co-workers.

The open letter complains that prisoners other than satyagrahis have not been released. I have explained the reason why it was impossible to insist on the release of the other prisoners. Personally, I want the release of all of them. I would make every effort to secure their release. I am aware that some of them ought to have been discharged long ago. The Congress has a resolution in that behalf. Sjt. Nariman (a Congress leader) has been appointed by the Working Committee to collect all names. As soon as he has got the list, steps will be taken to secure their release. But those who are out must help by preventing revolutionary murder. We may not have the cake and also eat it. Of course, there are political prisoners, who should be discharged in any case. I can only give the assurance to all concerned that the delay is due not to want of will but due to want of ability. Let it be also remembered that when the final settlement comes, if it does, in the course of a few months, all political prisoners must be discharged. If it does not come, those who are trying to secure the release of the other political prisoners will find themselves in prison.

Epilogue

Bhagat Singh ke khoon ka asar dekh lena!
Mitadenge zaalim ka ghar dekh lena.!

AWASH WITH SUNLIGHT, WASHINGTON WAS BRIGHT AND CLEAN in November,1981. Even the cloistered chambers of the Congressmen and senators were bathed in light. But one room in 1088, Westside Drive had its curtains drawn, as if the occupant preferred to live in the dark. Of course, this was no surprise to the neighbours who always found the shutters of the house closed.

Few people had anything to do with the brooding occupant, a tall man, tense and tentative in his behaviour. He always shunned company. For the last several months he had confined himself to his room.

Now old and drooping, Hans Raj Vohra liked to stay indoors all by himself. He was often drowned in his thoughts. Why had he turned official approver against his comrades, the revolutionaries? He had been wanting to tell his side of the story for many years. But every time he felt the need to do so he held back. He had convinced himself that nobody would care to give him a hearing. After all, his testimony had been crucial to the death sentence given to three of his ex-comrades – Bhagat Singh, Sukhdev and Rajguru. People would shun him when they heard who he was.

The manner in which he was boycotted even by his friends after he turned approver had made him believe that he would be a social pariah all his life. Even the people closest to him had doubts about him. He had learnt to live with the odium. It had been a hard and lonely life but he had come to terms with it.

After the trial, the British had whisked Vohra off to the UK where he joined London University. But for their help, he would not have got a job.

The first job he held, after a stint in London, was with the English-owned newspaper, *Civil and Military Gazette,* in Lahore itself. A senior government official spoke to editor F.W. Bustin who hired him as a reporter. Even at that time Vohra knew that he would have to carry the stigma of betraying his friends and harming the revolutionaries' cause for the rest of his life.

He had never forgotten the contempt on Bhagat Singh's face when he saw him in court. Though Sukhdev had recruited him to the HSRA it was Bhagat Singh who had grown close to him. Like Bhagat Singh, Vohra too had once run away from home to escape his father's wrath for associating with the revolutionaries.

Was he to blame for the hanging of the three? He had convinced himself that he'd paid enough for sins he had not committed. A few months before Partition, he had joined the *Statesman*, a Calcutta daily owned by a Britisher. Bustin had spoken to Editor Arthur Moore, who made him a special correspondent in Delhi. Though his position gave him an opportunity to meet with senior politicians, he always had a nagging feeling that they did not confide in him. His past always caught up with his present.

He took the first opportunity to get a posting abroad. *The Times of India* hired him as its Washington correspondent. After retirement he did not come back to India and became a representative of *Deccan Herald* in the US. Subsequently, he started his own feature service, an inconsequential venture that didn't fare well.

The passage of time dimmed the memory of Bhagat Singh's execution. But whenever his sacrifice was recalled, Vohra's name cropped up as the person who had given evidence against Bhagat Singh and betrayed him and the cause.

A letter he received from India, fifty years after the hangings, shook Vohra. It was a letter from Sukhdev's brother, Mathura Das Thapar, an engineer. Thapar said that history would want to know why he had let down his comrades.

Vohra had decided to die in America, unnoticed and unheard. The letter accused him of what he thought was not true. Thapar's insinuation hurt him deeply: 'Why did you forget that foreign rulers of our country, in collusion with their administrative machinery, which included Indians, followed a policy of suppression of the people?'

Thapar still seemed to have faith in him; he reminded Vohra of the time he had stood firm even at the age of seventeen after a bomb explosion at the Dussehra ground in Lahore in 1926. The authorities could not make him speak. Sukhdev had praised him then. Why then did he break when he was arrested in the Lahore Conspiracy Case, Thapar asked.

Thapar had placed the blame squarely on him. Vohra felt he must explain his side of the story. In any case, he did not have many days to live. Doctors had diagnosed a malignancy made worse by heavy drinking.

Vohra was a stickler for form. Even during the height of summer in Delhi, he wore a jacket with a necktie. He looked at the typewriter in the corner of his room for a long time. He could not decide whether he should type out his reply or write it in longhand. Finally he picked up his pen; if it was a confession, it should be handwritten.

In his letter, Vohra said:

I was moved by your letter and your overflowing affection which I do not in the least deserve. I regret we did not meet. In retrospect, who knows, it was probably a good thing. If we had met, we would have talked of old times and what happened in the twenties when I was only 17 years old. I understand you have researched the episode very thoroughly. I have often thought of doing it myself and also about writing a book on it. But second thoughts have deterred me. Anything I wrote would be treated as biased and self-serving. It would be a waste of time, although I still believe a factual account would be a helpful contribution to the history of the period...

You have every right to be proud of Sukhdev. He was the soul of the party, a real organizer. I guess he is your hero. But I explained to Balbir (Vohra's cousin) how my views changed and what in fact happened. Probably he has conveyed my version of events to you. That is why I hold that our non-meeting was a good thing...

It has been a most difficult life, full of risks, but so far, touch-wood, I have emerged virtually unscathed at least physically. But the memory of the twenties accompanies me doggedly, teasingly, hauntingly, painingly. I have adopted a semi-public career as a journalist. I had to steer through the 44 years of a writing career like a fish in murky waters, seeking professional success while avoiding public recognition. It is amazing and extremely satisfying that, despite unavoidable handicaps, I have achieved the utmost professional success in my line of journalism.

...I still earn my living purely by wielding my pen, which is a clean way to spend my remaining years particularly because my profession imbibes expression with thinking, art with craft and reading with writing. I hope by the time I die, I would have been fully forgotten. This is my ambition.

Thapar replied to Vohra's letter dated 7 October, 1980 nearly a year later, on 9 September, 1981 and sought 'elaboration and more information'.

He wrote:

> It gratified me to know that you have now achieved the utmost professional success in your line of journalism after having passed through a life of struggle and uncertainties... But, in the midst of those dulcet notes I also heard discordant ones: that in spite of utmost professional success, you have been avoiding public recognition, and that (to quote your own concluding words) 'I hope by the time I die I would have been fully forgotten. This is my only ambition'... Fatalism may be a piece of ill-advised philosophy where it leads to inaction, to an endless wait for the happy chance to fall from heavens above; but it is, without any reservations, commendable where merit and efforts, for one reason or the other, don't bear the desired fruit; it is a balm of all hurt minds. You seem to have yielded to self-mortification which, to my mind, is a temptation breeding ill-humour and which bedins life's serenity and sunshine.
>
> What in fact happened (to quote your own words) is my genuine curiosity to know. And, it is raised to such an extent that I may even make bold to ask that if you thought that Sukhdev yielded to weakness or some such thing when the conspiracy was unearthed, why you didn't remain firm as you had been on the earlier occasion, and why you have been harbouring an aversion for him when he, till his last, ever held you in esteem...

Could Sukhdev have made a 'confession' to gain the confidence of the police? Vohra wondered. Sukhdev wanted access to comrade Jai Gopal, who had become an official approver. Sukhdev had chosen him as a messenger to inform Bhagat Singh, Rajguru and Azad about the arrival of Scott at his office. Jai Gopal identified Saunders as Scott. He was the police's key witness, who had witnessed the murder of Saunders. Did Sukhdev confess only to get close to Jai Gopal and kill him?

Vohra thought he would tell all. He said in the second letter: 'My Guru (Sukhdev), I felt, had let me down. Together with the rest of the public, I could not go down with the people I no longer respected.'

Below is Vohra's letter dated 27 November, 1981, three months after Thapar's reply:

Hans R. Vohra,
Editor, US Feature Service

My dear Mathuradasji,

I must ask your forgiveness for the delay in answering your affectionate letter.
Your affection is so overwhelming and unexpected that I continue to be surprised by it for I prefer to label myself as a political leper. Perhaps this little poem would explain the situation:

Once I had a friend,
A leper friend was he
Could you shake him by the hand,
Chorus: Oh, No.
Could you look him in the eye,
Chorus: Oh, No.
Could you sleep with him,
Chorus: Oh No, No.

That was the tragedy.

I am not much of a poet, but I hope this stanza does explain my true feeling about myself. That is why I wonder whether you are not wasting your sentiments on a person consumed by grief over the turn his life has taken. As I have told you, it would be very inappropriate for me to talk about the Sukhdev case and the role he played after his arrest. I had the relevant bits read to me. Since you compel me, I cannot in all honesty say that I agree with your conclusions.

I shall deliberately confine this letter to my personal reactions to the events.

I was arrested on the eve of Saunders' murder. This did not surprise me. I was the most important and the most well-known student leader in town. At the age of 17 or so, I became the first Secretary of the Punjab Students movement which I tried to convert into a public forum for our revolutionary movement.

I called a Punjab Students' conference which was astonishingly well attended. I proposed a resolution for complete independence for India when the Indian National Congress was comtemplating Dominion Status. So I put the students ahead of the elders.

After my arrest, *the burden of concealing the murder conspiracy,* about which I knew everything, fell on my shoulders. When I was released on bail several weeks after the arrest, I had carried out my responsibility to the party successfully. The secret remained locked in my chest. I do not want to write about the ordeal in the police lock-up lest you should construe that I am asking for mercy or that I am flattering myself.

However, when I was arrested a second time, soon after the rounding up of Sukhdev and some other party members, I was presented a statement by Sukhdev which ran, I believe, into probably 100 or (50) pages, typewritten and foolscap.

Secondly, I found that about eight or ten members of the party, and every senior members at that, had become the King's witnesses or approvers as (they) call them.

So I had to think things anew in the light of the following facts: Sukhdev at whose command I had given up my family and whom I had accepted as my guru had wrecked the party which he had done so much to create.

It was an inexplicable situation, totally disappointing and terribly shattering of morale or the common purpose we had set out to serve.

I cannot accept your explanation that he became nervous *(ghabra gaya)*. This is so inadequate for a would-be hero of a story that it mocks his better side. He was a great organizer. He was selflessly devoted to the cause. He was a ceaseless worker. He was a convincing talker which is apparent as I joined the party at his behest.

To this day, I do not know what precisely went through his mind that he burst like a Diwali cracker within hours of being arrested. I am absolutely sure that the police did not use any high-handed methods. If anything, the investigators were very respectful and kind.

Sukhdev voluntarily divulged every secret of the party. There was nothing important to keep although I did find a few things which he had forgotten to mention and which, therefore, I also withheld in my statement.

Sukhdev's performance presents two problems, none of which you have solved; (a) if he had no axe to grind, why did he make the statement?; (b) having made the statement why did he not take some advantage of it?

As I have said, there is no rational reason for (a) except that his mind was like a tumbler of water. The tumbler cracked and the water overflowed.

Having thus mentally evacuated himself, I guess, he was at peace. But his overflowing knowledge about the party, which he freely cast away, created problems for others. Mine has remained my companion throughout my life.

My life is stunted and stained and there is nothing I can do to wash away the horrible marks so deeply etched in history.

I gave up the resistance to the investigating police for the following reasons: (a) My guru, I felt, had let me down together with the rest of the party. My portion of the story was relatively small and inconsequential as compared with what had been given away.

I was consumed by helplessness and although it is easy to say .that I would have received a light punishment, I could not risk going down with people I no longer respected.

Secondly, it would have meant a total disruption of my life as I was in my final year of education.

So I tried very deftly, without doing the least possible additional harm to the party, to extricate myself so that I could pick up the remaining pieces as best as I could.

(1)   I was able to abstain from giving any personal evidence of the murder, which I had seen organized and which I had seen being readied a few minutes before the execution.

I said nothing about it. So I was neither a witness to the conspiracy of the murder nor of the murder.

(2)   I also take such credit as I can for abstaining to mention anything about Durga Das whom I had recruited.

I was able to do both because I found that Sukhdev's statement had omitted them.

You must also remember that I was the youngest member of the party. But I did understand the legal consequences of actions. Even while giving evidence, I tried to do the least harm, and possibly some good as Durga Das has often acknowledged to me.

I would be grateful if you give copies of our correspondence to Balbir as he is interested in the case.

Once again, I must seek your pardon if I have unwittingly written anything derogatory of Sukhdev. You have every reason to treat him as a hero. He was your brother. I have written this letter about my experience of the case much against my wishes.

With kind regards,

Yours affectionately,
(H.R. Vohra)

Thapar took nearly five months to reply to Vohra's letter. It was a long 14-page reply typed in single space.

Thapar summarized Vohra's reply – 'Your grudge,' as he put it into four points:

(1) That after your third and the last arrest on May, 1929, you were shown about a hungred-page statement (alleged to have been made) by Sukhdev; (2) that Sukhdev being an important leader, let you and others down, and destroyed the party which he so much laboured to create; (3) that eight or 10 senior members of the party had become King's witnesses; and (4) you wondered that, having made the statement, why Sukhdev did not take advantage unto himself.

Thapar argued that the statement 'which was shown to you was concocted by the police…' He contradicted Vohra's allegation that the Punjab police did not use any high-handed methods against Sukhdev. Thapar said that,

> the police had resorted to third degree methods in trying to break him and bend him. But his spirits remained undaunted and firm in resolve, though his body bore marks of cruelty… Now, what actually happened was that Jai Gopal's statement must have upset Sukhdev. As soon as he came to know of it, he told the investigating police that instead of demanding from Jai Gopal, they should better ask him for details, he being in the know of every thing as an important leader. In assuming this posture, which caused much misunderstanding in the minds of his associates, Sukhdev's purpose was to, somehow take the police into confidence and gain their favour so that he could get access to Jai Gopal in order to strangle him to death. This was what Sukhdev confessed to some of us of the family when we met him while he was in the custody of Aziz Ahmad, who was in charge of the Conspiracy Case, and Sardar Gopa, Singh, Deputy Superintendent.

Thapar alleged that Yashpal, the Hindi writer, was a police informer. 'He used to gather all information from Jai Gopal and then pass it on to the police. Though now dead a few years, he is fondly remembered by his admirers as a great revolutionary and a Hindi writer of no mean significance.' What an irony!

In his reply dated 9 October, 1982, Vohra said:

> I cannot for the life of me agree that Sukhdev's actions after arrest were guided by the motive you have

attributed. It is too fantastic to be credible. Nor can I accept the thesis that his long statement was a police concoction. This is at variance with his effort to guide the police to some of the party's hideouts even if he did not show all of them. Nor did I find any substance in your assumption of torture by the police who used the more powerful weapon of politeness, respect and indulgence.

Vohra concluded the correspondence by saying: 'The best thing we can do is to agree amiably to disagree or that we can meet in a friendly way when I visit India in December.' He never returned to his country.

Thapar too closed the correspondence by writing on 19 November, 1982: 'Yes, there seems to be cleavage in our views which, as you say, cannot be closed. Hence it would be proper if we do no more talking on this affair.'

∽◌◌◌∾

'How do I check Vohra's version?' I asked myself. Thapar did not say anything beyond what the letter said when I sought more information from him. He died before I could meet him. He did not publicize Vohra's letter as he did not believe him. But Thapar was fair: he sent Vohra's letter to his family members in New Delhi.

One person, Durga Devi, widow of Bhagwati Charan, Bhagat Singh's close associate, would know the truth. I checked with her too. She was living in Ghaziabad with her son Sachin when I met her. She suffered from frequent memory lapses at the time. But she recalled Vohra whom she dismissed as 'a small functionary in the party'. Regarding Vohra's allegation, she said: 'We suspected Sukhdev all along.'

Still suspicion cannot change the facts. Sukhdev was hanged along with Bhagat Singh and Rajguru. There is no evidence that he faltered during the trial or later. He was as defiant as he was in school – when he was caned for refusing to salute visiting white military officers. If he was the person who had divulged everything to the police, why was he not pardoned in place of Vohra? Sukhdev knew far much more than Vohra.

Vohra probably fell prey to the usual tactics of the police. Even today the ruse commonly employed by them is: 'Your comrade has already told us every thing. You may as well tell your side and we would try to get you a pardon.' Something like that might have happened. The truth is, Vohra's version lacks conviction. How could a person with even a grain of commitment to the revolution turn into a stool-pigeon?

During his lifetime Vohra must have often recalled the years when his involvement in the revolution was above question. When he was steadfast in his commitment to the cause and his comrades all respected and trusted him. He was not a Marxist. But the thought of emancipation from the British animated him. He was present at every closed-door meeting and not once did he give the impression of being the kind of person who would desert the ranks of the revolutionaries.

Vohra died on 13 September, 1985, in his room in Washington, with the shutters down. He could keep the light out but not the darkness. He was cremated in Washington with just a clutch of family members in attendance.

The difference between Sukhdev and Vohra is underlined by the people's response to them both.

The ashes of Bhagat Singh, Sukhdev and Rajguru were consigned to a shrine near Ferozepur where a memorial came up and where thousands of people flock to pay their homage all through the year. The crematorium where Vohra's body was put to fire is not even known. Sukhdev is a hero. How big the difference between the hero and the betrayer. The first lives in the hearts of the people the other in their curses. History remembers both, one because he sacrificed his own life, the second because he sacrificed the lives of his friends.

Faiz Ahmed Faiz described the death of Bhagat Singh, Sukhdev and Rajguru in these lines:

Jis dhaj se koi maqtal mein gaya, woh shaan salamat rehti hai
yeh jaan to aani jaani hai, is jaan ki koi baat nahin.

(It is the dignity with which one goes to his death that is remembered by all,
What of life, it comes and goes...)

Annexure – I

Mr. Kuldip Nayar,
D-7/2, Vasant Vihar,
New Delhi-110057.

My dear Mr Nayar,

I am in receipt of your letter of 22nd October, 1992 and am sorry for the delay in reply. Many factors are responsible for the delay including my failing health – being 82 years old and having eye trouble requiring operation of both the eyes. Besides failing physical health I am without a proper shelter after retirement as cold storage expert. I have worked in such an organisation in Hapur since 1940. Before this I was in Saharanpur from 1936 to 1940 in a ice factory of L., Ram Labhaya Chanaan of Lyallpur, one amongst the family of old Congress politicians of Punjab. The reason I came away from Lyallpur was due to the constant troubles created against me by the Punjab Police on account of my being the blood brother of Sukhdev – the BRAIN BEHIND THE CONSPIRACY as per the notings of the British Police Officer in Punjab Police, the TRIO combine of Sukhdev, Bhagat Singh and Rajguru. I always acted like a carrier of letters exchanged by the head of the conspirators named above (Sukhdev) – letter by Sukhdev to Mahatma Gandhi – that he wrote just before being HANGED on 23rd March, 1931. No one from amongst the Congress leaders of Punjab cared to accept the letter to be carried to Karachi Congress Session held there by 31st March, 1931 (sic). L. Chint Ram, our uncle, a very big Congress leader of Punjab could not go as he was to reach Lyallpur to be present there to sit as the HEAD of the Thapar clan to receive the mourners who were to reach Lyallpur to mourn the sad end of Sukhdev. L.Pindi Das and other Congress leaders heading for the Karachi Session refused to carry the letter to Mahatma Gandhi for the fear of being

REBUKED and branded by the Mahatama as hand in glove with conspirator to indicate any kind of link or association with the above TERRORISTS. I was therefore asked by L. Chint Ram – our uncle and HEAD OF THE THAPAR clan, to proceed to Karachi to carry the letter to be delivered to Gandhiji. I reached by the train carrying the Congress leaders to Karachi and in spite of all the beating and insulting offensive attitude of Congress volunteers, I could after all meet the P.A. to Gandhiji's, Shri Mahadev Desai, and delivered the letter. Gandhiji being awfully busy at that very important session after the HANGING of the THREE HEROES, Mr. Desai told me to CONVEY IT TO L. CHINT RAM that the letter will be replied by Gandhi Jee only after the session and its reply can be seen in *Navjivan* (Hindi) and *Young India* (English) after Gandhi Jee returns to Wardha.

Before this also I was twice jailed in the years 1927-28 and 1930-31, once when Sukhdev wrote a letter addressed to 'BIRATHER-AE-MUN' and was to be posted at my address in Lahore; and before that in Lyallpur when a BOMB exploded in Company Bagh Club of the British officers. Many others were arrested in Lyallpur but they were all let off but I was held for being the nephew of L. Chint Ram and the real younger brother of SUKHDEV and imprisoned for FOUR MONTHS in Qilla Gujar Singh, Lahore. It will not be out of place to add that I suffered most when my brother was in the process of writing the above entitled letter to my address in Lahore, which my brother wrote from BORSTAL JAIL, Lahore. This he did after he was condemned along with others (Bhagat Singh and Rajguru). Immediately Police rushed to Borstal Jail and snatched the letter that was half finished and Aziz Ahmed, the head of police party questioned SUKHDEV as to whom this letter was to be sent. He said this is for my comrades-other party KRANTIKARIES WHOSE NAME HE refused to disclose. He *(AZIZ AHMED)* then told him that under the circumstances your brother Mathura Das Thapar will be taken into custody and jailed and suffer police torture. He replied, 'so what, he has been always suffering from Police Excesses in the past as well' 'and will once again face the police torture. But under no circumstances the names of his comrades will be disclosed to whom this letter was meant.' The Police party had gone to Borstal Jail to transfer him to Central Jail to be lodged in the cell meant for condemned convicts. The death sentence had just been passed and all condemned were transferred immediately to Central Jail cells meant for housing the condemned.

I was again under the GRIP of Punjab Police and suffered jail torture for many months to come.

Allow me the indulgence to add further that other Political sufferers like Dr. Kitchloo's son got a monthly packet of Rs.5000-00 plus a lump sum compensation of Rs.50,000-00 and also a DDA flat free of cost. As compared to Dr. Kitchloo's son compare our Clan's sacrifices – L. Chint Ram (my uncle)went to Jail several times from 1907 onwards in the struggle for FREEDOM of the country and my elder brother was hanged along with Bhagat Singh and Rajguru and I was also a victim of Police torture repeatedly and this was the main reason, I moved out of Punjab at the advice of our Uncle L. Chint Ram as said above.

Now coming to the main point about the material for your proposed book on BHAGAT SINGH TRIAL, I may again draw your kind attention to PROCEEDINGS BOOK of LAHORE CONSPIRACY CASE, that I have presented to the National Archives in New Delhi. This is the only document I had compiled which runs into more than 400 pages. I may tell you that I collected the entire case documents from Lahore High Court and other relevant documents that in itself are the HISTORY of National Importance. The case – the Lahore Conspiracy Case reads in Govt. records as 'SUKHDEV VS KING AND OTHER ACCUSED.' The English version and the judgement in English, comprising of the 'PROCEEDINGS BOOK' are in the National Archives and its version in Urdu in three volumes is with me. I have also many more documents of interest to a WORLD FAME writer like your goodself. I can place at your disposal for some time all these documents in my possession that I have collected from Lahore High Court by spending time and money to obtain these records. Please note that as and when I go to Delhi I stay with my daughter Mrs. Lata Gujral at No.L-15, First Floor, South Extension, Part (II), New Delhi. They are on telephone and shall give you the telephone number later if you feel further interested to have a look at the other relative papers and documentary proof available with me.

With best regards and hoping to be of use in your GREAT TASK of writing another masterpiece of great HISTORIC IMPORTANCE.

Sincerely Yours,

Sd/-

(M.D. Thapar)

Annexure-II
Why I Am an Atheist

Bhagat Singh

A NEW QUESTION HAS CROPPED UP, IS IT DUE TO VANITY THAT I do not believe in the existence of an omnipotent, omnipresent and omniscient God? I had never imagined that I would ever have to confront such a question. But conversation with some friends has given me a hint that certain of my friends – if I am not claiming too much in thinking them to be so – are inclined to conclude from the brief contact they have had with me, that it was too much on my part to deny the existence of God and that there was a certain amount of vanity that actuated my disbelief. Well, the problem is a serious one. I do not boast to be quite above these human traits. I am a man and nothing more. None can claim to be more. I also have this weakness in me. Vanity does form a part of my nature. Amongst my comrades I was called an autocrat. Even my friend Mr. B.K. Dutt sometimes called me so. On certain occasions I was decried as a despot. Some friends do complain, and very seriously too, that I involuntarily thrust my opinions upon others and get my proposals accepted. That this is true up to a certain extent, I do not deny. This may amount to egotism. There is vanity in me inasmuch as our cult as opposed to other popular creeds is concerned. But that is not personal. It may be, it is only legitimate pride in our cult and does not amount to vanity. Vanity, or to be more precise 'Ahankar' is the excess of undue pride in one's self. Whether it is such an undue pride that has led me to atheism or whether it is after very careful study of the subject and after much consideration that I have come to disbelieve in God, is a question that I intend to discuss here. Let me first make it clear that egotism and vanity are two different things.

In the first place, I have altogether failed to comprehend as to how undue pride or vaingloriousness could ever stand in the way of a man in believing in God. I can refuse to recognize the greatness of a really great man, provided, I have also achieved a certain amount of popularity without deserving it or without having possessed the qualities really essential or indispensable for the same purpose. That much is conceivable. But in what way can a man believing in God cease believing due to his personal vanity? There are only two ways. The man should either begin to think himself a rival of God or he may begin to believe himself to be a God. In neither case, can he become a genuine atheist. In the first case he does not even deny the existence of his rival. In the second case as well, he admits the existence of a conscious being behind the screen guiding all the movements of nature. It is of no importance to us whether he thinks himself to be that supreme being or whether he thinks the supreme conscious being to be somebody apart from himself. The fundamental is there. His belief is there. He is by no means an atheist. Well, here I am. I neither belong to the first category nor to the second. I deny the very existence of that Almighty Supreme Being. Why I deny it, shall be dealt with later on. Here I want to clear one thing, that it is not vanity that has actuated me to adopt the doctrines of atheism. I am neither a rival nor an incarnation, nor the Supreme Being Himself. One point is decided, that it is not vanity that has led me to this mode of thinking. Let me examine the facts to disprove this allegation. According to these friends of mine, I have grown vainglorious perhaps due to the undue popularity gained during the trials – both Delhi Bomb and Lahore Conspiracy Cases. Well, let us see if their premises are correct. My atheism is not of so recent origin. I had stopped believing in God when I was an obscure young man, of whose existence my above-mentioned friends were not even aware. At least a college student cannot cherish any short of undue pride which may lead him to atheism. Though a favourite with some professors and disliked by certain others. I was never an industrious or a studious boy. I could not get any chance of indulging in such feelings as vanity. I was rather a boy with a very shy nature, who had certain pessimistic dispositions about the future career. And in those days, I was not a perfect atheist. My grandfather under whose influence I was brought up is an orthodox Arya Samajist. An Arya Samajist is anything but an atheist. After finishing my primary education I joined the D.A.V. School of Lahore and stayed in its Boarding House for full one year. There, apart from morning and evening prayers, I used to recite 'Gayatri Mantra' for hours and hours. I was a perfect devotee in those days. Later on I began to live with my father. He is a liberal in as much as the orthodoxy of religions is concerned. It was through his teachings that I aspired to devote my life to the cause of freedom. But he is not an atheist. He is a firm believer. He used to encourage me for offering prayers daily. So this is how I was brought up. In the Non-Cooperation days I joined the National College. It was there that I began to think liberally and discuss and criticise all the religious problems, even about God. But still I was a devout believer. By that time I had begun to preserve the unshorn and unclipped long hair but I could never believe in the mythology and doctrines of Sikhism or any other religion. But I had a firm faith in God's existence.

Later on I joined the revolutionary party. The first leader with whom I came in contact, though not convinced, could not dare to deny the existence of God. On my persistent inquiries about God, he used to say: 'Pray whenever you want to.' Now this is atheism less courage required for the adoption of that creed. The second leader with whom I came in contact was a firm believer. Let me mention his name – respected Comrade Shachindra Nath Sanyal, now undergoing life transportation in connection with the Kakori Conspiracy Case. From the very first page of his famous and only book, *Bandi Jivan* (or Incarcerated Life), the Glory of God is sung vehemently. On the last page of the second part of that beautiful book, his mystic – because of vedantism – praises showered upon God form a very conspicuous part of his thoughts. 'The Revolutionary leaflet' distributed throughout India on January 28th, 1925, was, according to the prosecution story, the result of his intellectual labour. Now, as is inevitable in the secret work, the prominent leader expresses his own views which are very dear to his person, and the rest of the workers have to acquiesce in them, in spite of differences which they might have. In that leaflet one full paragraph was devoted to praise the Almighty and His rejoicing and doings. That is all mysticism. What I wanted to point out was that the idea of disbelief had not even germinated in the revolutionary party. The famous Kakori martyrs – all four of them passed their last days in prayers. Ram Prasad Bismil was an orthodox Arya Samajist. Despite his wide studies in the field of socialism and communism, Rajen Lahiri could not suppress his desire of reciting hymns of the Upanishads and the Gita. I saw only one man amongst them, who never prayed and used to say: 'Philosophy is the outcome of human weakness or limitation of knowledge.' He is also undergoing a sentence of transportation for life. But he also never dared to deny the existence of God.

Up to that period I was only a romantic idealist revolutionary. Up till then we were to follow. Now came the time to shoulder the whole responsibility. Due to the inevitable reaction for some time the very existence of the party seemed impossible. Enthusiastic comrades- nay, leaders- began to jeer at us. For some time I was afraid that some day I also might not be convinced of the futility of our own programme. That was a turning point in my revolutionary career. 'Study' was the cry that reverberated in the corridors of my mind. Study to enable yourself to face the arguments advanced by opposition. Study to arm yourself with arguments in favour of your cult. I began to study. My previous faith and convictions underwent a remarkable modification. The romance of the violent methods alone which was so prominent amongst our predecessors, was replaced by serious ideas. No more mysticism, no more blind faith. Realism became our cult. Use of force justifiable when resorted to as a matter of terrible necessity: non-violence as policy indispensable for all mass movements. So much about methods. The most important thing was the clear conception of the ideal for which we were to fight. As there were no important activities in the field of action I got ample opportunity to study various ideals of the world revolution. I studied Bakunin, the anarchist leader, something of Marx, the father of communism, and much of Lenin, Trotsky and others – the men who had successfully carried out a revolution in their country. They were all atheists. Bakunin's God and State, though only fragmentary, is an interesting study of the subject. Later still I came across a book entitled *Common Sense* by Nirlamba Swami. It was only a sort of mystic atheism. This subject became of utmost interest to me. By the end of 1926 I had been convinced as to the baselessness of the theory of existence of an almighty supreme being who created, guided and controlled the universe. I had given out this disbelief of mine. I began discussion on the subject with my friends. I had become a pronounced atheist. But what it meant will presently be discussed.

In May 1927 I was arrested at Lahore. The arrest was a surprise. I was quite unaware of the fact that the police wanted me. All of a sudden, while passing through a garden, I found myself surrounded by police. To my own surprise, I was very calm at that time. I did not feel any sensation, nor did I experience any excitement. I was taken into police custody. Next day I was taken to the Railway Police lock-up where I was to pass full one month. After many days' conversation with the police officials I guessed that they had some information regarding my connection with the Kakori party and my other activities in connection with the revolutionary movement. They told me that I had been to Lucknow while the trial was going on there, that I had negotiated a certain scheme about their rescue, that after obtaining their approval, we had procured some bombs, that by way of test one of the bombs was thrown in the crowd on the occasion of Dussehra 1926. They further informed me, in my interest, that if I could give any statement throwing some light on the activities of the revolutionary party, I was not to be imprisoned but on the contrary set free and rewarded, even without being produced as an approver in the court. I laughed at the proposal. It was all humbug. People holding ideas like ours do not throw bombs on their own innocent people. One fine morning Mr Newman, the then Senior Superintendent of C.I.D., came to me. And after much sympathetic talk with me, imparted- to him the extremely sad-news that if I did not give any statement as demanded by them, they would be forced to send me up for trial for conspiracy to wage war in connection with Kakori Case and for brutal murders in connection with Dussehra bomb outrage. And he further informed me that they had evidence enough to get me convicted and hanged. In those days I believed – though I was quite innocent – the police could do it if they desired. That very day certain police officials began to persuade me to offer my prayers to God regularly, both the times. Now I was an atheist. I wanted to settle for myself whether it was in the days of peace and enjoyment alone that I could boast of being an atheist or whether during such hard times as well, I could stick to those principles of mine. After great consideration I decided that I could not lead myself to believe in and pray to God. No, I never did. That was the real test and I came out successful. Never for *a* moment did I desire to save my neck at the cost of certain other things. So I was a staunch disbeliever; and have ever since been. It was not an easy job to stand that test. 'Belief softens the hardships, even can make them pleasant. In God man can find very strong consolation and support. Without Him man has to depend upon himself. To stand upon one's own legs amid storms and hurricanes is not a child's play. At such testing moments, vanity – if any – evaporates, and man cannot dare to defy the general beliefs. If he does, then we must conclude that he has got certain other strength than mere vanity. This is exactly the situation now. Judgement is already too well known. Within a week it is to be pronounced. What is the consolation with the exception of the idea that I am going to sacrifice my life for a cause? A God-believing Hindu might be expecting to be reborn as a king, a Muslim or a Christian might dream of the luxuries to be enjoyed in paradise and the reward he is to get for his suffering and sacrifices. But, what am I to expect? I know the moment the rope is fitted round my neck and rafters removed from under my feet, that will be the final moment – that will be the last moment. I, or to be more precise, my soul as interpreted in the metaphysical terminology shall all be finished there. Nothing further. A short life of struggle with no such magnificent end, shall in itself be the reward, if I have the courage to take it in that light. That is all. With no selfish motive or desire to be awarded here or hereafter, quite disinterestedly, have I devoted my life to the cause of independence, because I could not do otherwise. The day we find a great number of men and women with this psychology, who cannot devote themselves to anything else than the service of mankind and emancipation of the suffering humanity, that day shall inaugurate the era of liberty. Not to become a king, nor to gain any other rewards here, or in the next birth or after death in paradise, shall they be inspired to challenge the oppressors, exploiters, and tyrants, but to cast off the yoke of serfdom from the neck of humanity and to establish liberty and peace shall they tread this- to their individual selves perilous and to their noble selves the only glorious imaginable- path. Is the pride in their noble cause to be misinterpreted as vanity? Who dares to utter such an abominable epithet? To him I say either he is a fool or a knave. Let us forgive him for he cannot realize the depth, the emotion, the sentiment and the noble feelings that surge in that heart. His heart is dead as a mere lump of flesh, his eyes are weak, the evils of other interests having been cast over them. Self-reliance is always liable to be interpreted as vanity. It is sad and miserable but there is no help.

You go and oppose the prevailing faith, you go and criticise a hero, a great man who is generally believed to be above criticism because he is thought to be infallible, the strength of your argument shall force the multitude to decry you as vainglorious. This is due to the mental stagnation. Criticism and independent thinking are the two indispensable qualities of a revolutionary. Because Mahatmaji is great, therefore none should criticise him. Because he has risen above, therefore everything he says-may be in the field of Politics or Religion, Economics or Ethics – is right. Whether you are convinced or not you must say: 'Yes, that's true'. This mentality does not lead towards progress. It is rather too obviously reactionary.

Because our forefathers had set up a faith in some supreme being – the Almighty God – therefore, any man who dares to challenge the validity of that faith, or the very existence of that supreme being, he shall have to be called an apostate, a renegade. If his arguments are too sound to be refuted by counter-arguments and spirit too strong to be cowed down by the threat of misfortunes that may befall him by the wrath of the Almighty, he shall be decried as vainglorious, his spirit to be denominated as vanity. Then, why to waste time in this vain discussion? Why try to argue out the whole thing? This question is coming before the public for the first time, and is being handled in this matter of fact way for the first time, hence this lengthy discussion.

As for the first question, I think I have cleared that it is not vanity that has led me to atheism. My way of argument has proved to be convincing or not, that is to be judged by my readers, not me. I know in the present circumstances my faith in God would have made my life easier, my burden lighter, and my disbelief in Him has turned all the circumstances too dry, and the situation may assume too harsh a shape.

A little bit or mysticism can make it poetical. But I do not want the help of any intoxication to meet my fate. I am a realist. I have been trying to overpower the instinct in me by the help of reason. I have not always been successful in achieving this end. But man's duty is to try and endeavour, success depends upon chance and environments.

As for the second question that if it was not vanity, then there ought to be some reason to disbelieve the old and still prevailing faith in the existence of God. Yes, I come to that now. Reason there is. According to me, any man who has got some reasoning power at his command always tries to reason out his environments. Where direct proofs are lacking philosophy occupies the important place. As I have already stated, a certain revolutionary friend used to say that philosophy is the outcome of human weakness. When our ancestors had leisure enough to try to solve out the mystery of this world, its past, present and the future, its whys and wherefores, they having been terribly short of direct proofs, everybody tried to solve the problem in his own way. Hence we find the wide differences in the fundamentals of various religious creeds, which sometimes assume very antagonistic and conflicting shapes. Not only the Oriental and occidental philosophies differ, there are differences even amongst various schools of thought in each hemisphere. Amongst Oriental religions, the Moslem faith is not at all compatible with Hindu faith. In India alone Buddhism and Jainism are sometimes quite separate from Brahmanism, in which there are again conflicting faiths as Arya Samaj and Sanatan Dharma. Charwak is still another independent thinker of the past ages. He challenged the authority of God in the old times. All these creeds differ from each other on the fundamental question; and everybody considers himself to be on the right. There lies the misfortune. Instead of using the experiments and expressions of the ancient Savants and thinkers as a basis for our future struggle against ignorance and to try to find out a solution to this mysterious problem, we, lethargical as we have proved to be, raise the hue and cry of faith, unflinching and unwavering faith to their versions and thus are guilty of stagnation in human progress.

Any man who stands for progress has to criticise, disbelieve and challenge every item of the old faith. Item by item he has to reason out every nook and corner of the prevailing faith. If after considerable reasoning one is led to believe in any theory or philosophy, his faith is welcomed. His reasoning can be mistaken, wrong, misled, and sometimes fallacious. But he is liable to correction because reason is the guiding star of his life. But mere faith and blind faith is dangerous: it dulls the brain, and makes a man reactionary. A man who claims to be a realist has to challenge the whole of the ancient faith. If it does not stand the onslaught of reason it crumbles down. Then the first thing for him is to shatter the whole down and clear a space for the erection of a new philosophy. This is the negative side. After it begins the positive work in which sometimes some material of the old faith may be used for the purpose of reconstruction. As far as I am concerned, let me admit at the very outset that I have not been able to study much on this point. I had a great desire to study the Oriental philosophy but I could not get any chance or opportunity to do the same. But so far as the negative study is under discussion, I think I am convinced to the extent of questioning the soundness of the old faith. I have been convinced as to non-existence of a conscious supreme being who is guiding and directing the movements of nature. We believe in nature and the whole progressive movement aims at the domination of man over nature for his service. There is no conscious power behind it to direct. This is what our philosophy is.

As far the negative side, we ask a few questions from the 'believers'.

(1) If, as you believe, there is an almighty, omnipresent, omniscient and omnipotent God, who created the earth or world, please let me know why did he create it? This world of woes and miseries, a veritable, eternal combination of numberless tragedies: Not a single soul being perfectly satisfied.

Pray, don't say that it is His Law. If he is bound by any law, he is not omnipotent. He is another slave like ourselves. Please don't say that it is his enjoyment. Nero burnt one Rome. He killed a very limited number of people. He created very few tragedies, all to his perfect enjoyment. And, what is his place in History? By what names do the historians mention him? All the venomous epithets are showered upon him. Pages are blackened with invective diatribes condemning Nero, the tyrant, the heartless, the wicked. One Changez Khan sacrificed a few thousand lives to seek pleasure ' in it and we hate the very name.

Then, how are you going to justify your almighty, eternal Nero, who has been, and is still causing numberless tragedies every day, every hour and every minute? How do you think to support his misdoings which surpass those of Changez every single moment? I say why did he create this world – a veritable hell, a place of constant and bitter unrest? Why did the Almighty create man when he had the power not to do it? What is the justification for all this? Do you say, to award the innocent sufferers hereafter and to punish the wrongdoers as dare to inflict wounds upon your body to apply a very soft and soothing ointment upon it afterwards? How far the supporters and organizers of the Gladiator institution were justified in throwing men before the half-starved furious lions to be cared for and well looked after if they could survive and could manage to escape death by the wild beasts? That is why I ask: Why did the conscious supreme being create this world and man in it? To seek pleasure? Where, then, is the difference between him and Nero?

You Mohammadans and Christians: Hindu philosophy shall still linger on to offer another argument. I ask you, what is your answer to the above-mentioned question? You don't believe in previous birth. Like Hindus, you cannot advance the argument of previous misdoings of the apparently quite innocent sufferers. I ask you, why did the omnipotent labour for six days to create the world through word and each day to say that all was well? Call him today. Show him the past history. Make him study the present situation. Let us see if he dares to say: 'All is well'.

From the dungeons of prisons, from stores of starvation consuming millions upon millions of human beings in slums and huts, from the exploited labourers, patiently or say apathetically watching the procedure of their blood being sucked by the capitalist vampires, and the wastage of human energy that will make a man with the least common sense shiver with horror, and from the preference of throwing the surplus of production in oceans rather than to distribute amongst the needy producers- to the places of kings built upon the foundation laid with human bones... let him see all this and let him say: 'All is well.' Why and wherefore? That is my question. You are silent. All right then, I proceed.

Well, you Hindus, you say all the present sufferers belong to the class of sinners of the previous births. Good. You say the present oppressors were saintly people in their previous births, hence they enjoy power. Let me admit that your ancestors were very shrewd people, they tried to find out theories strong enough to hammer down all the efforts of reason and disbelief. But let us analyse how far this argument can really stand.

From the point of view of the most famous jurists, punishment can be justified only from three or four ends, to meet which it is inflicted upon the wrongdoer. They are retributive, reformative and deterrent. The retributive theory is now being condemned by all the advanced thinkers. Deterrent theory is also following the same fate. Reformative theory is the only one which is essential and indispensable for human progress. It aims at returning the offender as a most competent and a peace-loving citizen to the society. But what is the nature of punishment inflicted by God upon men, even if we suppose them to be offenders? You say he sends them to be born as a cow, a cat, a tree, a herb or a beast. You enumerate these punishments to be 84 lakhs. I ask you: what is its reformative effect upon man? How many men have met you who say that they were born as a donkey in previous birth for having committed any sin? None. Don't quote your Puranas. I have no scope to touch your mythologies. Moreover, do you know that the greatest sin in this world is to be poor? Poverty is a sin, it is a punishment. I ask you how far would you appreciate a criminologist, a jurist or a legislator who proposes such measures of punishment which shall inevitably force men to commit more offences? Had not your God thought of this, or he also had to learn these things by experience, but at the cost of untold sufferings to be borne by humanity? What do you think shall be the fate of a man who has been born in a poor and illiterate family of, say, a chamar or a sweeper? lie is poor, hence he cannot study. He is hated and shunned by his fellow human beings who think themselves to be his superiors having been born in say, a higher caste. His ignorance, his poverty and the treatment meted out to him shall harden his heart towards society. Suppose he commits a sin, who shall bear the consequences? God, he or the learned ones of the society? What about the punishment of those people who were deliberately kept ignorant by the haughty and egotist Brahmans, and who had to pay the penalty by bearing the stream of being led (not lead) in their ears for having heard a few sentences of your Sacred Books of learning – the Vedas? If they committed any offence, who was to be responsible for them and who was to bear the brunt? My dear friends, these theories are the inventions of the privileged ones; they justify their usurped power, riches and superiority by the help of these theories. Yes, it was perhaps Upton Sinclair that wrote at some place that just make a man a believer in immortality and then rob him of all his riches and possessions He shall help you even in that ungrudgingly. The coalition among the religious preachers and possessors of power brought forth jails, gallows, knots and these theories.

Annexure-III
The Philosophy of the Bomb

Bhagat Singh

RECENT EVENTS, PARTICULARLY THE CONGRESS RESOLUTION ON the attempt to blow up the Viceregal Special on the 23 December, 1929, and Gandhi's subsequent writings in *Young India*, clearly show that the Indian National Congress, in conjunction with Gandhi, has launched a crusade against the revolutionaries. A great amount of public criticism, both from the press and the platform, has been made against them. It is a pity that they have all along been, either deliberately or due to sheer ignorance, misrepresented and misunderstood. The revolutionaries do not shun criticism and public scrutiny of their ideals or actions. They rather welcome these as chances of making those understand, who have a genuine desire to do so, the basic principles of the revolutionary movement and the high and noble ideals that are a perennial source of inspiration and strength to it. It is hoped that this article will help the general public to know the revolutionaries as they are and will prevent it from taking them for what interested and ignorant persons would have it believe them to be.

VIOLENCE OR NON-VIOLENCE

LET US, first of all, take up the question of violence and non-violence. We think that the use of these terms in itself, is a grave injustice to either party, for they express the ideals of neither of them correctly. Violence is physical force applied for committing injustice, and that is certainly not what the revolutionaries stand for. On the other hand, what generally goes by the name of non-violence is in reality the theory of soul force, as applied to the attainment of personal and national rights through courting, suffering and hoping thus to finally convert your opponent to your point of view. When a revolutionary believes certain things to be his right he asks for them, pleads tor them, argues for them, wills to attain them with all the soul-force at his command, stands the greatest amount of suffering for them, is always prepared to make the highest sacrifice for their attainment, and also backs his efforts with all the physical force he is capable of. You may coin what other word you like to describe his methods but you cannot call it violence, because that would constitute an outrage on the dictionary meaning of that word. Satyagraha is insistence upon truth. Why press, for the acceptance of truth, by soul-force alone? Why not add physical force also to it? While the revolutionaries stand for winning independence by all the forces, physical as -well as moral, at their command, the advocates of soul-force would like to ban the use of physical force. The question really, therefore, is not whether you will have violence, but whether you will have soul-force plus physical force or soul-force alone.

OUR IDEAL

THE REVOLUTIONARIES believe that the deliverance of their country will come through revolution. The revolution, they are constantly working and hoping for, will not only express itself in the form of an armed conflict between the foreign government and its supporters and the people, it will also usher in a new social order. The revolution will ring the death knell of capitalism and class distinctions and privileges. It will bring joy and prosperity to the starving millions who are seething today under the terrible yoke of both foreign and Indian exploitation. It will bring the nation into its own. It will give birth to a new state – a new social order. Above all, it will establish the dictatorship of the proletariat and will for ever banish social parasites from the seat of political power.

TERRORISM

THE REVOLUTIONARIES already see the advent of the revolution in the restlessness of youth, in its desire to break free from the mental bondage and religious superstitions that hold them. As the youth will get more and more saturated with the psychology of revolution, it will come to have a clearer realisation of national bondage and a growing, intense, unquenchable thirst for freedom. It will grow, this feeling of bondage, this insatiable desire for freedom, till, in their righteous anger, the infuriated youth will begin to kill the oppressors. Thus has terrorism been born in the country. It is a phase, a necessary, an inevitable phase of the revolution. Terrorism is not the complete revolution and the revolution is not complete without terrorism. This thesis can be supported by an analysis of any and every revolution in history. Terrorism instils fear in the hearts of the oppressors, it brings hopes of revenge and redemption to the oppressed masses, it gives courage and self-confidence to the wavering, it shatters the spell of the superiority of the ruling class and raises the status of the subject race in the eyes of the world, because it is the most convincing proof of a nation's hunger for freedom. Here in India, as in other countries in the past, terrorism will develop into the revolution and the revolution into independence, social, political and economic.

REVOLUTIONARY METHODS

THIS THEN is what the revolutionaries believe in, that is what they hope to accomplish for their country. They are doing it both openly and secretly, and in their own way. The experience of a century long and world-wide struggle, between the masses and the governing class, is their guide to their goal, and the methods they are following have never been known to have failed.

THE CONGRESS AND THE REVOLUTIONARIES

MEANWHILE, WHAT has the Congress being doing? It has changed its creed from Swaraj to Complete Independence. As a logical sequence to this, one would expect it to declare a war on the British government. Instead, we find, it has declared war against the revolutionaries. The first offensive of the Congress came in the form of a resolution deploring the attempt made on the 23 December,1929, to blow up the Viceroy's Special. It was drafted by Gandhi and he fought tooth and nail for it, with the result that was passed by a trifling majority of 81 in a house of 1,713. Was even this bare majority a result of honest political convictions? Let us quote the opinion of Sarla Devi Chaudharani who has been a devotee of the Congress all her life, in reply. She says: 'I discovered in the course of my conversations with a good many of the

Mahatma's followers that it was only their sense of personal loyalty to him that was keeping them back from an expression of the independent views and preventing them from voting against any resolution whatsoever that was fathered by Mahatmaji.' As to Gandhi's arguments in favour of his proposition, we will deal with them later, when we discuss his article The Cult of the Bomb which is more or less an amplification of his speech in the Congress. There is one fact about this deplorable resolution which we must not lose sight of, and that is this. In spite of the fact, that the Congress is pledged to non-violence and has been actively engaged in carrying on propaganda in its favour for the last ten years, and in spite of the fact also that the supporters of the resolution indulged in abuse, called the revolutionaries 'cowards' and described their actions as 'dastardly' – and one of them even threateningly remarked that if they wanted to be led by Gandhi, they should pass this resolution without any opposition – in spite of all this, the resolution could only be adopted by a dangerously narrow majority. That demonstrates, beyond the shadow of a doubt, how solidly the country is backing the revolutionaries. In a way Gandhi deserved our thanks for having brought the question up for discussion and thus having shown to the world at large that even the Congress – that stronghold of non-violence – is at least as much, if not more, with the revolutionaries as with him.

GANDHI ON WAR PATH

HAVING ACHIEVED a victory which cost him more than a defeat, Gandhi has returned to the attack in his article The Cult of the Bomb. We will give it our closest attention before proceeding further. That article consists of three things – his faith, his opinion and his arguments. We will not discuss what is a matter of faith with him because reason has little in common with faith. Let us then take such of his opinion as are backed by arguments and his arguments proper, against what he calls violence and discuss them one by one.

DO THE MASSES BELIEVE IN NON-VIOLENCE

HE THINKS that on the basis of his experience during his latest tour in the country, he is right in believing that the large masses of Indian humanity are yet untouched by the spirit of violence and that non-violence has come to stay as a political weapon. Let him not delude himself on the experiences of his latest tour in the country. Though it is true that the average leader confines his tours to places where only the mail train can conveniently land him while Gandhi has extended his tour limit to where a motorcar can take him, the practice of staying only with the richest people in the places visited, of spending most of his time on being complimented by his devotees in private and public, and of granting Darshan now and then to the illiterate masses whom he claims to understand so well, disqualifies him from claiming to know the mind of the masses. No man can claim to know a people's mind by seeing them from the public platform and giving them Darshan and Updesh. He can at the most claim to have told the masses what he thinks about things. Has Gandhi, during recent years, mixed in the social life of the masses? Has he sat with the peasant round the evening fire and tried to know what he thinks? Has he passed a single evening in the company of a factory labourer and shared with him his vowes? (sic). We have, and therefore we claim to know what the masses think. We assure Gandhi that the average Indian, like the average human being, understands little of the fine theological niceties about *Ahimsa* and loving one's enemy. The way of the world is like this. You have a friend: you love him, sometimes so much that you even die for him. You have an enemy: you shun him, you fight against him and, if possible, kill him. The gospel of the revolutionaries is simple and straight. It is what has been since the days of Adam and Eve, and no man has any difficulty about understanding it. We affirm that the masses of India are solidly with us because we know it from personal experience. The day is not far off when they will flock in their thousands to work the will of the Revolution.

THE GOSPEL OF LOVE

GANDHI DECLARES that his faith in the efficacy of non-violence has increased. That is to say, he believes more and more, that through his gospel of love and self-imposed suffering, he hopes someday to convert the foreign rulers to his way of thinking. Now, he has devoted his whole life to the preaching of his wonderful gospel and has practised it with unwavering constance, (sic) as few others have done. Will he let the world know how many enemies of India he has been able to turn into friends? How many O'Dwyers, Readings and Irwins has he been able to convert into friends of India? If none, how can India be expected to share his 'growing faith' that he will be able to persuade or compel England to agree to Indian Independence through the practice of non-violence?

WHAT WOULD HAVE HAPPENED

IF THE bomb, that burst under the Viceroy's Special, had exploded properly, one of the two things suggested by Gandhi would have surely happened. The viceroy would have either been badly injured or killed. Under such circumstances there certainly would have been no meeting between the leaders of political parties and the viceroy. The uncalled for and undignified attempt on the part of these individuals, to lower the national prestige by knocking at the gates of the government house with the beggar's bowl in their hands and dominion status on their lips, in spite of the clear terms of the Calcutta Ultimatum, would have been checkmated and the nation would have been the better off for that. If, fortunately, the explosion had been powerful enough to kill the viceroy, one more enemy of India would have met a well deserved doom. The author of the Meerut prosecutions and the Lahore and Bhusawal persecutions can appear a friend of India only to the enemies of her freedom. In spite of Gandhi and Nehru and their claims to political sagacity and statesmanship, Irwin has succeeded in shattering the unity between different political parties in the country, that had resulted from the boycott of the Simon Commission. Even the Congress today is a house divided against itself. Who else, except the viceroy and his olive tongue, have we to thank for our grave misfortunes? And yet, there exist people in our country who proclaim him a Friend of India.

THE FUTURE OF THE CONGRESS

THERE MIGHT be those who have no regard for the Congress and hope nothing from it. If Gandhi thinks that the revolutionaries belong to the category, he wrongs them grievously. They fully realize the part played by the Congress in awakening among the ignorant masses a keen desire for freedom. They expect great things of it in the future. Though they hold firmly to their opinion, that so long as persons like Sen Gupta whose wonderful intelligence compels him to discern the hand of the CID in the late attempt to blow up the Viceroy's Special,, and persons like Ansari, who think abuse the better part of argument and know so little of politics as to make the ridiculous and fallacious assertion that no nation had achieved freedom by the bomb, have a determining voice in the affairs of the Congress, the country can hope little from it; they are hopefully looking forward to the day, when the mania of non-violence would have passed away from the Congress, and it would march arm in arm-with the revolutionaries to their common goal of complete Independence. This year, it has accepted the ideal which the revolutionaries have preached and lived up to more than a quarter of a century. Let us hope the next year will see it endorse their methods also.

VIOLENCE AND MILITARY EXPENDITURE

GANDHI IS OF opinion that as violence has been practised in the country, it has resulted in an increase of military expenditure. If his reference is to revolutionary activities during the last twenty-five years we dispute the accuracy of his statement and challenge him to prove his statement with facts and figures. If, on the other hand, he had the wars that have taken place in India since the British came here in mind, our reply is that even his modest experiment in Ahimsa and Satyagraha which had little to compare in it with the wars for independence produced its effect on the finances of the bureaucracy. Mass action, whether violent or non-violent, whether successful or unsuccessful, is bound to produce the same kind of repercussion on the finances of a state.

THE REFORMS

WHY SHOULD Gandhi mix up the revolutionaries with the various constitutional reforms granted by the government? They never cared or worked for the Morely-Minto Reforms, Montague Reforms and the like. These the British government threw before the constitutionalist agitators to lure them away from the right path. This was the bribe paid to them for their support to the government in its policy of crushing and uprooting the revolutionaries. These toys – as Gandhi calls them – were sent to India for the benefit of those, who, from time to time, raised the cry of 'Home Rule', 'Self-Government', 'Responsible', 'Full

Responsible Government', 'Dominion Status' and such other constitutional names for slavery. The revolutionaries never claim the Reforms as their achievements. They raised the standard of independence long ago. They have lived for it. They have ungrudgingly laid their lives down for the sake of this ideal. They claim that their sacrifices have produced a tremendous change in the mentality of the people. That their efforts have advanced the country a long way on the road to independence, is granted by even those who do not see eye to eye with them in politics.

THE WAY OF PROGRESS

As to Gandhi's contention that violence impedes the march of progress and thus directly postpones the day of freedom, we can refer him to so many contemporary instances where violence has led to the social progress and political freedom of the people who practised it. Take the case of Russia and Turkey for example. In both countries the party for progress took over the state orgnisation through an armed revolution. Yet social progress and political freedom have not been impeded. Legislation, backed by force, has made the masses go 'double march' on the road of progress. The solitary example of Afghanistan cannot establish a political formula. It is rather the exception that proves the rule.

FAILURE OF NON-COOPERATION

GANDHI IS of opinion that the great awakening in the people, during the days of non-cooperation, was a result of the preaching of non-violence. It is wrong to assign to non-violence the widespread awakening of the masses which, in fact, is manifested wherever a programme of direct action is adopted. In Russia, for instance, there came about widespread awakening in the peasants and workers when the communists launched forth their great programme of Militant Mass Action, though nobody preached non-violence to them. We will even go further and state that it was mainly the mania for non-violence and Gandhi's compromise mentality that brought about the disruption of the forces that had come together at the call of Mass Action. It is claimed that non-violence can be used as a weapon for righting political wrongs. To say the least, it is a novel idea, yet untried. It failed to achieve what were considered to be the just rights of Indians in South Africa. It failed to bring 'Swaraj within a year' to the Indian masses in spite of the untiring labours of an army of national workers and one and a quarter crores of rupees. More recently, it failed to win for the Bardoli peasants what the leaders of the Satyagraha movement had promised them – the famous irreducible minimum of Gandhi and Patel. We know of no other trials non-violence has had on a country-wide scale. Up to this time non-violence has been blessed with one result – Failure. Little wonder, then, that the country refuses to give it another trial. In fact Satyagraha as preached by Gandhi is a form of agitation – a protest, leading up invariably, as has already been seen, to a compromise. It can hardly be of any use to a nation striving for national independence which can never come as the result of a compromise. The sooner we recognize that there can be no compromise between independence and slavery, the better.

IS IT A NEW ERA

'WE ARE entering upon a new era', thinks Gandhi. The mere act of defining Swaraj as Complete Independence, this technical change in the Congress constitution, can hardly constitute a new era. It will be a great day indeed when the Congress will decide upon a country-wide programme of Mass Action, based on well recognized revolutionary principles. Till then the unfurling of the flag of Independence is a mockery and we concur with the following remarks of Sarla Devi Chaudharani which she recently made in a press interview.

'The unfurling of the Flag of Independence', she says, 'at just one minute after midnight of the 31 December, 1929, was too stagy for words- just as the GOC and the assistant GOC and others in gaudy uniforms were card board Grand Officers Commanding.

'The fact that the unfurling of the flag of Independence lay hanging in the balance till midnight of that date, and that the scales might have been turned at even the eleventh hour fiftyninth minute had a message from the viceroy or the secretary of state come to the Congress granting Dominion Status, proves that Independence is not a heart hunger (sic) of the leaders but that the declaration of it is only like a petulant child's retort. It would have been a worthy action of the Indian National

Congress if Independence was achieved first and declared afterwards.' It is true that the Congress orators will henceforth harangue the masses on Complete Independence instead of Dominion Status. They will call upon the people to prepare for a struggle in which one party is to deliver blows and the other is simply to receive them, till beaten and demoralised beyond hope of recovery. Can such a thing be named a struggle and can it ever lead the country to Complete Independence? It is all very well to hold fast to the highest ideal worthy of a nation, but it is nonetheless necessary, to adopt the best, the most efficacious and tried means to achieve it, are you became the laughing stock of the whole world.

NO BULLYING PLEASE

GANDHI HAS called upon all those who are not past reason to withdraw their support from the revolutionaries and condemn their actions so that 'our deluded patriots may, for want of nourishment to their violent spirit, realize the futility of violence and the great harm that violent activities have every time done'. How easy and convenient it is to call people deluded, to declare them to be past reason, to call upon the public to withdraw its support and condemn them so that they may get isolated and be forced to suspend their activities, specially when a man holds the confidence of an influential section of the public. It is a pity that Gandhi does not and will not understand revolutionary psychology in spite of the life-long experience of public life. Life is a precious thing. It is clear to everyone. If a man becomes a revolutionary, if he goes about with his life in the hollow 'of his hand ready to sacrifice it at any moment, he does not do so merely for the fun of it. He does not risk his life merely because sometimes, when the crowd is in a sympathetic mood, it cries 'Bravo' in appreciation. He does it because his reason forces him to take that course, because his conscience dictates it. A revolutionary believes in reason more than anything. It is to reason, and reason alone, that he bows. No amount of abuse and condemnation, even if it emanates from the highest of the high can turn him from his set purpose. To think that a revolutionary will give up his ideas if public support and appreciation is withdrawn from him, is the highest folly. Many a revolutionary has, ere now, stepped on the scaffold and laid his life down for the cause, regardless of the curses that the constitutionalist agitators rained plentifully upon him. If you will have the revolutionaries suspend their activities, reason with them squarely. That is the one and the only way. For the rest let there be no doubt in anybody's mind. A revolutionary is the last person on earth to submit to bullying.

AN APPEAL

WE TAKE this opportunity to appeal to our countrymen – to the youth, to the workers and peasants, to the revolutionary intelligentsia – to come forward and join us in carrying aloft the banner of freedom. Let us establish a new order of society in which political and economic exploitation will be an impossibility. In the name of those gallant men and women who willingly accepted death so that we, their descendants, may lead a happier life, who toiled ceaselessly and perished for the poor, the famished, and exploited millions of India, we call upon every patriot to take up the fight in all seriousness. Let nobody toy with the nation's freedom which is her very life, by making psychological experiments in non-violence and such other novelties. Our slavery is our shame. When shall we have courage and wisdom enough to be able to shake ourselves free of it? What is our great heritage of civilisation and culture worth if we have not enough self-respect left in us to prevent us from bowing surveillance to the commands of foreigners and paying homage to their flag and kind?

VICTORY OR DEATH

THERE IS no crime that Britain has not committed in India. Deliberate misrule has reduced us to paupers, has 'bled us white'. As a race and a people we stand dishonoured and outraged. Do people still expect us to forget and to forgive? We shall have our revenge – a people's righteous revenge on the tyrant. Let cowards fall back and cringe for compromise and peace. We ask not for mercy and we give no quarter. Ours is a war to the end – to Victory or Death.

LONG LIVE REVOLUTION

President,
Hindustan Socialist Republican Association.

Annexure-IV
To the Young Political Workers

Bhagat Singh

Dear Comrades,

Our movement is passing through a very important phase at present. After a year's fierce struggle, some definite proposals regarding the constitutional reforms have been formulated by the Round Table Conference and the Congress leaders have been invited to give this...* think it desirable in the present circumstances to call off their movement. Whether they decide in favour or against is a matter of little importance to us. The present movement is bound to end in some sort of compromise. The compromise may be effected sooner or later. And compromise is not such ignoble and deplorable a thing as we generally think. It is rather an indispensable factor in the political strategy. Any nation that rose against the oppressors was bound to fail in the beginning, and to gain partial reforms during the medieval period of its struggle through compromises. And it is only at the last stage-having fully organized all the forces and resources of the nation-that it could possibly strike the final blow in which it might succeed to shatter the ruler's government. But even then it might fail, which made some sort of compromise inevitable. Bhagat Singh illustrated his point by the Russian example. In 1905 a revolutionary movement broke out in Russia. All the leaders were very hopeful. Lenin had returned from the foreign countries where he had taken refuge. He was conducting the struggle. People came to tell him that a dozen landlords were killed and a score of their mansions were burnt. Lenin responded by telling them to return and to kill twelve hundred landlords and burn as many of their palaces. In his opinion that would have meant something if revolution failed. Duma (parliament) was introduced. The same Lenin advocated the view of participating in the Duma. This was what happened in 1907. In 1906 he was opposed to the participation in the second one whose rights had been curtailed. Reaction was gaining the upper hand and Lenin wanted to use the floor of the Duma as a platform to discuss socialist ideas.

After the 1917 revolution, when the Bolsheviks were forced to sign the Brest Litovsk Treaty, everyone except Lenin was opposed to it. But Lenin said: 'Peace'. 'Peace and again peace: peace at any cost – even at the cost of many of the Russian provinces to be yielded to German War Lord'. When some anti-Bolshevik people condemned Lemin for this treaty, he declared frankly that the Bolsheviks were not in a position to face the German onslaught and they preferred the treaty to the complete annihilation of the Bolshevik government.

The thing that I wanted to point out was that compromise is an essential weapon which has to be wielded every now and then as the struggle develops. But the thing that we must keep always before us is the idea of the movement. We must always maintain a clear notion as to the aim for the achievement of which we are fighting. That helps us to verify the success and failures of our movements and we can easily formulate the future programme. Tilak's policy, quite apart from the ideal, i.e. his strategy, was the best. You are fighting to get sixteen annas from your enemy, you get only one anna. Pocket it and fight for the rest. What we note in the moderates is of their idea'. They start to achieve one anna and they can't get it. The revolutionaries must always keep in mind that they are striving for a complete revolution. Complete mastery of power in their hands. Compromises are dreaded because the conservatives try to disband the revolutionary forces after the compromise. But able and bold revolutionary leaders can save the movement from such pitfalls. We must be very careful at such junctures to avoid any sort of confusion of the real issues, especially the goal. The British Labour leaders betrayed their real struggle and have been reduced to mere hypocrite imperialists. In my opinion the diehard conservatives are better to us than these polished imperialist Labour leaders. About the tactics and strategy one should study tha life-work of Lenin. His definite views on the subject of compromise will be found in 'Left Wing' Communism.

I have said that the present movement, i.e. the present struggle, is bound to end in some sort of compromise or complete failure.

I said that, because in my opinion, this time the real revolutionary forces have not been invited into the arena. This is a struggle dependent upon the middle class, shopkeepers and a few capitalists. Both these, and particularly the latter, can never dare to risk its property or possessions in any struggle. The real revolutionary armies are in the villages and in factories, the peasantry and the labourers. But our bourgeois leaders do not and cannot dare to tackle them. The sleeping lion once awakened from its slumber shall become irresistible even after the achievement of what our leaders aim at. After his first experience with the Ahmedabad labourers in 1920 Mahatma Gandhi declared: 'We must not tamper with the labourers. It is dangerous to make political use of the factory proletariat' (The Times, May 1921). Since then, they never dared to approach them. There remains the peasantry. The Bardoli resolution of 1922 clearly defines the horror the leaders felt when they saw the gigantic peasant class rising to shake off not only the domination of an alienation but also the yoke of the landlords.

It is there that our leaders prefer a surrender to the British than to the peasantry. Leave alone Pt. Jawaharlal. Can you point out any leader who made any effort to organize the peasants or the labourers? No, they will not run the risk. There they lack. That is why I say they never meant a complete revolution. Through economic and administrative pressure they hoped to get a few more reforms, a few more concessions for the Indian capitalists. That is why I say that this movement is doomed to die, may be after some sort of compromise or even without. The young workers who in all sincerity raise the cry 'Long Live Revolution,' are not well organized and strong enough to carry the movement themselves. As a matter of fact, even our great leaders, with the exception of perhaps Pt. Motilal Nehru, do not dare to take any responsibility on their shoulders, that is why every now and then they surrender unconditionally before Gandhi. In spite of their differences, they never oppose him seriously and the resolution have to be carried for the Mahatma.

In these circumstances, let me warn the sincere young workers who seriously mean a revolution, that harder times are coming. Let them beware lest they should get confused or disheartened. After the experience made through two struggles of the Great Gandhi, we are in a better position to form a clear idea of our present position and the future programme.

Allow me to state the case in the simplest manner. You cry, Long Live Revolution.' Let me assume that you really mean it. According to our definition of the term, as stated in our statement in the Assembly Bomb Case, revolution means the complete overthrow of the existing social order and its replacement with the socialist order. For that purpose our immediate aim is the achievement of power. As a matter of fact, the state, the government machinery is just a weapon in the hands of the ruling class to further and safeguard its interest. We want to snatch and handle it to utilize it for the consummation of our ideal, i.e., the social reconstruction on new, i.e. Marxist basis. For this purpose we are fighting to handle the government machinery. All along we have to educate the masses and to create a favourable atmosphere for our social programme. In the struggles we can best train and educate them.

With these things clear before us, i.e. our immediate and ultimate object having been clearly put, we can now proceed with the examination of the present situation. We must always be very candid and quite business-like while analyzing any situation.

We know that since a hue and cry was raised about the Indian's participation in and share in the responsibility of the Indian government, the Minto-Morley Reforms were introduced, which formed the viceroy's council with consultation rights only. During the Great War, when the Indian help was needed the most, promises about self-government were made and the existing reforms were introduced. Limited legislative powers have been entrusted to the Assembly but subject to the goodwill of the viceroy. Now is the third stage.

Now reforms are being discussed and are to be introduced in the near future. How can our young men judge them? This is a question; I do not know by what standard are the Congress leaders going to judge them. But for us, the revolutionaries, we can have the following criteria:

1. Extent of responsibility transferred to the shoulders of the Indians.
2. Form of the Government institutions that are going to be introduced and the extent of the right of participation given to the masses.
3. Future prospects and the safeguards.

These might require a little further elucidation. In the first place, we can easily judge the extent of responsibility given to our people by the control our representatives will have on the executive. Up till now, the executive was never made responsible to the Legislative Assembly and the viceroy had the veto power, which rendered all the efforts of the elected members futile. Thanks to the efforts of the Swaraj party, the viceroy was forced every now and then to use these extraordinary powers to shamelessly trample the solemn decisions of the national representatives under foot. It is already too well known to need further discussion.

Now in the first place we must see the method of the executive formation: Whether the executive is to be elected by the members of a popular assembly or is to be imposed from above as before, and further, whether it shall be responsible to the house or shall absolutely affront it as in the past?

As regards the second item, we can judge it through the scope of franchise. The property qualifications making a man eligible to vote should be altogether abolished and universal suffrage be introduced instead. Every adult, both male and female, should have the right to vote. At present we can simply see how far the franchise has been extended.

As for the form, we have the bicameral government. In my opinion the upper house is much a bourgeois superstition or trap. According to me unicameral government is the only best we can expect.

I may here make a mention about provincial autonomy. But from whatever I have heard, I can only say that the Governor imposed from above, equipped with extraordinary powers, higher and above the legislative, shall prove to be no less than a despot. Let us better call it the 'provincial tyranny' instead of 'autonomy'. This is a strange type of democratisation of the state institution.

The third item is quite clear. During the last two years the British politicians have been trying to undo Montague's promise for another dole of reforms to be bestowed every ten years till the British Treasury exhausts.

We can see what they have decided about the future.

Let me make it clear that we do not analyse these things to rejoice over the achievement, but to form a clear idea about our situation, so that we may enlighten the masses and prepare them for further struggle. For us, compromise never means surrender, but a step forward and some rest. That is all and nothing else.

HAVING DISCUSSED the present situation, let us proceed to discuss the nature programme and the line of action we ought to adopt.

As I have already stated, for any revolutionary party, a definite programme is very essential. For, you must know that revolution means action. It means a change brought about deliberately by an organized and systematic work, as opposed to sudden and unorganized or spontaneous change or breakdown. And for the formulation of a programme, one must necessarily study:

1. The goal,
2. The premises from where we are to start, i.e. the existing conditions;
3. The course of action, i.e. means and methods.

Unless one has a clear notion about these three factors, one cannot discuss anything about programme.

We have discussed at present situation to some extent. The goal has been slightly touched. We want a socialist revolution, the indispensable preliminary to which is the political revolution. That is what we want. The political revolution does not mean the transfer of state for more crudely, the power, from the hands of the British to the Indians, but to those Indians who are at one with us as to the final goal, or to the more precise, the power to be transferred to the revolutionary party through popular support. After that, to proceed in right earnest is to organize the reconstruction of the whole society on the socialist basis. If you do not mean this revolution, then please have mercy. Stop shouting, 'Long

Live Revolution.' The term revolution is too sacred, at least to us, to be so lightly used or misused. But if you say you are for the national revolution and the aims of your struggle is an Indian republic of the type of the United States of America, then I ask you to please let me know on what forces you rely that will help you bring about that revolution. The only forces on which you can rely to bring about any revolution, whether national or the socialist, are the peasantry and the labour. Congress leaders do not dare to organize those forces. You have seen it in this movement. They know it better than anybody else that without these forces they are absolutely helpless. When they passed the resolution of complete independence – that really meant a revolution – they did not mean it. They had to do it under pressure of the younger element, and then they wanted to use it as a threat to achieve their hearts' desire – Dominion Status. You can easily judge it by studying the resolutions of the last three sessions of the Congress. I mean Madras, Calcutta and Lahore. At Calcutta, they passed a resolution asking for Dominion Status within twelve months, otherwise they would be forced to adopt complete independence as their object, and in all solemnity waited for some such gift till midnight after the 31st December, 1929. Then they found themselves 'honour bound' to adopt the Independence resolution, otherwise they did not mean it. But even then Mahatmaji made no secret of the fact that the door (for compromise) was open. That was the real spirit. At the very outset they knew that their movement could not but end in some compromise. It is this half-heartedness that we hate, not the compromise at a particular stage in the struggle. Anyway, we were discussing the forces on which you can depend for a revolution. But if you say that you will approach the peasants and labourers to enlist their active support, let me tell you that they are not going to be fooled by any sentimental talk. They ask you quite candidly: what are they going to gain by your revolution for which you demand their sacrifices, what difference does it make to them whether Lord Reading is the head of the Indian government or Sir Purshotamdas Thakordas? What difference for a peasant if Sir Tej Bahadur Sapru replaces Lord Irwin? It is useless to appeal to his national sentiment. You can't 'Use' him for your purpose; you shall have to mean seriously and to make him understand that the revolution is going to be his and for his good. The revolution of the proletariat and for the proletariat.

When you have formulated this clear-cut idea about your goals, you can proceed in right earnest to organize your forces for such an action. Now there are two different phases through which you shall have to pass. First, the preparation; second, the action.

After the present movement ends you will find disgust and some disappointment amongst the sincere revolutionary workers. But you need not worry. Leave sentimentalism aside. Be prepared to face the facts. Revolution is a very difficult task. It is beyond the power of any man to make a revolution. Neither can it be brought about on any appointed date. It is brought about by special environments, social and economic. The function of an organized party is to utilize any such opportunity offered by these circumstances. And to prepare the masses and organize the forces for the revolution is a very difficult task. And that requires a very great sacrifice on the part of the revolutionary workers. Let me make it clear that if you are a businessman or an established wordly or family man, please don't play with fire. As a leader you are of no use to the party. We have already very many such leaders who spare some evening hours for delivering speeches. They are useless. We require – to use the term so dear to Lenin – the 'professional revolutionaries'. The whole-time workers who have no other ambitions or life-work except the revolution. The greater the number of such workers organized into a party, the greater the chances of your success.

To proceed systematically, what you need the most is a party with workers of the type discussed above with clear-cut ideas and keen perception and ability of initiative and quick decisions. The party shall have iron discipline and it need not necessarily be an underground party, rather the contrary. Though the policy of voluntarily going to jail should altogether be abandoned. That will create a number of workers who shall be forced to lead an underground life. They should carry on the work with the same zeal. And it is this group of workers that shall produce worthy leaders for the real opportunity.

The party requires workers who can be recruited only through the youth movement. Hence we find the youth movement as the starting point of our programme. The youth movement should organize study circles, class lectures and publication of leaflets, pamphlets, books and periodicals. This is the best recruiting and training ground for political workers.

Those young men who may have matured their ideas and may find themselves ready to devote their life to the cause, may be transferred to the party. The party workers shall always guide and control the work of the youth movement as well. The party should start with the work of mass propaganda. It is very essential. One of the fundamental causes of the failure of the Ghadar Party (1914-15) was the ignorance, apathy and sometimes active opposition of the masses. And apart from that, it is essential for gaining the active sympathy of and organising the peasants and workers. The name of party or rather,[+] a communist party. This party of political workers, bound by strict discipline, should handle all other movements. It shall have to organize the peasants and workers' parties, labour unions, and may even venture to capture the Congress and kindred political bodies. And in order to create political consciousness, not only of national politics but class politics as well, the party should organize a big publishing campaign. Subjects on all proletens (;) enlightening the masses of the socialist theory shall be within easy reach and distributed widely. The writings should be simple and clear.

There are certain people in the labour movement who enlist some absurd ideas about the economic liberty of the peasants and workers without political freedom. They are demagogues or muddle-headed people. Such ideas are unimaginable and preposterous. We mean the economic libert, of the masses, and for that very purpose we are striving to win the political power. No doubt in the beginning, we shall have to fight for little economic demands and privileges of these classes. But these struggles are the best means for educating them for a final struggle to conquer political power.

Apart from these, there shall necessarily be organized a military department. This is very important. At times its need is felt very badly. But at that time you cannot start and formulate such a group with substantial means to act effectively. Perhaps this is the topic that needs a careful explanation. There is very great probability of my being misunderstood on this subject. Apparently I have acted like a terrorist. But I am not a terrorist. I am a revolutionary who has got such definite ideas of a lengthy programme as is being discussed here. My 'comrades in arms' might accuse me, like Ram Prasad Bismil, for having been subjected to certain sort of reaction in the condemned cell, which is not true. I have got the same ideas, same convictions, same zeal and same spirit as I used to have outside, perhaps – nay, decidedly – better. Hence I warn my readers to be careful while reading my words. They should not try to read anything between the lines. Let me announce with all the strength at my command that I am not a terrorist and I never was, except perhaps in the beginning of my revolutionary career. And I am convinced that we cannot gain anything through those methods. One can easily judge it from the history of the Hindustan Socialist Republican Association. All our activities were directed towards an aim, i.e. identifying ourselves with the great movement as its military wing. If anybody has misunderstood me, let him amend his ideas. I do not mean that bombs and pistols are useless, rather the contrary. But if mean to say that mere bomb-throwing is not only useless but sometimes harmful. The military department of the party should always keep ready all the war-material it can command for any emergency. It should back the political work of the party. It cannot and should not work independently.

On these lines indicated above, the party should proceed with its work. Through periodical meetings and conferences they should go on educating and enlightening their workers on all topics.

If you start the work on these lines, you shall have to be very sober. The programme requires at least twenty years for its fulfilment. Cast aside the youthful dreams of a revolution within ten years of Gandhi's Utopian promises of Swaraj in One Year. It requires neither the emotion nor the death, but the life of constant struggle, suffering and sacrifice. Crush your individuality first. Shake off the dreams of personal comfort. Then start to work. Inch by inch you shall have to proceed. It needs courage, perseverance and very strong determination. No difficulties and no hardships shall discourage you. No failure and betrayals shall dishearten you No travails (!) imposed upon you shall snuff out the revolutionary will in you. Through the ordeal of sufferings and sacrifice you shall come out victorious. And these individual victories shall be the valuable assets of the revolution.

LONG LIVE REVOLUTION

2nd February, 1931.

Bibliography

Andrews, Charles Freer, *India and the Simon Report*, London, George Allen, 1930.

Andrews, Charles Freer, *Mahatma Gandhi at Work: His Own Story Continued*, London, George Allen & Unwin Ltd., 1931.

Bardhan, A.S., *Bhagat Singh: Pages from the Life of a Martyr.*

Chandra, Bipan, *India's Struggle for Independence, 1857-1947*, New Delhi, India, Viking, 1988.

Chandra, Bipan, *Nationalism and Colonialism in Modern India*, New Delhi, Orient Longman, 1981.

Chatterjee, J.C., *Indian Revolutionaries in Conference*, Calcutta, 1960.

Deol, Gurdev Singh, *Shaheed-e-Azam Sardar Bhagat Singh,* Patiala, 1978.

Deol, Gurdev Singh, *The Role of the Ghadar Party in the National Movement*, Delhi, Sterling Publishers, 1969.

Dublish, Kaushalya Devi, *Revolutionaries and Their Activities In Northern India*, New Delhi, B.R. Pub. Corporation, 1982.

Ghosh, Ajoy, *Bhagat Singh and his Comrades,* Calcutta, 1945.

Ghosh, Kalichan, *Roll of Honour.*

Gupta, Manmathnath, *Bhagat Singh and His Times,* 1st ed, New Delhi, Lipi Prakashan, 1977.

Josh, Sohan Singh, *Tragedy of Komagata Maru*, New Delhi, People's Publishing House, 1975.

Khullar, K.K., *Shaheed Bhagat Singh*, New Delhi, Hem Publishing, 1981.

Laushey, David M, *Bengal Terrorism & the Marxist Left: Aspects of Regional Nationalism in India, 1905-1942*, Calcutta, 1975.

Nath, Shaileshwar, *Terrorism in India Left.*

Rahbar, Hansraj, *Bhagat Singh and His Thought*, 1990.

Rao, Niraja, '*Bhagat Singh and the Revolutionary Movement*', Revolutionary Democracy, *April, 1997.*

Samanta, Amiya K, *Terrorism in Bengal: A Collection of Documents* (Vol. 2), Calcutta, Government of West Bengal, 1995.

Sandhu, Virendra *(ed), Bhagat Singh Letters and Documents*

Sanyal, Jatindranth, *Sardar Bhagat Singh.*

Sanyal, Sachindranath, *Bandi Jibon.*

Sarkar, Sumit. *Modern India, 1885-1947,* Delhi, Macmillan, 1983.

Sharma, I. Mallikarjuna, *Role of Revolutionaries in the Freedom Struggle: A Critical History of the Indian Revolutionary Movements,* 1918-1934, Hyderabad, Marxist Study Forum, 1987.

Sinha, S.N., ed. *Simon Commission in U.P.: Documents Preserved in the U.P. State Archives.* India: Dept. of Cultural Affairs, U.P., 1987.

Sitaramayya, Pattabhi, *The History of the Indian National Congress,* Vol. 2 (1935-47).

Vaishampayan, Vishwanath, *Chandrashekhar Azad,* Vol I, II, III.

Vajpeyi, J. N., *The Extremist Movement in India,* Chugh Publications, Allahabad, 1974.

Verma, Shiv, *Selected Writings of Shaheed Bhagat Singh,* New Delhi, 1986.

Wolpert, Stanley A, *Jinnah of Pakistan,* New York, Oxford University Press, 1984.

Index

All India Congress Committee, 26, 34, 99

Asaf Ali, 75, 78, 79, 144, 145

Asaf Ali, Aruna, 144, 145

Azad, Chandra Shekhar, 6, 15, 16, 25, 26, 27, 33, 49, 136, 160, 190

Aziz, Khan Bahadur Abdul, 105, 106, 129

Bagha Jatin, (Jatindra Nath Mukherjee), 24, 25

Bajaj, Jamnadas, 181

Baker, Herbert, 69

Bakshi, Dina Nath, 100

Bakshi, S.R. 13,

Bannerjee, Man Mohan, 132

Barkat, 1, 2, 162

Barkat Ali 100, 101, 115

Bhai Parmanand, 13, 65

Bishan Nath, 100

Bismil, Ram Prasad, 167, 208, 237

Bose, Subhash, Chandra, 7, 94, 95, 149, 172

Bose, Rash Behari, 42, 56

Bustin, F.W., 188

Carden-Noad, C.H., 100,101, 102,103, 115- 117

Chakraborti, Trailokyanath, 43, 45, 46

Chapekar Brothers, 44

Chatterjee, Bankim Chandra 44, 144

Chatterji, Ramanand, 164, 165

Chittagong Armoury Raid Case, 137

Coldstream, Justice, 112-115, 117, 121-123, 130

Crerar, Sir James, 47

Das, Chhabil, 13, 14, 37

Das, Jatindra Nath, 44, 46, 49, 91, 94, 95, 96, 97

Das, Ram Saran, 61, 67, 129

Desai, Mahadev, 173, 181, 202

Dhingra, Madan Lal, 75, 76

Dunedin, Viscount, 139

Duni Chand, 92, 100, 101, 107, 115, 120

Durga Devi, 25, 26, 32-34, 36-41, 65, 67, 198

Dutt, Batukeshwar (B.K.), 15, 42, 61, 63, 67, 68, 69, 70, 72, 73, 76, 77, 78, 79, 81, 84, 85, 88, 89, 95, 96, 98, 99, 100, 103, 105, 116, 117, 120, 121, 123, 130, 132, 134, 135, 205

Dutt, Prem, 132

Dutt, W.C., 100
Dyer, Reginald, 21, 22, 24, 96

Emerson, Herbert, 151

Faiz, Faiz Ahmed, 29,100
Fern, W.J.C., 29, 119
Fourier, Charles 136
Fuller, Barnfield, 168

Gandhi, Mohandas
   Karamchand, 5, 17, 18, 19,
   23-25, 36, 39, 56, 58, 64, 66,
   76, 79, 83, 86, 96, 98, 110,
   125, 137, 141, 142, 148, 150,
   151-153, 156, 157, 158, 159,
   163, 167, 171-174, 176-181,
   184, 201, 202, 217, 219-226,
   230, 231, 237, 239
Ganguli, Prafulla, 43
Ghadar party, 12, 51- 57, 182,
   236, 239
Ghalib, Mirza, 162, 163
Gidwani, Choithram, P., 172
Ghosh, Ajoy, 15, 16, 134
Ghosh, Aurobindo, 42, 143
Ghosh, Barindra Kumar, 42,
   144
Ghosh, Jyotish, 43, 46
Ghosh, Motilal, 144
Ghosh, Phonindro Nath, 43,
   123
Ghosh, Sisir Kumar, 144
Gopal Lal, 100, 113
Gorky, Maxim, 64
Gupta, Jaidev, 3, 14

Haider, Agha, 113, 122, 127, 130
Hansraj, 239
Harding, Hamilton 100, 116
Hilton, J.C, 113, 122, 127, 130
Hindu Sanrakshani Samiti, 44
Hindustan Socialist Republican
   Association, 6, 24, 71, 74,
   101, 227, 237
HSRA 6, 24-26, 28, 35, 46, 59-61,
   65, 105, 106, 124, 137, 147, 188
Hume, Allan Octavian, 18
Hugo, Victor, 38

Irwin, Lord 108, 150, 151, 234

Jai Gopal, 27, 28, 30, 84, 104,
   119, 120, 123-127, 129, 131-
   133, 135, 192, 197
Jinnah, Mohammad Ali, 70, 88,
   89
Josh, Sohan Singh 33

Kakori Case, 16, 82, 83, 167,
   209
Kaur, Amar, 155
Kaur, Shakuntala, 155
Kaur, Sumitra, 155
Kaur, Vidyavati, 5, 149, 155
Kapur, Amolak Ram 100, 103,
   132
Khan, Ashfhaqullah, 12, 167,
   168
Khan, Kalandar Ali 100
Khan, Maulana Zafar Ali, 11
Khanna, Durga Das, 102
Kidwai, Rafi Ahmed, 105

Lahore Conspiracy Case, 2, 27, 93, 105, 109, 110, 113, 116, 129, 182, 189, 203, 206
Lal, Gopal, 113,
Kishori, Lal, 135
Lal Kundan, 132,
Lall, Chaman, 73, 75
Lenin, 3, 4, 7, 15, 64, 68, 80, 103, 167, 208, 228, 229, 235
Lowell, James Russell, 170
Lutyens, Edwin, 69

Malviya, Madan Mohan, 149, 179
Marx, Karl, 5, 15, 163
Mehta, Amin Chand 100, 115
Mehta, Pran Nath, 6, 7
Mehta, Puran Chand, 100, 103
Middleton, Judge Leonard 78, 81
Mitra, Krishna Kumar 143
Moore, Arthur 188
Mulla, Sir Dinshah 139
Mukherji, Lalit, 49

Nehru, Jawaharlal, 7, 18, 19, 23, 24, 58, 88, 96, 171, 178, 179, 181, 222
Nehru, Motilal, 49, 70, 88, 96, 105, 172, 230
Naujawan Bharat Sabha, 15, 45, 65, 129
Newman, 82

O' Dwyer, Michael, 22, 87

Pal, Bipin Chandra, 143
Pandey, Surendra 134,
Patel, Vallabhbhai, 172, 173, 174
Patel, Vithalbhai, 69
Peace Treaty of Brest-Litovsk, 4
Petrie, Sir David, 47
Pool, P.B., 76, 81
Pran Nath Mehta, 6
Prashad, Gaya, 116, 117, 121, 135
Pritt, D.N., 138
Public Safety Bill, 59, 69, 71, 72
Punjab Quami Vidya Pith, 13

Qadir, Abdul, 130

Rajguru, Hari Shivaram, 1, 6, 7, 9, 10, 11, 24, 26-29, 32-35, 41, 49, 50, 114-116, 121, 126, 131, 135, 140, 145, 147, 149, 150, 154, 160, 172, 179, 180, 187, 192, 199, 200, 201, 202, 203
Rai, Lala Lajpat, 12, 13, 19, 20, 21, 23, 24, 25, 26, 30, 43, 72, 125, 128, 137, 163, 169
Rai Sahib Pandit Sri Kishen, 93
Ram, Agya, 116, 120, 130, 134
Ramatirtha, Swami, 40
Russell, Bertrand, 3, 163, 169

Sachar, Bhimsen, 2, 37
Sanyal, Jatinder Nath, 24, 95, 134
Sanyal, Sachindranath, 15
Saunders, J.P., 10, 28-30, 35, 41, 44, 49, 58, 59, 62, 65, 67, 73,

84, 87, 106, 116, 119, 120,
124, 126, 128, 129, 134, 135,
160, 192, 193
Savarkar, Vir, 44
Scott, J.A., 21
Shadi Lal, Sir 106
Shastri, Lal Bahadur, 180
Simon Commission, 19, 21, 71,
240
Simon, John Allsbrook, 17
Sinha, Bijoy Kumar, 3, 97, 116,
132, 133, 135
Singh, Ajit, 12, 13, 156
Singh, Arjun, 14, 155
Singh, Babu, 129
Singh, Baba Randhir, 165, 166
Singh, Baba Sohan, 88
Singh, Chanan, 29, 32, 84
Singh, Charat, 1, 2, 6, 8, 11, 154,
160, 161, 163
Singh, Gurdit, 53
Singh, Kishen, 12, 113, 156,
179, 180
Singh, Kulbir, 3, 155
Singh Kultar, 155, 161, 162,
163, 170
Singh, Mahabir, 116, 117, 121,
135
Singh, Mewa, 53, 54
Singh, Udham, 87, 88
Suryanarayan, Rai Bahadur 76

Tandon, Purshottam Das, 49
Tapp, J.K., 130
Tawney, R.H., 63

Tewari, Kamalnath, 135
Thapar, Mathura Das 189, 191,
196, 197, 198, 202
Thapar, Sukhdev, 1, 6, 7, 9, 10,
11, 24, 26, 27, 32, 34, 38, 39,
49, 60, 64, 65-68, 97, 110,
116, 120-129, 131, 132, 135,
136, 140, 145, 147, 149, 150,
154, 160, 172, 179, 180, 181,
184, 187, 188-194, 196, 197,
198-203
Tilak, Bal Gangadhar, 18, 52
Trade Disputes Bill, 59, 69, 71,
72, 79

Upadhayaya, Brahmomadhab,
143

Verma, Prem Dutt, 103, 104,
Verma, Shiv, 15, 68, 116, 121, 135
Viceroy Irwin, 59, 141
Viceroy Lord Curzon, 42
Vidyalankar, Jai Chandra, 14, 46
Vidyarthi, Ganesh Shankar 14,
15
Vivekananda, Swami, 40, 44
Vohra, Bhagwati Charan, 25,
34, 40, 41, 45, 84, 117, 141,
147, 198
Vohra, Hans Raj, 28, 84, 124,
125, 126, 127, 128, 129, 132,
135, 187-200

William Curzon Wyllie, 75

Yashpal, 37, 197

Scoop!

Inside Stories from the Partition to the Present

Kuldip Nayar

A candid collection of riveting news-stories that brings alive the political history of the Indian subcontinent and the noble—and not-so-noble—men and women who shaped it...

In a distinguished career spanning sixty years, veteran journalist, political commentator and author Kudip Nayar has seen and reported it all. From his vantage point at the forefront of every ground-breaking news event, in close proximity to and in close confidence of the people in power, Kuldip Nayar's articles are all the more fascinating as they give us a first-hand account of historic political events, along with personal insights into the motives and machinations that conspired to bring them about.

From personal encounters with Gandhi, Jinnah and Nehru, and interviews with Mountbatten and Radcliffe, to the controversy surrounding Shastri's death in Tashkent, the 1965 Indo-Pak war and its aftermath, the 1969 Congress split, the liberation of Bangladesh, the assassination of Zulfikar Ali Bhutto and the imposition of the Emergency in India—Kuldip Nayar's scoops are as much a testament of the times as they are of his uncanny reporter's gift for anticipating the news.

Also from HarperCollins *Publishers* India

India 60:

Towards a New Paradigm

2007 marks 60 years of India's independence from colonial rule. Traditionally, in India, the attainment of 60 years, called *shashtipoorti*, is an important milestone in the life of an individual. It is a time to reflect on one's past and start planning for the future.

This volume brings together a brilliant posse of writers, including academicians, journalists and activists, who took up the challenge of such stocktaking, of assessing the achievements and failures of these six decades across a range of issues and concerns. The result is a lively collection of essays which examine the problems, solutions and debates which move contemporary India. From democracy, elections, agriculture, economy, education, human rights and reservations—areas where no single voice or solution seems to be the answer—to literature, art, cinema and urban life—where the eye cannot keep pace with the flashing images-writers range at will, differing from one another in tone and opinion, but allied in the clarity and sharpness of their perspective.

A thoughtful compendium of elegantly presented arguments supported by facts and, more importantly, a real understanding of the way things work in this country of a billion ideas, *India 60* is a must-read for all those who seek to know India. For, more than any other book in recent times, it captures for us, truthfully and without artifice, the shifting boundaries of ideology and creativity that continue to shape a nation at once old and young.

Ira Pande worked as a university teacher for 15 years, and then as an editor at *Seminar*, *Biblio*, Dorling Kindersley and Roli Books. She is currently Chief Editor, IIC Publications. She is also the author of *Diddi: My Mother's Voice*.

Also from HarperCollins *Publishers* India